Paris Monographs in America

Chichén Itzá, Yucatán, México

Sylvanus G. Morley 1946

Edited by

John M. Weeks
Nuria Matarredona Desantes

BAR International Series 2718
2015

Since 1974

British Archaeological Reports

First published in 2015
BAR International Series 2718

Paris Monographs in American Archaeology 39
Chichén Itzá, Yucatán, México: Sylvanus G. Morley 1946

ISBN: 978 1 4073 1371 9

Printed in England

All BAR titles are available from:

British Archaeological Reports Ltd
Oxford
United Kingdom
Phone +44 (0)1865 310431
Fax +44 (0)1865 316916
Email: info@barpublishing.com
www.barpublishing.com

Originally published by Archaeopress in conjunction with British Archaeological Reports (Oxford) Ltd//Hadrian Books Ltd the Series principal publisher, in 2015

Table of Contents

List of Figures

List of Maps

PREFACE

Chichén Itzá is a UNESCO-designated World Heritage site, one of the largest and most accessible Maya archaeological areas in southern Mexico. It is a major destination for tourists from the Cancún and Cozumel coastal resorts, and from the colonial capital city of Mérida. The densely clustered architecture of the site core covers an area of at least 6.5 square kilometers, and smaller scale residential architecture extends for an unknown distance beyond the site core. The site contains many elaborate stone buildings in various states of preservation, consolidation, or restoration.

The architecture represents several styles, including the Puuc[1] and Chenes[2] styles of northern Yucatán. The buildings are assembled in a series of groups, and each at one time separated from the other by a series of low walls. The three best known of these complexes are the Great North Platform, which includes El Castillo (Str. 2D5), Temple of Warriors (Str. 2D8) and Great Ball Court (Str. 2D1), the Osario Group, which includes the pyramid of the same name as well as the Temple of Xtoloc; and the Central Group, which includes the Caracol (Str. 3C15), Las Monjas (Str. 4C1), and Akab Dzib (Str. 4D1). South of Las Monjas, in an area known as Chichén Viejo (Old Chichén) are several other complexes, such as the Group of the Initial Series, Group of the Lintels, and Group of the Castillo. Many of these buildings were connected by a dense network of more than 80 paved causeways radiating in all directions from the site core (see site plan in Appendix 3).

[1] The Puuc style of architecture originated in the Puuc hills region of southern Campeche and western Quintana Roo and then spread across much of the Yucatán Peninsula during the Late and Terminal Classic. This style is recognized by elaborate stone mosaics that decorated building façades with geometric motifs, the presence of stone masks, usually representing the rain deity Cha'ac, located at the external corners of the structures. Inward and outward friezes and moldings were also common. The Maya sites that represent the Puuc architectural style are Chacmultún, Kabáh, Labná, Oxkintok, Sayil, Uxmal, and Xlapac.

[2] The Chenes Style of architecture incorporates one or more sculpted heads of the rain deity Cha'ac in the façades of buildings. The Maya sites that represent the Chenes architectural style are Edzná, Hochob, Tabasqueño, Uxmal, and Xtampak.

Although the history of archaeological study of the site extends back over a century, the most significant and productive effort was that directed between 1924 and 1940 by Sylvanus G. Morley under the sponsorship of the Carnegie Institution of Washington[3] (now Carnegie Institution for Science).

Sylvanus Griswold Morley[4]

The study of the ancient Maya was dominated for most of the first half of the twentieth-century by Sylvanus G. Morley, a scholar associated with the Carnegie Institution of Washington (CIW). This organization was active in the Maya region beginning in 1913, when it agreed to fund a 40 year research program on the Maya, until the late 1950's, when the archaeology program was gutted to better support such war-related initiatives as the development of radar (Weeks and Hill 2003).

Morley was born in Chester, Pennsylvania, and studied at Pennsylvania Military College (now Widener University, West Chester, Pennsylvania) and Harvard University. He did most of his archaeological work under the auspices of the School of American Research at Quirigua in

[3] The Carnegie Institution of Washington (Carnegie Institution for Science) was founded in 1902 as an organization for scientific discovery by industrialist Andrew Carnegie. Today the Carnegie Institution directs programs in six main areas: plant molecular biology at the Department of Plant Biology (Stanford University); developmental biology at the Department of Embryology (Baltimore); global ecology at the Department of Global Ecology (Stanford University); Earth and planetary sciences, and astronomy, at the Department of Terrestrial Magnetism (Washington, DC); and at the observatories of the Carnegie Institution of Washington (Pasadena, CA and Las Campañas, Chile). Initially, the president and trustees devoted much of the institution's budget to individual grants in various fields, including astronomy, anthropology, literature, economics, history and mathematics. Under the leadership of Robert Woodward, who became president in 1904, the board changed its course, deciding to provide major support to departments of research rather than to individuals. This approach allowed them to concentrate on fewer fields and support groups of researchers in related areas over many years.

[4] There are several biographical treatments of Morley, including those by Barrera Rubio 1992; Brunhouse 1971; Harris and Sadler 2003; *Morleyana* 1950; Pollock 1950.

Guatemala, and with the Carnegie Institution of Washington elsewhere in the Maya region. He was largely responsible for the excavation and restoration at Chichén Itzá, and wrote several popular books synthesizing his Maya research. Morley's *The Ancient Maya,* was first published in 1946, has been revised and reprinted in English and Spanish (1947a, b, 1956, 1961, 1963, 1972); a franchise continued by George Brainerd (Morley and Brainerd 1968, 1987), and Robert J. Sharer (Morley, Brainerd, and Sharer 1983; Morley and Sharer 1994a, b, 1998; Sharer and Traxler 2006).

Morley was a man of great energy, who had an affection for the indigenous people of southern Mesoamerica, or more specifically, the Maya people in the Mexican states of Campeche, Chiapas, Quintana Roo, and Yucatán, as well as Guatemala and Belize, and the western parts of Honduras and El Salvador. His work in the study of ancient hieroglyphic inscriptions helped to establish generally the broad historical outlines of Maya culture and to convey the excitement of Maya civilization to a public eager for tales of adventure and the exotic. He formulated and promoted an integrated vision of Maya civilization that became widely accepted during the first half of the twentieth century (Brunhouse 1971:158).

Although Morley was awarded funding from the Carnegie Institution of Washington in 1913 and was granted a permit for long-term archaeological research at Chichén Itzá from the Mexican government, excavation was delayed by World War I (1914-1918) and the Mexican Revolution (1910-1920) (Brunhouse 1971:76-77). By 1922 the turbulent political situation in Mexico had stabilized somewhat, clearing the way for excavation and restoration to begin at the site. In February of 1923 Morley and Charles Merriam, then President of the Carnegie Institution, visited the site and Morley identified the area he believed would be best for excavation and restoration, a mound complex then known as the Group of One Thousand Columns (including the Temple of Warriors). Later that year the Carnegie Institution of Washington and the Mexican government began a collaborative program of excavation and restoration at Chichén Itzá (Weeks and Hill 2006). The Mexican government was by then already at work restoring the massive pyramid, El Castillo.

In 1924, armed with a renewable ten-year digging concession from the Mexican government, Morley, Earl H. Morris, his field director, and archaeologists Oliver G. Ricketson, and Munroe Amsden, began their first explorations of the Northeast Colonnade (Str. 3E1). Much to their surprise they uncovered a series of rows of free-standing columns; an architecture feature rare in Classic Maya architecture. This complex (now called the Complex of a Thousand Columns) confirmed earlier speculations that Chichén Itzá was something of an archaeological enigma. This arrangement had much more in common with the architectural styles of central Mexico cultures than that of the Preclassic or Classic Maya. In particular, this complex and others appeared to have much in common with structures built at Tula, believed to be the capital of the Toltecs and which was located north of present-day Mexico City (Brunhouse 1971:206).

Over the next few seasons excavations were expanded. In 1925, work was initiated at the Northwest Colonnade (Str. 2D8) and the Temple of the Warriors (Str. 2D8) by Morris and Gustav Strömsvik, the Temple at Cenote Xtoloc by Ann Axtell Morris, and the Temple of the Four Lintels by Oliver G. Ricketson (see Appendix I). Gradually earthen mounds revealed structures, such as the Temple of the Jaguar (Str. 2D1) and the Temple of the Warriors (Str. 2D8). In 1927 an older structure buried beneath the Temple of the Warriors was discovered, and named Temple of the Chacmool (Str. 2D8) after a further example found of this distinctive statuary. These structures had frescoes recorded by artists Ann Axtell Morris and Jean Charlot which again exhibited a non-Maya style, or at least a blending of Maya and non-Maya. They also worked on the reconstruction of El Caracol, a unique circular building believed to be an astronomical observatory. A separate archaeological project, this one under the Mexican government, had also commenced working the site; the two projects divided the areas to excavate, continuing side-by-side for several years, in a somewhat guarded but nonetheless cooperative fashion.

While Morris oversaw daily operations, Morley continued to record inscriptions, particularly the date portions. Since most of these inscription dates at the site were recorded in an abbreviated form known as the "Short Count", which only identified an event within a span of about 260 years, it was difficult to pin down in which particular span an event referred to in the inscriptions occurred. Towards the end of the project Morley's work on these was to be superseded somewhat by a more-comprehensive analysis made by Hermann Beyer in 1937.

The later years of the Chichén Itzá project would concentrate increasingly on completing the restoration work on principal structures, for Morley always had an eye on the dual purpose of the project: to research, but also rebuild to generate the promised revenue from tourism.

Despite the success of his work as an epigrapher, Morley's administrative weaknesses as a leader of the large-scale archaeological project at Chichén Itzá became increasingly obvious as the excavation project developed. In 1928 Morley's subordinate Karl Ruppert was chosen to assume all administrative duties at Chichén Itzá, and in 1930 his close friend Alfred V. Kidder, a prominent Southwestern archaeologist, replaced Morley as Director of the Division for Historical Research. Three years' later excavations were suspended at Chichén Itzá. In many ways the site remains an enigma because of the emphasis on consolidation and reconstruction of buildings rather constructing an accurate culture history (Coe 1999). Several monographs summarizing some of the architectural achievements of the site were eventually published although a general synthesis of the overall excavation program was never formulated.

Morley and Ancient Maya Society

There is no doubt that Morley had a profound influence of the development of Maya studies. From the late 1920s through to the mid-1970s, Morley's reconstruction of ancient Maya society and history constituted the traditional interpretation against which competing views were measured. However, major advances made in the decipherment of Maya hieroglyphic writing and refinements in archaeological data analysis made since that time have now called into question much of this former standard interpretation, significantly revising the Maya historical account. Seduced by the spectacular architectural remains of the Maya, these early scholars ignored much information in their search for objects originally manufactured for the ruling elite.

Morley (1946:159) maintained that ancient Maya society was essentially a theocracy, one which was devoted almost exclusively to astronomical observations and the passage of time. These ideas are now hopelessly dated, and although astronomical and calendrical observations were important, the Maya are now seen in more objective terms, concerned also with dynastic succession, political conquests, and the lives and achievements of actual personages.

He also argued that the great southern centers such as Copán in Honduras, and Quiriguá in Guatemala, had been united in the Classic period (200-1000 CE) under what he termed the "Old Empire". This empire suddenly collapsed, and the surviving remnants later migrated to the northern sites in Yucatán (such as Chichén Itzá) to form a "New Empire." It is now generally accepted that at no time was the Maya region united under a single polity, but rather that individual "city-states" maintained a somewhat independent existence, albeit one with its fluctuating conquests and local subservience to more dominant centers. In support of his view, Morley devised a classification system of relative importance, which he ascribed to all of the then-known Maya sites; more sites have now been discovered, and his classification system is now seen as arbitrary, contradicted in places by the sites' hieroglyphic inscriptions which can now be substantially read.

The ancient Maya, in contrast to the militaristic cultures of central Mexico, were believed by Morley to have been one of the world's least warlike people. In actuality, warfare was endemic throughout the region and probably contributed in some way to the collapse of Classic period Maya civilization in the southern lowlands. The great Maya centers with their complicated site plans and stunning architecture were the remains of ceremonial gathering places and not cities where people actually lived. More recent investigations by the University of Pennsylvania Museum at Tikal and work at other centers indicate that some of these settlements were indeed urban centers with significant residential populations.

Morley (1956:138-140) proposed that the ancient Maya were the first people in Mesoamerica to domesticate maize (*Zea mays* spp.), with the wild variety known as *teosinte* being its progenitor. Recent genetic studies have shown Morley to be largely correct in this, although the beginnings of its domestication (12,000 to 7,500 years ago) pre-date the establishment of Maya society. Slash and burn (swidden) agriculture was believed to have been the only agricultural system known to the ancient Maya. This reinforced the argument that the great sites were not true urban centers because it was reasoned that slash-and-burn agricultural could not support substantial population density. However recent studies clearly indicate that intensive methods of agricultural production, including irrigation and crop diversification, were also employed.

Finally, the Postclassic period (1000-1697 CE) Maya were seen as a people whose culture had deteriorated to a "decadent" level (Morley 1956:94-97). This belief reinforced the conceptualization of a sudden cataclysmic collapse. In reality, Maya society continued to evolve during the Postclassic period and continues today. That the period produced fewer elaborate objects and more mass-produced works may suggest a political evolution toward more complex political structures and away from more rigid hierarchies controlled by a small royal caste. Mass-production can be seen as a sign that more goods were being made for comparatively lower social classes.

Thus, a new construct of the ancient Maya has emerged in the past half century. Perhaps this was inevitable, since the pioneers like Morley started from a point at which so little was known.

Morley and Maya Hieroglyphic Writing

Morley (1956:262-265) was particularly interested in the nature of Maya writing and between 1915 and 1923 made annual expeditions in search of hieroglyphic inscriptions. These explorations resulted in the publication of two important works, *Inscriptions at Copán* (1920), and the massive five volume *Inscriptions of Petén* (1937). The essentials of the calendrical notation and astronomical data had been worked out by the early twentieth century, and by the 1930s John E. Teeple (1931) demonstrated that the glyphs known as the "Supplementary Series," referred to the lunar cycle and could be used to predict lunar eclipses. However, most of the texts and inscriptions still defied all attempts at decipherment. It was the view of Morley and other of his contemporaries, such as J.E.S. Thompson, that these undeciphered portions would contain only more of the same astronomical, calendrical and perhaps religious information, but not actual historical data. He argued strenuously that the Maya writing system was ideographic or pictographic, without any phonetic components.

The convincing evidence which was to overturn this view became known only after Morley's death, starting with Russian scholar Yuri Knorosov's work in the 1950s. Over the next decades other Mayanists such as Tatiana Proskouriakoff, and David H. Kelley would further expand upon this phonetic line of inquiry, which ran counter to the accepted view but would prove to be ever more fruitful as their work continued. By the mid-1970s, it had become increasingly clear to most that the Maya writing system was a logosyllabic one, a mixture of logograms and phonetic components that included a fully functional syllabary.

These realizations led to the successful decipherment of many of the texts which had been dismissed by Morley and others. In retrospect, these breakthroughs could probably have been realized earlier had it not been for Morley's, and later Thompson's, position against the phonetic approach. Consequently, most of Morley's attempts to advance understanding of the Maya script have not stood the test of time, and are now superseded (Coe 1999).

Morley however did make some useful observations that have withstood subsequent examination. His talent was not so much to make innovations, but rather to publicize and explain the workings of the various systems. He was particularly proficient at recovering calendar dates from eroded and weathered inscriptions, owing to his great familiarity with the various glyphic styles of the *tzolk'in*, *haab'* and Long Count elements.[5] Yet in his focus on calendrical details, he would often overlook or even neglect the documentation of other non-calendrical aspects of the Maya script; the comprehensiveness of some of his publications suffered much as a result.

Morley and Maya Archaeology

As the director of the archaeological excavation project at Chichén Itzá, Morley was well-regarded and liked by his colleagues and his Carnegie board employers. The reconstructions of Chichén Itzá and other sites are widely admired; but in terms of the research output and the resulting documentation produced, the legacy of these projects did not quite amount to what might have been expected to come from such a lengthy investigation. For some later Maya researchers Chichén Itzá remains comparatively little-understood given the amount of work which had gone into it under Morley's direction. The Yale University Mayanist Michael D. Coe (1999) notes that many talented people such as Thompson spent more time in restoring the site for later tourism than in actual research.

Morley and His Legacy

Despite the later reassessments with the benefit of hindsight, Morley remains a remarkable figure in Maya scholarship (*Morleyana* 1950). His research brought him many honors, including the Order of the Quetzal, Franklin Medal, and the Loubat Prize, as well as honorary doctorates from the Pennsylvania Military Academy and from Tufts University. His publications are now generally superseded, except for his calendrical compilations. His epigraphic work is also generally outdated, although it was widely supported for several decades after his death. Perhaps the contributions that today remain the most relevant arise from his developing of the Carnegie Maya research program, his enthusiasm and support shown to other scholars, and the undeniable successes in the restorative efforts that have made Maya sites famous. He had particular talents in communicating his fascination for the subject to a wider audience, and in his lifetime became quite widely known as perhaps the quintessential model of an early twentieth-century Central American scholar and explorer. Morley was also to be remembered as a spokesman and representative of the Maya peoples, among whom he spent so much of his time, and who otherwise lacked the means to directly address some of their concerns with the wider public.

Several volumes have been published which detail the architectural restoration efforts of Morley and his colleagues at Chichén Itzá. These include the Caracol (Ruppert and Morley 1935), Casa Redonda (Pollock 1936); Mercado (Ruppert 1943), Monjas (Bolles 1976), Temple of the Wall Panels (Ruppert 1931), and Temple of the Warriors (Morris 1931; Morris, Charlot, Morris 1931), as well as studies of the pottery (Brainerd 1958; Smith 1971), lithics (Beyer 1931; Sievert 1992; Stromsvik 1931, 1937), and objects retrieved from the Sacred Cenote (Coggins 1992; Coggins and Shane 1984; Tozzer 1957), including metals (Lothrop 1952), jade (Proskouriakoff 1974), lithics (Sievert 1992), and skeletal material (Hooton 1940).

In addition, numerous buildings were excavated and consolidated by the Instituto Nacional de Antropologia e Historia, including the Great Ball Court, Platform of the Skulls, Platform of the Eagles, Platform of the Cones, and the Castillo (Ruppert 1952:1).

Chichén Itzá and Tula

Despite extensive investigation of Chichén Itzá by the Carnegie Institution of Washington, some fundamental issues associated with site still remain in dispute. One of these is the relationship between Chichén Itzá, in the southern Mexican state of Yucatán, and Tula, in the central Mexican state of Hidalgo. Both have clear architectural similarities in several of their constructions. This Toltec-Maya connection is considered unique in Mesoamerica. Unlike most Maya sites, some of Chichén Itzá's buildings have Toltec traits, an historically powerful group from central Mexico. The explanation of these similarities remains a point of controversy among scholars. Certain historical records caused many early scholars of the region to assume that a Toltec invasion from Tula, Hidalgo, usually placed in the ninth or tenth centuries, was responsible for a new wave of Mexican-style Maya buildings after the rest of the buildings in Chichén Itzá were built. Other historical accounts imply a migration from Tula to Chichén Itzá. An account of Tula records a ruler of the Toltecs travelling east, which, paired with another account of Chichén that records a ruler from the west coming and teaching the Maya of that

[5] The Mesoamerican Long Count calendar is a non-repeating vigesimal (base-20) and base-18 calendar. Using a modified vigesimal tally, the Long Count calendar identifies a day by counting the number of days passed since a mythical creation date (August 11, 3114 BCE). The Long Count calendar was widely used on monuments.

city many things, supported a direct influence of the Toltecs on the Maya around 900-1000 CE. However, recent radiocarbon dating suggests that Chichén Itzá's 'Mexicanized' and pure Maya constructions were built at the same time, and that both were built previous to any recorded Toltec invasion, and previous to the banishing of the semi-historical ruler. The precise connection between these two groups is unknown, and fiercely contested among scholars of Toltecs and Maya, but it is not disputed that no other counterparts to these two cities are found in the 800 mile distance between them. Established contradicting theories and a lack of information cause the precise relationship between Chichén Itzá and Tula to be fervently contested.

Tula and Chichén Itzá share numerous architectural similarities not found in other Maya or Toltec sites. The Temples of the Warriors, two corresponding buildings in each site, are of equivalent style, they both have pillars inscribed with warriors, and the warriors in Chichén Itzá portray a possible invasion by Toltecs. A nearby Chac Mool, or sacrificial altar, outside each of the temples confirms again a direct correlation between the two sites. There is also a large series of columns, which originally supported a tremendous enclosed space, surrounding the Temples of the Warriors in both of the two sites, and in other areas. A now ruined Castillo in Tula, of similar construction to Chichén Itzá, and the fact both sites have very large ballcourts set in a similar architectural context further argue that there is some connection between Chichén and Tula. These bases of comparison are undisputed. However, the exact relationship between the two sites remains unknown. This connection between the two is significant in part because Chichén Itzá and Tula were both the seats of large Mesoamerican empires. That they share such constructions is unique and startling. No other Toltec or Maya site has an equivalent set of buildings in a different city, and in a different culture. This distinctive trait, and the huge historical power of each of these two sides, makes this argument a tremendous one in Mesoamerican studies.

The religious iconography of Chichén Itzá is unusual for a Maya site. The numerous depictions of Quetzalcoatl (Kukulkan), or feathered serpent deities, are more consistent with Toltec ideology than with that of the Maya. Though the Maya did worship the Feathered Serpent, it was typically much less common. There is also a greater persistence of weapons and shields in the Maya site than is typical.

Originally, there was a majority consensus that the Toltecs militarily exerted power over the Maya and conquered them. This caused a shift in their architectural style, which creates the Toltec-Maya incongruity within the construction of Chichén Itzá. Usually it was assumed that the pure Maya constructions had been constructed previous to the 'Mexicanized,' or Toltecized, buildings. Many theories were established explaining the precise nature of this connection by well-known scholars (of the time), but these early efforts were directly contradicted by later information.

Morley proposed that after the Maya buildings in Chichén Itzá were constructed, the leaders of Chichén Itzá, the Itzá, abandoned the center and "wandered" for a while before subsuming a group of Toltecs lead by Kukulcan, learning new crafts and traditions in the processes. The Itzá then returned to Chichén Itzá and constructed the 'Mexicanized' sites of Chichén Itzá, which were based on Tula. By migration, the Toltecs supposedly became the kings of Chichén Itzá, leading to similarities between the two sites.

Alfred M Tozzer, a Harvard-based authority in Maya studies during the first half of the twentieth century, proposed that the Maya at Chichén Itzá were overcome by the Toltecs three times, which subverted the development of their culture. The first invasion supposedly was of Toltecs, and was led by the mythological figure Kukulkan. The second was an invasion of Toltecized Itzá (the founding royal family of Chichén Itzá) and was led by Kukulkan II. The third invasion was of Mexican mercenaries from Tabasco. Tozzer argued that the Maya ruled between these three waves of violence, and that this creates the dichotomy within Chichén Itzá architecture. There is no strong evidence that there was a Toltec dominance of Chichén Itzá outside of the buildings in question, and so Tozzer's work remains mainly within the boundary of speculation.

The British Mayanist J. Eric S. Thompson has argued that the Itzá Maya were powerful warriors and merchants who led Chichén Itzá. Thompson proposed that they held a massive commercial empire and that when a Toltec ruler, Kukulkan, was taken in and supported by the Itzá; it led Chichén Itzá to become the center of a new Toltec empire. While there is some similarity in Thompson's theory to that of Morley's, his proposal placed more significance on the Itzá than had been proposed before.

Evidence for the influence of Tula upon Chichén Itzá was mainly based upon the assumption that Tula was older than Chichén, and that Chichén's 'Mexicanized' structures were built long after its Maya structures. Recent radiocarbon dating of the ceramics of Chichén Itzá shed new light upon this subject, and invalidated many of the older arguments. First, it was learned that the 'Mexicanized' and pure Maya sites had been constructed at about the same time. Second, it was also learned that most of these sites were constructed before any recorded major Toltec influence occurred. And third, Chichén Itzá's 'Mexicanized' architecture seems to be older than the corresponding architecture at Tula. The unanticipated results of the dating of Chichén Itzá and Tula cause many of the older theories explaining the similarities to be entirely discredited. More recent theories have incorporated age into their considerations.

There is no widely accepted explanation for how Tula came to mirror the Toltec architecture present in Chichén Itzá. However, a few theories do present arguments that propose Chichén Itzá's connection to the Toltec. The Maya at Chichén Itzá, who were the center of a great empire, traded with the Toltecs. It is known that the Chichén Itzá did have trade networks extending into the present-day areas of New Mexico and Arizona, because of certain commodities, such as turquoise mosaics, present in Chichén that can only be found in these far-off regions. It is theorized that the Maya, envious of Toltec culture, came to adopt certain aspects of them into certain buildings, while maintaining some pure Maya construction. Another theory, similar to Sylvanus Morley's years earlier, is that the people of Chichén Itzá were of two ethnicities: Toltec and Maya, and that this led to the duality of style within the site.

Rooted primarily in the seniority of Chichén Itzá is a modern-day counter-argument to the Tula's influence of the Maya of Chichén Itzá. Because of the greater age of Chichén Itzá, and the lack of direct evidence of Toltec control over Chichén, there is some argument that it was the Maya who were influencing the Toltecs. Despite the fairly concrete evidence of Chichén Itzá's seniority, this theory is not widely accepted. This is due in large part because the architecture of the Temple of the Warriors and other areas are of Toltec style, not Maya style. Thus, even if Chichén Itzá is a central influence for the construction Tula, and not the other way around, it can be argued that Chichén Itzá was still originally affected by the Toltecs, even if there is no evidence to support that theory.

While these and other hypotheses cannot be contradicted with known evidence, no evidence links the Toltecs and Chichén Itzá prior to the construction of the buildings that are the source of this controversy.

The fall of Chichén Itzá was approximately 800-1000 years ago. Because of this, information about Chichén Itzá is mostly drawn through the analysis of its art and architecture. This, and the scarcity of texts prior to the Spanish conquest of Mesoamerica, led to a lack of historical information about Chichén Itzá. The gaps in information that exist in the history both of Chichén and of Tula are often filled with speculative migrations, invasions, and other events. It is in large part because of this that no consensus can be drawn as to the reason for this connection. There are enough gaps in information that many different theories can 'answer' why there is this connection.

While the presence of a relationship is not under any dispute, the extent of the relationship between Chichén Itzá and Tula is entirely unknown. While buildings in each of the two sites may have intense similarities, and seem similar, this does not mean that each of the buildings in one site contained the same ritual significance as the other site's equivalent building. Not only the source of the relationship is in dispute, but its extent is equally unknown.

Chichén Itzá and a Century of Controversy

Chichén Itzá, perhaps more than any other Mesoamerican ruin, has been mired in controversy for many years. Francisco de Montejo y León, the Younger,[6] conquered the city in 1532 and renamed it *Ciudad Real*. Several months later the Maya rebelled and forced Montejo and his conquistadors out of the city, and eventually entirely out of Yucatán. When the conquest resumed several years later, the Montejo family instead took the Maya settlement of *T'ho*, renamed it Mérida. From there the subjugation of the remainder of the peninsula was based.

Chichén Itzá became part of a Spanish land grant, and by the 1580s was a cattle ranch. The ruins, for the most part, were ignored, both by the Spanish government and by the owners of the property, except as a source of stone for the hacienda buildings and as a place for cattle to forage.

In 1894 the United States Consul to Yucatán, Edward H. Thompson, purchased the Hacienda Chichén, including the ruins of Chichén Itzá. For the next 30 years Thompson explored the ruins, and his discoveries included an early dated carving on a lintel in the Temple of the Initial Series (Str. 5C4), and the excavation of several burials in the High Priest's Temple (*Osario*; Str. 3C1). Thompson is best remembered for dredging the Sacred Cenote (*Cenote Sagrado*) from 1904 to 1910, where he recovered artifacts of gold, copper, and carved jade, as well as examples of Maya cloth and wooden weapons. Thompson clandestinely shipped the bulk of the artifacts to the Peabody Museum of Archaeology and Ethnology at Harvard University. The disposition of these objects has remained in contention ever since. In the 1960s and 1970s the Peabody Museum returned two sets of artifacts, and in 2008 William Fash, then Director of the Peabody Museum, indicated he would support further returning a collection of jades. However, such a decision would require approval by the university officials (US Museum 2008). By 1926, Mexican federal authorities had charged Thompson with the theft of artifacts, and seized Hacienda Chichén. Thompson, who was in the United States at the time, never returned to Yucatán. He died in New Jersey in 1935. He wrote about his experiences in Yucatán in *People of the Serpent* (1932). His case finally reached the Mexican Supreme Court in 1944, which ruled that Thompson had broken no laws, and the property reverted to Thompson's heirs, who in turn sold the Hacienda Chichén to tourism entrepreneur Fernando Barbachano Peón (Usborne 2007). There have been other attempts to further recover artifacts from the Sacred Cenote, in 1961 and 1967. The first was sponsored by the National Geographic Society, and the second by private interests. Both projects were supervised by Mexico's Instituto Nacional de Antropologia e Historia (INAH). In addition, INAH has conducted ongoing efforts to excavate and restore other buildings at the site, including the *Osario* (Str. 3C1), *Akab D'zib* (Str. 4D1), and several structures in Chichén Viejo. In 2009 Mexican

[6] Francisco de Montejo the Younger, son of the Adelantado Francisco de Montejo (c. 1479-c. 1548), was a Spanish conquistador who was entrusted by his father with the conquest of the Maya of Yucatán. In 1542 he subdued the western part of the peninsula, founding Villa de San Francisco de Campeche, Mérida, and other settlements. After a general uprising had been quelled, he finally conquered the eastern portion in 1546.

archaeologists began excavations to investigate construction that predated El Castillo.

In 1923 the Mexican government awarded the Carnegie Institution of Washington a ten year permit to allow U.S. archaeologists to conduct excavation and restoration at Chichén Itzá (Weeks and Hill 2006:111). Through Thompson, the Carnegie Institution established its first head-quarters at Hacienda Chichén in 1923. Rustic cottages were built to house the archaeologists and their research teams. Carnegie researchers excavated and restored the Temple of the Warriors (Str. 2D8), the Caracol (Str. 3C15), and other major structures. At the same time the Mexican government archaeologists excavated and restored El Castillo (Str. 2D5) and the Great Ball Court (Str. 2D1) (Weeks and Hill 2006:577-653).

In the early 1920s a group of Yucatecans businessmen, led by writer and photographer Francisco Gómez Rul, began working toward expanding tourism to Yucatán. They urged Governor Felipé Carrillo Puerto to build roads to the more famous site areas, including Chichén Itzá. In 1923, the highway to Chichén Itzá was officially opened. Gómez Rul published one of the first guidebooks to Yucatán and the ruins (1920).

Gómez Rul's son-in-law, Fernando Barbachano Peón, began the first official tourism business in Yucatán. He began in the 1920s by meeting steamship passengers at Progreso and convincing them to spend a week in Yucatán. In the mid-1920s Barbachano Peón persuaded Edward Thompson to sell five acres (20,000 m^2) next to Chichén Itzá for a hotel. In 1930 the Mayaland Hotel opened, just north of the Hacienda Chichén, which was now occupied by the archaeologists of the Carnegie Institution of Washington (Madeira 1931:108-109), and a few hundred meters from the monuments of El Castillo (Str. 2D5), Caracol (Str. 3C15), and the Temple of the Warriors (Str. 2D8). He and his wife, Carmen Gómez Rul de Barbachano, also built tourist lodges and hotels near the Maya site of Uxmal.

In 1944 Barbachano Peón purchased all of the Hacienda Chichén, including Chichén Itzá, from the heirs of Edward Thompson. About this time the Carnegie Institution completed its investigations at Chichén Itzá and abandoned the Hacienda Chichén, which Barbachano Peón turned into another seasonal hotel.

Over the years, the property has been passed down within the Barbachano family and was recently in the hands of three members. The very northern section, including the Sacred Well (Cenote Sagrado), was owned by Hans Jürgen Thies Barbachano, grandson of the former owner, Fernando Barbachano Gómez Rul; Fernando Barbachano Herrero, son of Fernando, owned the section that includes El Castillo (Str. 2D5) and the Great Ball Court (Str. 2D1). This is the part that includes the Mayaland Resort; and Carmen Barbachano Gómez Rul owned the southern portion of Chichén Itzá, including Chichén Viejo. She is the sister of Fernando, the aunt of Fernando Barbachano Herrero, and the great aunt of Hans Thies Barbachano. She also owns the Hacienda Chichén, which is managed by her niece, Belisa Barbachano Herrero.

In 1972, Mexico enacted the *Ley Federal Sobre Monumentos y Zonas Arqueologicas, Artisticas e Historicas* that put all the nation's prehispanic monuments, including those at Chichén Itzá, under federal ownership (Breglia 2006:45-46). With the touristic development of the Cancún resort area to the east, Chichén Itzá experienced a massive increase of visitors each year.

Designated a UNESCO World Heritage Site in 1988, Chichén Itzá has become the second most visited of Mexico's archaeological sites (*Compendio* 2006). In 2007, El Castillo was named one of the New Seven Wonders of the World after a worldwide vote. Soon thereafter, debate was renewed in Mexico over the ownership of the site. During much of the tenure of Barbachano ownership, the relationship between the owners and the government was somewhat problematic. The Instituto Nacional de Antropologia y Historia (INAH), the federal government's agency that oversees archaeological zones, managed the site and conducted archaeological investigations. The Barbachano family was permitted to operate the Mayaland and the Hacienda Chichén as profit-making tourist enterprises.

In 2007 the federal government investigated taking the property through expropriation, the same process that was used to seize the oil industries in Mexico from foreign interests in the 1930s, and a move which deterred foreign investment in Mexico until NAFTA. By law, the federal government in an expropriation can only pay what the property is valued. Chichén Itzá is officially listed as "agricultural" land, and valued at $5 million Mexican (approximately $400,000 US).

Discord broke out sometime after the turn of the century when state militia prevented Barbachano Gómez Rul at gunpoint from bringing guests into the archaeological zone. By that time relations between the state and Barbachano had already degraded as Barbachano was criticizing the governor, Patricio Patrón Laviada, in the press. The state began withholding his percentage of ticket receipts. In retaliation, the Barbachano took over operation of two large *palapas*[7] inside the archaeological zone. For years the families of the men who provided security and maintenance at Chichén Itzá, most if not all descended from the indigenous Maya, had operated these *palapas*, selling snacks and trinkets to tourists visiting the site.

With the *palapas* at Chichén Itzá now run by Barbachano's organization, the Maya vendors invaded the archaeological zone. But this time the president of

[7] A *palapa* (a Spanish word of Mayan origin, meaning "pulpous leaf") is an open-sided dwelling with a thatched roof made of dried palm leaves. It is very useful in hot weather and common in Mexican beaches. *Palapas* are commonly used to shelter vendors at Chichén Itzá and other touristic sites.

Mexico was Vicente Fox Quesada, the first opposition candidate to win election since the Revolution of 1910. He had won, in part, on his pledge to respect indigenous rights. This time there would be no army to drive the Maya out of Chichén Itzá. The leaders of the vendors announced they had organized into a union called New Kukulcan. They made numerous demands, one of them being the "expropriation" of Chichén Itzá.

In 2006, the federal government had appropriated $14 million Mexican to enable INAH to purchase land under archaeological sites. The Instituto Nacional de Antropologia e Historia made a formal offer for Chichén Itzá of $8 million Mexican, but received no response. Fernando Barbachano Gómez Rul died the same year, and he had deeded his Chichén Itzá property to his grandson, Hans Jürgen Thies Barbachano. Since the passing of his grandfather, Thies Barbachano took several controversial steps to protect his property rights at Chichén Itzá. He installed two small trailers at the site to sell snacks to tourists; he began charging the vendors every day to enter the archaeological zone to sell their wares; there were charges that his *palapa* was discharging septic waste into the Cenote Sagrado, which, if true, was actually a practice that predated his management of them. As a result of these actions and others, the Barbachano name began appearing on banners hoisted by the vendors to protest what they perceive as oppression. The voices grew louder for expropriation.

On March 29, 2010, Hans Jürgen Thies Barbachano, owner of 200 acres upon which some of the world's most recognizable monuments rest, El Castillo, Great Ball Court, Caracol, Temple of Warriors, agreed to sell his property to the state of Yucatán for $220 million Mexican ($17.6 million US). The Chichén Itzá transaction ends more than a decade of controversy between the property's owners, the state and federal governments, and various stakeholder groups, all of which have been vying for control of the restored ancient city.[8]

Guidebook to the Ruins at Chichén Itzá

On February 2, 1948, nearly seven months before his death in Santa Fe, New Mexico, Sylvanus G. Morley wrote a letter to F.C. Fassett, editor for publications at the Carnegie Institution of Washington, summarizing his publication legacy. Morley wrote:

> *I have gradually formed the ambition to leave behind as my published contribution to the [Carnegie] Institution a trilogy of books on the Maya inscriptions: 1. The Inscriptions of Copán, published in 1920; 2. The Inscriptions of Petén, published in 1937-1938; and 3. All other Maya inscriptions, a project now abandoned because [Alfred V.] Kidder informs me that the President [of CIW, Vannevar Bush] is against the publication of large monographs. Much as I regret this, I have abandoned this subject. In addition to the foregoing, I have contemplated four popular guidebooks as follows: 1. Guide Book to the Ruins of Quirigua, published and I understand already in its second edition; 2. Guide Book to the Ruins of Chichén Itzá; 3. Guide Book to the Ruins of Copán, and 4. Guide Book to the Ruins of Uxmal, Kabah, and Labna.*

The *Guide Book to the Ruins of Quirigua* was published in 1935 by the Carnegie Institution of Washington as its Supplementary Publication, 16. In 1946 Gustav Strömsvik, who had worked at Copán for decades, published *Guia de las ruinas de Copán* (Tegucigalpa: Talleres Tipo-Lito Ariston), and the following year an English language translation, *Guide Book to the Ruins of Copán*, was issued by the Carnegie Institution of Washington as its Publication, 577. The Copán guide book was reprinted again in 1952.

Morley's series of guide books to Chichén Itzá, and Uxmal, Kabah, and Labna, were never published. However, Morley did prepare a draft of a *Guide Book to the Ruins of Chichén Itzá* in 1946, which has since languished in the archaeological archives of the Carnegie Institution at the Peabody Museum of Archaeology and Ethnology, Harvard University, in Cambridge, Massachusetts. Although dated and probably considered quaint by modern standards, Morley's guide book to Chichén Itzá, remains the only synthesis of the site based on almost 20 years of excavation, consolidation, and restoration of the ruins by the project director.

In the 1940s Kidder pressed upon Morley the idea of completing the remaining work on inscriptions not covered in the Copán and Petén volumes, but in February of 1948, Morley abandoned the project after he realized that the Carnegie Institution was unwilling to publish it. In the interim he made progress on one of his proposed guides. Morley's rationale for publishing a guidebook to Chichén Itzá is clear. In a letter dated June 2, 1948, to F.G. Fassett at the Carnegie Institution in Washington, DC, Morley made his argument for publishing the volume:

> *So far as I know, a chronological summary of the [Carnegie] Institution's Chichén Itzá Project has never appeared and indeed its yearly chronicle has only been covered in our Year Books which have a limited circulation ... after the hundreds of thousands of dollars the Institution has spent at Chichén Itzá it seems only fair to me that the resulting guide book on this site should give us due credit for all we did there.*

To this he added, "I am convinced that a guide book ... will have a considerable demand, especially among the thousands of tourists who visit Yucatán annually."

He submitted the manuscript of the guide to Chichén Itzá about three months before his death, and was spared the

[8] In addition to the sources given, further information on Morley, the Maya, and the litigation over Chichén Itzá may be found on various websites, including http://en.wikipedia.org/wiki/Sylvanus_Morley; http://en.wikipedia.org/wiki/Maya_civilization; http://en.wikipedia.org/wiki/Chichen_Itzá; and http://carnegiescience.edu/auburn_university_montgomery_carnegie_explorer_0.

knowledge of its fate. Kidder, Fassett, and Pollock could not bring themselves to publish it because the weaknesses were obvious. The text was repetitious, it was filled with unnecessary descriptions, and the author injected opinions that other scholars did not accept, a practice not consistent with a guidebook (Brunhouse 1971).

Morley died on September 2, 1948, before any decision had been made about his book. In a letter dated September 17, 1948, to F.G. Fassett, Alfred V. Kidder expressed his thoughts about Morley. He writes:

> *He [Morley] was a very remarkable person and did more to advance the study of his beloved Maya than almost anyone else. His death was a great blow to me personally as we had been close friends and associates for forty-one years. His enthusiasm for the Maya was unbounded and I know that as soon as he had got by St. Peter he made a bee-line for the Maya quarter.*

The decision whether to publish the book posthumously was based on the critical evaluations by Fassett, an editor at the Carnegie Institution, Kidder, emeritus director of the Division of Historical Research, H.E.D. Pollock, then current director of the Division of Historical Research, and some input from Karl Ruppert, an archaeologist who had worked for Morley at Chichén Itzá since the 1925. After reviewing the manuscript Kidder was concerned that the historical section repeated what Morley had written erroneously in his *Ancient Maya*. Karl Ruppert, a Carnegie archaeologist who was at the time working in Chichén Itzá, read the sections on the architecture and noted that these were full of mistakes and other errors, and added that many of Morley's insights about the architecture at the site would be obvious to visitors. Fassett added that "the writing is terribly repetitious." Kidder's final observation to Fassett was recommending "the shelving of Morley's last piece of work ... it is not worthy either of him or the Institution." Fassett believed the manuscript to require a thorough revision, if not a complete rewrite, and the Chichén guide was shelved for the time being. There was full agreement among Kidder, Pollock, and Fassett that the Chichén guidebook should be written by someone other than Morley with a statement that it is based on materials prepared by Morley.

Our interest in publishing Morley's manuscript so many years after its completion was based on several factors: it was Morley's last written work; it was the only synthesis of Morley's work at Chichén Itzá; and, quite simply, it is a work important to the history of the study of Maya archaeology. Several modifications have been made to the manuscript. We have attempted to leave as much of the original text as written by Morley. Sections that have been corrected by more recent research are amended and included as notes. Repetitious text has been removed, and obvious errors in spelling and punctuation have been corrected. All distance measurements in feet have been converted to the metric system, the present standard. Chronology has been modified from AD/BC to BCE/CE. Notes have been added by the editors [ed] to explain or amplify statements in the manuscript. In addition, written commentary on the original manuscript by Karl Ruppert (KR) has been included as notes.[9]

Unpublished

American Philosophical Society, Philadelphia, PA
- Sylvanus Griswold Morley diaries, 1905-1947. Mss B.M828.

Carnegie Institution of Washington, Archives, Washington, DC
- Letter, F.G. Fassett, to S.G. Morley, February 26, 1948
- Letter, F.G. Fassett to A.V. Kidder, October 8, 1948
- Letter, F.G. Fassett to A.V. Kidder, October 13, 1948
- Letter, A.V. Kidder to F.G. Fassett, September 12, 1948
- Letter, S.G. Morley to F.G. Fassett, February 13, 1948
- Letter, S.G. Morley to F.G. Fassett, June 4, 1948
- Letter, A.V. Kidder to F.G. Fassett, October 18, 1948

Massachusetts Historical Society, Boston, MA
- Charles P. Bowditch Family Papers, 1849-1952. Ms. N-846.

Peabody Museum Archives, Harvard University, Cambridge, MA
- Chichén Itzá Expedition Records: A Finding Aid, 2009. No. 47-52.

Records of the Archaeology Division of the Carnegie Institution of Washington, 1919-1958. No. 58-34.

Published

BARRERA RUBIO, A. 1992. *Coloquio en torno a la obra de un Mayista: Sylvanus G. Morley, 1883-1948.* Mexico: Instituto Nacional de Antropología e Historia; Mérida: Universidad Autónoma de Yucatán.

BEYER, H. 1937. Studies on the Inscriptions of Chichén Itzá. *Contributions to American Archaeology* 4(21):29-175. Washington, DC: Carnegie Institution of Washington.

BOLLES, J.S. 1976. *Las Monjas: A Major Pre-Mexican Architectural Complex at Chichén Itzá.* Norman: University of Oklahoma Press.

BRAINERD, G.W. 1958. *The Archaeological Ceramics of Yucatán.* Anthropological Records, 19. Berkeley: University of California, Berkeley.

---

[9] This project has taken a long time and benefitted from many people along its journey. Permission to prepare the manuscript for publicatioin was given by Patricia Kervick, Peabody Museum Archives, Harvard University. Patricia Craig and Tina McDowell, archivists at the Carnegie Insctitutioin of Science, Washington, DC, have been suuportive of all our efforts to republish Carnegie Institution Maya material for another generation of students and scholars. The photograph of the 1925 field season staff was genrously provided by Dr. Terance L. Winemiller, Auburn University Carnegie Explorer, and Carnegie Institution for Science. Jacquelyn Battel, University of Pennsylvania Museum Library considerally improved the image quality of the photographs included in Morley's manuscript. These were discovered by Nuria Matarredona in the Carnegie Institution archives in Wsashington, DC.

Breglia, L. 2006. *Monumental Ambivalence: The Politics of Heritage*. Austin: University of Texas Press.

Brunhouse, R.L. 1971. *Sylvanus G. Morley and the World of the Ancient Mayas*. Norman: University of Oklahoma Press.

Carnegie Institution for Science. http://carnegiescience.edu/

Chichén Itzá World Heritage Site. http://.whc.unesco.org/en/list/483.

Coe, M.D. 1999. *Breaking the Maya Code*. Rev. ed. New York: Thames and Hudson.

Coggins, C.C. 1992. *Artifacts from the Cenote of Sacrifice, Chichén Itzá, Yucatan: Textiles, Basketry, Stone, Bone, Shell, Ceramics, Wood, Copal, Rubber, Other Organic Materials, and Mammalian Remains*. Memoirs, 10(3). Cambridge: Peabody Museum of Archaeology and Ethnology, Harvard University.

Coggins, C.C., and O.C. Shane. 1984. *Cenote of Sacrifice: Maya Treasures from the Sacred Well at Chichén Itzá*. Austin: University of Texas Press.

Compendio Estadistico del Turismo en Mexico, 2006. Mexico: Secretaria de Turismo, 2006. Mexican State of Yucatán buys archaeological site from private landowner, 2011. http://www.artdaily.com/index.asp?int_new=37171&int_sec=11&int_modo=1.

Fry, S. 2008. The Casa Colorada Ball Court: INAH Turns Mounds into Monuments. http://www.americanegypt.com/feature/casacolorada.htm.

Gómez Rul, F. 1920. *Hand Book of Yucatán*. Mérida: Gamboa Guzmán.

Harris, C.H., and L.R. Sadler. 2003. *Archaeologist Was a Spy: Sylvanus G. Morley and the Office of Naval Intelligence*. Albuquerque: University of New Mexico Press.

Hooton, E.A. 1940. Skeletons from the Cenote of Sacrifice at Chichén Itzá. In *The Maya and Their Neighbors*. C. Hay, ed. pp. 272-280. New York: Appleton-Century.

Knorosov. I.V. 1967. *Selected Chapters From The Writing of the Maya Indians*. Sophie D. Coe, ed. Russian Translation Series, 4. Cambridge: Peabody Museum of Archaeology and Ethnology, Harvard University.

Lothrop, S.K. 1952. *Metals from the Cenote of Sacrifice, Chichén Itzá, Yucatan*. Memoirs, 10(2). Cambridge: Peabody Museum of Archaeology and Ethnology, Harvard University.

Madeira, P.C. 1931. An Aerial Expedition to Central America. *Museum Journal* 22(2):93-153.

Miller Llana, S. 2007. Ownership Fight Erupts Over Maya Ruins. http://www.csmonitor.com/2007/21017.p.20S01-woam.html.

Morley, S.G. 1935. *Guide Book to the Ruins of Quiriguá*. Supplementary Publication, 16. Washington, DC: Carnegie Institution of Washington.

Morley, S.G. 1946. *The Ancient Maya*. Stanford: Stanford University Press.

Morley, S.G. 1947a. *The Ancient Maya*. Stanford: Stanford University Press.

Morley, S.G. 1947b. *La Civilización Maya*. México: Fondo de Cultura Económica.

Morley, S.G. 1956. *The Ancient Maya*. Stanford: Stanford University Press.

Morley, S.G. 1961. *La Civilización Maya*. México: Fondo de Cultura Económica.

Morley, S.G. 1963. *The Ancient Maya*. Stanford: Stanford University Press.

Morley, S.G. 1972. *La Civilización Maya*. México: Fondo de Cultura Económica.

Morley, S.G., and G.W. Brainerd. 1968. *The Ancient Maya*. Stanford: Stanford University Press.

Morley, S.G., and G.W. Brainerd. 1987. *La Civilización Maya*. México: Fondo de Cultura Económica.

Morley, S.G., and R.J. Sharer. 1994a. *The Ancient Maya*. Stanford: Stanford University Press.

Morley, S.G., and R.J. Sharer. 1994b. *La Civilización Maya*. México: Fondo de Cultura Económica.

Morley, S.G., and R.J. Sharer. 1998. *La Civilización Maya*. México: Fondo de Cultura Económica.

Morley, S.G., G.W. Brainerd, and R.J. Sharer. 1983. *The Ancient Maya*. Stanford: Stanford University Press.

Morleyana: Collection of Writings in Memoriam Sylvanus Griswold Morley, 1883-1948. Santa Fe: School of American Research; Museum of New Mexico, 1950.

Morris, E.H. 1931. *The Temple of the Warriors; The Adventure of Exploring and Restoring a Masterpiece of Native American Architecture in the Ruined Maya City of Chichén Itzá, Yucatán*. New York, London: C. Scribner's Sons.

Morris, E.H. 1980. *Temple of the Warriors: The Adventure of Exploring and Restoring a Masterpiece of Native American Architecture in the Ruined Maya City of Chichén Itzá, Yucatán*. New York: AMS Press.

Morris, E.H., J. Charlot, and A.A. Morris. 1931. *The Temple of the Warriors at Chichén Itzá, Yucatán*. Publication, 406. Washington, DC: Carnegie Institution of Washington.

Ownership Fight Erupts Over Maya Ruins, 2007. http://csmonitor.com/2007/1017/p20s01-woqm.html.

Pollock, H.E.D. 1936. The Casa Redonda at Chichén Itzá, Yucatán. *Carnegie Institution of Washington, Contributions to American archaeology* 3(17):129-154.

Pollock, H.E.D. 1950. Dynamic Leader of the Chichén Itzá Project. In *Morleyana: A Collection of Writings in Memoriam, Sylvanus Griswold Morley 1883-1948*. Arthur J.O. Anderson, ed. pp. 203-207. Santa Fe:

School of American Research and the Museum of New Mexico.

POLLOCK, H.E.D. 1957. Review: The Ancient Maya. *American Anthropologist* 59(3):567-568.

PROSKOURIAKOFF, T. 1974. *Jades from the Cenote of Sacrifice, Chichén Itzá, Yucatan*. Memoirs, 10(1). Cambridge: Peabody Museum of Archaeology and Ethnology, Harvard University.

RAMÍREZ AZNAR, L. 1990. *El saqueo del cenote sagrado de Chichén Itz'a*. Mérida: Editorial Dane.

RUPPERT, K. 1931b. Temple of the Wall Panels, Chichén Itzá. *Carnegie Institution of Washington, Contributions to American archaeology* 1(3):117-140.

RUPPERT, K. 1935. *The Caracol at Chichén Itzá, Yucatan*. Publication, 454. Washington, DC: Carnegie Institution of Washington.

RUPPERT, K. 1943. Mercado, Chichén Itzá, Yucatán. *Contributions to American Anthropology and History* 8(43):223-260. Washington, DC: Carnegie Institution of Washington.

RUPPERT, K. 1952. *Chichén Itzá: Architectural Notes and Plans*. Publication, 595. Washington, DC: Carnegie Institution of Washington.

RUPPERT, K. and A.L. SMITH. 1955. Two New Gallery-Patio Type Structures at Chichén Itzá. *Notes on Middle American Archaeology and Ethnology* 5(122):59-62. Washington, DC: Carnegie Institution of Washington.

SHARER, R.J., and L.P. TRAXLER. 2006. *The Ancient Maya*. Stanford: Stanford University Press.

SIVERT, A.K. 1992. *Maya Ceremonial Specialization: Lithic Tools from the Sacred Cenote at Chichén Itzá, Yucatán*. Monographs in World Archaeology, 12. Madison: Prehistory Press.

SMITH, R.M. 1971. *The Pottery of Mayapán; Including Studies of Ceramic Material from Uxmal, Kabah, and Chichén Itzá*. Papers, 66. Cambridge, MA: Peabody Museum of Archaeology and Ethnology, Harvard University.

STEVENSON, M. 2008. US Museum head says Mexico should get Mayan jade. http://www.usatrpoday.com/news/topstories/2008-11-18-2204655354_x.htm

STRÖMSVIK, G. 1931. Notes on the Metates of Chichén Itzá, Yucatán. *Contributions to American Archaeology* 1(4):141-157. Washington, DC: Carnegie Institution of Washington.

STROMSVIK, G. 1937. Notes on Metates from Calakmul, Campeche, and from the Mercado, Chichén Itzá, Yucatan. *Contributions to American Archaeology* 3(16):121-128. Washington, DC: Carnegie Institution of Washington.

STRÖMSVIK, G. 1946. *Guía de las ruinas de Copán*. Tegucigalpa: Talleres Tipo-Lito Ariston.

STROMSVIK, G. 1947. *Guide Book to the Ruins of Copán*. Publication, 577. Washington, DC: Carnegie Institution of Washington.

STROMSVIK, G. 1952. *Guide Book to the Ruins of Copán*. Washington, DC: Carnegie Institution of Washington.

TEEPLE, J.E. 1931. *Maya Astronomy*. Contributions to American Archaeology 1(2):29-115. Washington, DC: Carnegie Institution of Washington.

THOMPSON, E.H. 1932. *People of the Srerpent: Life and Adventuire among the Mayas*. Boston: Houghton Mifflin.

THOMPSON, E.H. 1938. *The High Priest's Grave, Chichén Itzá, Yucatan, Mexico*. Fieldiana: Anthropology, 27(1). Chicago: Field Museum of Natural History.

THOMPSON, J.E.S. 1950. *Maya Archaeologist*. Norman: University of Oklahoma Press.

TOZZER, A.M. 1957. *Chichén Itzá and Its Cenote of Sacrifice: A Comparative Study of Contemporaneous Maya and Toltec*. Memoirs, 11, 12. Cambridge: Peabody Museum of Archaeology and Ethnology, Harvard University.

USBORNE, D. 2007. Mexican Standoff: the Battle of Chichén Itzá. http://www.Independent.co.uk/news/world/americas/mexican-standoff-the-battle-of-Chichén-Itzá-399310.html.

VOLTA, B., T.E. LEVY, and G.E. BRASWELL. 2009. The Virtual Chichén Itzá Project: Modelling an Ancient Maya City in Google SketchUp. http://antiquity.ac.uk/antiquityNew/projgall/levy321/.

WEEKS, J.M. and J. HILL. 2006. *Carnegie Maya: The Carnegie Institution of Washington Maya Research Program, 1913-1957*. Boulder: University Press of Colorado.

Figure 0.1. Carnegie Institution Staff at Chichén Itzá, 1925. From left, Earl H. Morris, Ann Axtell Morris, Karl Ruppert, Sylvanus G. Morley, Edith H. Bayles (Ricketson), Oliver G. Ricketson, and Jean Charlot (courtesy Carnegie Institution for Science and Auburn University Carnegie Explorer)

Chapter 1.
LOCATION, DISCOVERY, AND EXPLORATION OF CHICHÉN ITZÁ

The ruins of Chichén Itzá are located in the north central part of the peninsula of Yucatán (Fig. 1.1), more precisely in the municipality of Tinúm, Department of Valladolid, State of Yucatán, Mexico, at 20 degrees 41.0' north latitude, and 88 degrees 34.0' west longitude.

The northern half of the Yucatán peninsula is a flat, low, limestone plain with very little surface water, no rivers of any length, and only a few small lakes. There are several low ranges of limestone hills, rising in elevation from north to south, but never reaching higher than 150 m above sea level. This plain, in spite of its very shallow soil and ubiquitous outcropping of the native limestone, supports a dense and impenetrable growth of low trees and thorny bushes.

The water supply in ancient times, as well as it still is today, was derived for the most part, from large natural wells, formed by cave-ins which have occurred in the surface, or immediately sub-surface limestone, thus exposing the general subterranean water-table which everywhere underlies the peninsula. These great natural wells, called *cenotes* in Yucatec, vary in depth from 5 to 45 m; growing deeper as the surface stratum itself becomes thicker, proceeding from north to south, and in size from small holes in the surface-crust top great irregularly shaped openings, sometimes 60 m or more in diameter. In addition to the *cenotes*, the ancient Maya had wells and many cisterns called *chultunes*, artificially hollowed out in the limestone and, at a few cities, notably Uxmal, great man-made reservoirs.

The climate is one of the most delightful in the world, warm and mild in the winter, and nor excessively hot in the summer. There are two seasons, the dry and the rainy, the former runs from December to May, and the latter from May to December. The rainfall, like the elevation, also increases from north to south and, in the region of Chichén Itzá, averages 118 cm a year, most of which is concentrated in summer and early fall. A temperature record kept for the Carnegie Institution of Washington at Chichén Itzá from 1928 to 1938, showed extremes ranging from 39 degrees F in December to 107 degrees in May, with an average minimum temperature of 64 degrees F, and an average maximum of 91 degrees F, for the same period.

To this sunny, healthful region the Maya first brought their brilliant civilization, when they established themselves at Chichén Itzá in the early sixth century of the Christian era, while their descendants of the eleventh and twelfth centuries, developed the city into a sacred place, a center for pilgrimage from distant lands, and brought about the Maya Renaissance.

How to Reach Chichén Itzá[1]

A glance at the map in Figure 1.1 will immediately reveal that Mérida, the capital of Yucatán, stands at the aerial cross-roads of the Caribbean. Four air routes center at Mérida: one from the north, New Orleans; one from the east, Miami via Havana; one from the south, Central America and Guatemala City; and one from the west, Mexico City. The first three are operated by American World Airways and the last by the Compañia Mexicana de Aviación. These average more than ten flights daily. Flying time from New Orleans to Mérida is 3.5 hours; from Miami, five hours; from Guatemala City, 2.5 hours; and from Mexico City, 3.25 hours.

For the accommodation of travelers there are two first-class hotels in Mérida. The Hotel Mérida, a modern tourist hostelry, and the Hotel Itzá, a charming old Spanish palace, its face "lifted" with all the modern conveniences, as well as a number of other excellent hotels and pensions.

Chichén Itzá lies 125 km east-southeast of Mérida, with which it is connected by an excellent hard-surfaced, all-

[1] Morley's information on travel to Chichén Itzá is out-of-date and useless, but it does provide something of the travel conditions in the late 1930s and early 1940s [eds.].

Figure 1.1. Map of the Maya Region. Showing the location of Chichén Itzá [N. Matarredona]

weather highway. The Barbachano Tour Service maintains a service of automobiles and English-speaking guides for visiting the ruins, arrangements for trips to which may be made through the office of the Mayaland Tour Service in front of the Hotel Mérida in Mérida. In addition to this tourist agency there are many independent drivers with private cars for hire, and finally there are two public buses daily from Mérida and Chichén Itzá and return.

Mérida is possibly the most interesting city in Mexico. It was founded more than 500 years ago (January 6, 1542) by the conqueror of Yucatán Francisco de Montejo, and today is a fascinating blend of the Spanish colonial and modern against a strong Maya Indian background. The streets are spotless; the people, Yucatecans and Mayas, in their white or light colored clothing which always seems to be freshly laundered, are unusually friendly to foreigners, especially Americans; the old Spanish churches and palaces; the lofty Plateresque[2] cathedral, which was completed in 1598; the many beautiful parks and plazas, all combine to make the city an oasis of romantic charm and historic interest.

At Chichén Itzá there are two hotels: The Mayaland Lodge[3] and the less expensive Casa Victoria, the *fonda* or

[2] *Plateresque* (Spanish *plateresco*, "silversmith-like"), was the main architectural style in Spain during the late fifteenth and the sixteenth centuries, also used in Spain's American colonies. Cristóbal de Villalón first used the term in 1539 while comparing the richly ornamented facade of the Cathedral of León to a silversmith's intricate work [eds.].

[3] The Mayaland Lodge, now known as the Lodge at Chichén Itzá, offers the finest accommodations in the area. The lodge includes almost 40 bungalows clustered around swimming pools on 100 acres of landscaped gardens in the heart of the archaeological site. Other hotels and lodgings constructed since the 1940s include the following: Mayaland Hotel and Bungalows in the heart of the archaeological park, features extensive tropical gardens, three outdoor swimming pools, a hot tub, and spa treatments; Hotel Dolores Alba Chichén Itzá, a bungalow complex with two outdoor pools located five minute

inn of Doña Victoria Manjarrez de Marrufo. The former, operated by the Mayaland Tours, offers a superior tourist camp type of accommodations, a large central building with restaurant, office, lounge, gift-shop, post-office, some private rooms, and a number of detached cottages, each named after one of principal, ancient Maya cities: Chichén Itzá, Uxmal, Palenque, Mayapán, etc. It is necessary to make reservations for the Mayaland Lodge in Mérida at the offices of the Barbachano Tour Services, before going out to Chichén Itzá.

The inn of Doña Victoria Manjerrez is less expensive but equally comfortable and clean; the type of accommodation offered here is more Yucatecan than American in character, but is equally charming and comfortable.

The best months to visit Yucatán are December, January, and February. November is still apt to be somewhat rainy and by March the days are getting very warm. The summer months are more humid and rainy; but since the rains are usually confined to afternoon showers the summer also is an excellent time to visit Yucatán.

First Mention of Chichén Itzá in Modern Times and Its Post-Conquest History: 1532-1846

The first mention of Chichén Itzá in modern times is toward the end of 1532, or early in 1533, when Francisco de Montejo, the Younger, founded a royal city there. At that time the region around Chichén Itzá was occupied by a Maya group, called the *Cupules*. Montejo subdued the Cupules late in 1532 and divided them among his Spanish soldiers; the Maya were so numerous that each soldier was allotted the services of between 2,000 and 3,000 of them.

The Cupules did not take kindly to these exactions and the forced labor they were obliged to render the Spaniards, and about the middle of 1533, together with all the surrounding groups, they rose against their European oppressors and blockaded the small Spanish garrison in the newly founded royal city at Chichén Itzá.

Montejo, seeing that the countryside was thoroughly roused against him, decided to withdraw from Chichén Itzá, but the Maya so closely invested the Spanish camp that he was obliged to resort to a trick in order to make good his escape. An early chronicler describes his stratagem in the following words:

> *Finally one night they abandoned the town, leaving a dog attached to the clapper of a bell, and a little bread placed at one side so that he could not reach it; and the same day they wearied the Maya with skirmishes, so that they should not follow them. The dog rang the bell in his effort to reach the bread, which greatly astonished the Maya, who thought the Spaniards wished to attack them, later when they learned how they had been tricked they resolved to look for the Spaniards in all directions, as they did not know which road they had taken. And those who had taken the same road overtook the Spaniards, shouting loudly as at people who were running away because of which of the six horsemen awaited them in an open place and speared many. One of the Maya seized a horse by the leg and felled it as though it were sheep.*

As a result of his victory over a coalition of the western Maya in the summer of 1541, Montejo finally broke the will of native resistance in the west and, as already noted, founded the Very Loyal and Noble City of Mérida, the Spanish capital of the province of Yucatán on January 6, 1542, the Day of the Three Kings [*Dia de los Tres Magos*; Feast of the Epiphany]. And four years later, through a victory over a coalition of the eastern Maya chieftains, he finally brought the entire northern half of the Yucatán peninsula under the domination of the Spanish crown.

The first description of the ruins of Chichén Itzá is from Fray Diego de Landa (1941), the second Bishop of Yucatán, who wrote his famous *Relación de las cosas de Yucatán* in 1556; this is the Rosetta Stone of modern Maya research. Landa mentions the Castillo, the two dance platforms north and northwest of it, and the Sacred Cenote, or Well of Sacrifice. Landa has since left us the two earliest known maps of Yucatán, as well as the earliest known plan of a building at Chichén Itzá, i.e., that of the Castillo.

Fray Diego López de Cogolludo, another Franciscan priest, in his *Historia de Yucathan*, written almost a century later (1656), has left another early description of the site; although less complete than that of Landa, it gives additional important pre-conquest history and information (Lopez de Cogulludo 1867-1868).

That the *hacienda* of Chichén, on which the ruins of Chichén Itzá are located, was a flourishing cattle-ranch as early as the third decade of the eighteenth century, is proved by three different lines of evidence: 1. The title papers of the hacienda itself begin with the year 1734; 2. A coin of King Charles II of Spain minted that year was found in the garden of the hacienda during its occupation by the Carnegie Institution of Washington as headquarters for its archaeological staff; 3. The architecture of the sacristy of the church in the nearby

automobile drive from Chichén Itzá; Hotel Chichén Itzá, located in the village of Piste, is within walking distance of the ruins; Villas Arqueologicas Chichén Itzá, is located in nearby Tinúm. The Casa Mango is located 15 minutes' walk from the main plaza at Valladolid and 23.9 miles from Chichén Itzá; Hacienda Chichén Resort and Yaxkin Spa is located 300 m from the southeast entrance to Chichén Itzá. Hotel Okaan is situated 10 minutes' drive from the ruins and includes a spa and meditation area, as well as an outdoor pool. Real Mayab is set between Chichén Itzá and the colonial city of Valladolid, and offers a craft center, outdoor swimming pool, and extensive gardens with hammocks. Lemurian Embassy Eco Retreat Chichén Itzá is located at Tibolón, 16 miles from Chichén Itzá and features on-site yoga classes, temazcal treatments, and free coffee; Casa de los Pianos is in Uaymá, 16 miles from Chichén Itzá, offers air-conditioned rooms and a roof terrace with a BBQ, bar, views of the local parish church. Hacienda San Miguel, also located in Uaymá, is an historic building with an outdoor pool [eds.].

village of Piste, only two miles distant, has an inscription presenting this same year.

During the War of the Castes,[4] which devastated Yucatán a little more than a century later (1846-1847), between the Maya and the Spaniards, the hacienda of Chichén was seized by the Maya, and the Spanish owners, the Arce family, were obliged to flee to Mérida. The hacienda remained abandoned, with its buildings partly destroyed and roofless for another half century until it was purchased in the 1890s by Edward H. Thompson, then United States consul at Progresso, Yucatán.

Modern Study and Exploration

Although Thompson did not purchase the hacienda until the early nineties of the nineteenth century, the 50 years previous to his having acquired the property witnessed sporadic and unrelated attempts to explore this famous group of ruins.

To John Lloyd Stephens,[5] the American diplomat, traveler, and amateur archaeologist, should go credit for first having brought the ruins of Chichén Itzá to the attention of the outside world. Stephens, with the English artist Frederick Catherwood, first visited the site in 1842. Stephens' account of his visit to Yucatán (1841, 1843) and his earlier travels in Central America in 1839 and 1840, illustrated with Catherwood's drawings of the ruins of both regions, still remain, more than 100 years later, the most delightful book ever written about the Maya area.

The next traveler to leave an account of his visit was the French archaeologist, Claude Joseph Désiré Charnay,[6] who visited the Maya area several times between 1857 and 1882. Charnay's record of his travels in Yucatán is interesting, but adds nothing new to our knowledge of Chichén Itzá, and is about what might be expected from the pen of a rather pompous, French, mid-Victorian, amateur archaeologist.

Augustus LePlongeon,[7] another Frenchman, and his young English wife, visited Chichén Itzá in 1878 and practiced the first known excavations there in the two dance platforms north and northwest respectively of the Castillo. In the hearting of one of these he discovered the first and best preserved of the more than a dozen so-called Chac Mool figures that have been found at Chichén Itzá up to the present time. The Chac Mool found by Le Plongeon is now in the National Museum of Anthropology and History at Mexico City.

LePlongeon's conclusions about Chichén Itzá, and indeed about the whole Maya civilization, are so highly fanciful that they have been universally rejected. For example, he argued the Maya were the descendants of the fabled Atlantis and that the culture of ancient Egypt was founded 11,000 years ago by Maya emigrants from Yucatán (Le Plongeon 1896).

In 1892 Thompson did a little digging at Chichén Itzá to secure material for the World Columbian Exposition held at Chicago in 1893. His most important discovery was made in the pyramid called the High Priest's Grave where he found a series of five or six burials of high ranking personages, judging from the jade objects and pearls associated with the burials. These materials are now at the Chicago Museum of Natural History (i.e., Columbian Museum of Chicago or more recently, Field Museum of Natural History).

In 1895 William Henry Holmes,[8] Head Curator of Anthropology at the United States National Museum, visited Chichén Itzá on another expedition for the Field Columbian Museum (now the Chicago Museum of Natural History) and he has left us an excellent preliminary report on the ruins (Holmes 1895-1897), including one of his admirable panoramic sketches of the site, which he made long before the days of airplanes and aerial photography.

Big Four of Chichén Itzá Exploration

Easily the Big Four of Chichén Itzá exploration are, in order of their work at the site: 1. Alfred P. Maudslay in 1899; 2. E.H. Thompson, Representing the Peabody Museum of American Archaeology and Ethnology, at Harvard University, 1904-1907, 1910; 3. The Mexican government, 1906 forward); and 4. The Carnegie Institution of Washington, 1923-1940.

Alfred P. Maudslay, 1889

The English explorer and traveler Alfred P. Maudslay[9] spent five months at Chichén Itzá in 1889, leaving behind him, a monumental record of his visit to the site in the

[4] War of the Castes (1847-1901) was a rebellion by the indigenous Maya people of Yucatán against the population of European descent, who held political and economic control over the region. A lengthy war ensued between the non-Maya forces in the north-west of the Yucatán and the independent Maya in the south-east. It officially ended with the occupation of the Maya capital of Chan Santa Cruz by the Mexican army in 1901, although skirmishes with villages and small settlements that refused to acknowledge Mexican control continued for more than a decade [eds.].

[5] John Lloyd Stephens (1805-1852) was an American explorer, writer, and diplomat. He was important in the rediscovery of Maya civilization and in the planning of the Panama railroad [eds.].

[6] Claude-Joseph Désiré Charnay (1828-1915) was a French traveler and early archaeologist known for his explorations in Mexico and Central America. He was a pioneer in the use of photography to document his discoveries at sites such as Yaxchilan [eds.].

[7] Augustus LePlongeon (1825-1908) was a British-American photographer and antiquarian who studied ancient Maya ruins on the peninsula of Yucatán. LePlongeon proposed that the ancient Maya had been in touch with the lost continent of Atlantis and were ancestral to ancient Egyptian civilization. Morley identifies LePlongeon as French. However, he was born on the Isle of Jersey, officially the bailiwick of Jersey, a British Crown dependency [eds.].

[8] William Henry Holmes (1846-1933) was an American explorer, anthropologist, archaeologist, artist, scientific illustrator, cartographer, geologist, museum curator at the Field Museum of Natural History and the United States National Museum, and director of the Bureau of American Ethnology and the National Gallery of Art [eds.].

[9] Alfred P. Maudslay (1850-1931) was a British colonial diplomat, explorer, and archeologist. He was one of the first Europeans in the modern study of Maya ruins [eds.].

form of photographs, maps, plans, molds of the sculptures and hieroglyphic inscriptions, the first serious scientific study ever made of Chichén Itzá (Maudslay 1995-1902).

E.H. Thompson, 1904-1907, 1910

In 1906 E.H. Thompson[10] began dredging the Sacred Cenote, or Well of Sacrifice, at Chichén Itzá. This highly successful operation was inspired by the following passage to be found in Bishop Landa's *Relación de las Cosas de Yucatán*, written in 1566:

> *Into this well they have had, and then [middle 1500s] had the custom of throwing men alive, as a sacrifice to the gods in times of drought, and they believed that they did not die though they never saw them again. They also threw into it many other things, like precious stones and things that they prized, and so if this country had had gold, it would be this well that would have the greater part of it, so great was the devotion which the Maya showed for it.*

Acting on this clue Thompson, then owner of the hacienda of Chichén, began dredging the Well of Sacrifice with a small orange-sector dredge and a hand-winch. Thompson tried using a power-winch but the vibration of its motor shook loose more dust from the sides of the cenote, as well as under the sides, and the power-driven winch had to be abandoned in favor of a hand-operated one.

As Thompson told Morley afterward, during the first three weeks nothing of importance was brought up, only rotting trees and odd fragments of fallen rock, and then suddenly, he found himself in the midst of a veritable treasure trove: first several tons of copal incense, mostly held in small, shallow pottery bowls, the incense itself being painted a brilliant turquoise blue, the ancient Maya color of sacrifice; next objects of wood, such as carved knives with flint blades, throwing sticks; articles of jade, both plain and carved beads, ear-rings, plaques, and pendants; ornaments of metal, both of gold and of copper, as well as of all the intermediate alloys of the two, beads, bells, rings, bracelets, pendants, plaques, cups, saucers, and masks; human crania and bones; and pottery vessels of all sizes and shapes; but most frequent of all were bells of the hawk-bell variety, since these last were the chief ornaments of *Ah Puch*, the Maya deity of death in whose honor human victims of both sexes and of all ages were hurled to the Well of Sacrifice; all of which combined constitute a great archaeological treasure which has shed a flood on life on ancient Maya life.

These operations were continued for four years, 1905-1907, and 1910, and were finally suspended by order of the Mexican government, though Thompson, as he has often explained, believed that his casual dredging had scarcely touched the rich archaeological treasure which still lies buried in the black, muddy depths of the Well of Sacrifice. The Thompson collection, dredged from the Sacred Cenote, was purchased by Charles P. Bowditch[11] and was presented to the Peabody Museum of American Archaeology and Ethnology, Harvard University.

Mexican Government, 1906-

In 1906, on the occasion of the first visit of a President of Mexico, General José de la Cruz Porifio Diaz, to the State of Yucatán, the Ministry of Public Education of the Government of Mexico created an Inspection of Monuments for the State of Yucatán naming Señor Santiago Bolio as the first Inspector. Between 1906 and 1941 six different men have held this position: Santiago Bolio, Andrés Cámara Solís, Juan Martínez Hernández, Eduardo Martínez Cantón, Manuel Cirerol Sansores, and José Erosa Peniche.

The accomplishments of the Mexican government, through the Ministry of Public Education, and its local inspectors, in excavation, and especially in repair and stabilization, both at Chichén Itzá and at Uxmal, have set new standards of achievement in this highly difficult and specialized branch of archaeology.

Local caretakers were first installed at Chichén Itzá in 1906, but during the next forty years seven other archaeological sites in Yucatán, Uxmal, Kabah, Labná, Sayil, Chacmultún, and Izamal have been similarly protected.

At Chichén Itzá the principal buildings excavated and repaired by the Mexican government have been the Ball Court and associated structures including the Temple of the Jaguars, and the Castillo. The now famous Red Jaguar Throne was found in 1936 by the then inspector, José A. Erosa Peniche, walled up in the sanctuary of the temple buried beneath the Castillo. This is probably the most spectacular single archaeological find ever discovered in the Americas, ranking in relative importance with the Tutankhamun finds in Egypt a decade ago.

Carnegie Institution of Washington, 1923-1940

In the late summer of 1923, the Carnegie Institution of Washington, having signed a contract with the Mexican government to make a complete archaeological study of Chichén Itzá, began operations in that part of the city known as the Group of the Thousand Columns.

[10] Edward H. Thompson (1857-1935) was an American archaeologist and diplomat who devoted much of his career to the study of the ancient Maya, especially at Chichén Itzá [eds.].

[11] Charles P. Bowditch (1842-1921) was an American financier, archaeologist, and linguist who specialized in Mayan epigraphy. He was one of the founders of the American Anthropological Association, and an early contributor to the Peabody Museum of American Archaeology and Ethnology at Harvard University. Beginning in 1891 Bowditch funded numerous research expeditions to Mexico and Central America, including J.G. Owens, G.B. Gordon, M.H. Saville at Copán, T. Maler in the Petén region of Guatemala, E.H. Thompson at Chichén Itzá, A.M. Tozzer, R.E. Merwin, and C.L. Hay in British Honduras (Belize) and northern Guatemala, S.K. Lothrop in Honduras, S.G. Morley to Yucatán, and H.J. Spinden to southern Yucatán. On his death he left a large collection of books and other materials on the languages of Central America and Mexico to the museum, and endowed a professorship at Harvard University in archaeology [eds.].

Under the terms of the agreement, which was to run for a period of ten years with an option of renewal for another ten years, both the contracting parties bound themselves to devote certain specified sums annually, aggregating thousands of dollars, in excavation and repair-work at Chichén Itzá, a provision faithfully carried out by both parties throughout the life of the contract, 1923-1940.

The Mexican government undertook the study, excavation, and repair of the Ball Court and associated structures, and the Castillo. The Carnegie Institution, while centering its investigations at the Group of the Thousand Columns, during the eighteen years it carried on archaeological work at Chichén Itzá, excavated and repaired buildings in all parts of the site.

The three major architectural units excavated and stabilized by the Carnegie Institution of Washington were: 1. the Temple of the Warriors, and associated colonnades in 1925-1928 by Earl H. Morris and Gustav Strömsvik; 2. The Caracol or astronomical observatory and associated structures in 1926-1927, 1929-1931, by Oliver G. Ricketson, J. Eric S. Thompson, and Karl Ruppert; and the Monjas and associated structures by John S. Bolles and Russell T. Smith in 1932-1934.

In addition to the three major activities, each of which lasted several years, many other smaller buildings at Chichén Itzá were excavated and repaired by the Carnegie Institution of Washington; a list of these is provided in Appendix 1. Throughout the eighteen years the Carnegie Institution of Washington maintained field head-quarters at Chichén Itzá, this station was utilized as a base of operations, not only by other archaeological expeditions of the Institution itself, but also by a number of cooperative organizations, universities, and museums for related investigations in medicine and public health, botany, zoology, ethnology, linguistics, epigraphy, geology, geography, and museum studies. The purpose of these collateral studies was to clarify, to the extent possible, the background against which Maya civilization developed, flourished, and fell. For only by a thorough understanding of the environment which first permitted its origin, later conditioned its development, and finally brought about its decline and fall, could the Carnegie Institution of Washington hope to understand the complete story of Maya civilization, the most brilliant culture of ancient America.

Chapter 2.
ANCIENT HISTORY OF CHICHÉN ITZÁ

The Beginnings of Maya History

Ancient Maya history may be divided into two general periods: 1. The Old Empire, which extended from 317 BCE to 987CE and covered the entire peninsula of Yucatán from the highlands of Guatemala and eastern Chiapas in the south to the Yucatán channel in the north; and, 2. The New Empire, which extended from 987 to 1542, but which included only the northern half of the peninsula.[1]

The Maya story does not begin at Chichén Itzá, or anywhere in northern Yucatán. It has been shown elsewhere (Morley 1935) in this series of guide books to different Maya cities that the Maya civilization began to form in what is now the north central section of the Department of Petén, Guatemala, probably at the city of Tikal, during the first three centuries immediately preceding and following the beginning of the Christian Era (353 to 317 BCE).

---

[1] In the early twentieth century Maya culture was divided into Old and New Empires. The Old Empire, in analogy to ancient Egypt, originated in the fourth century BCE and terminated in the tenth century CE. The New Empire or Florescence existed from the end of the tenth century CE until the Spanish conquest. The chronological framework for the Maya region has become increasingly refined and is currently divided into several periods:

Postclassic	1000-1697 CE
Classic	200-1000 CE
Preclassic	2000-200 CE
Archaic	3500-2000 BCE

The Paleo-Indian period spans from the earliest evidence for humans in the region to the establishment of agriculture and subsistence techniques. During the Archaic period agriculture was developed and permanent villages were established, and class divisions begin to appear. The Preclassic or Formative period brought the rise of large-scale ceremonial architecture, writing systems, urbanization, and state-level government. Many of the distinctive elements of Mesoamerican civilization can be traced to this period. The Classic Period saw the development of high achievement in stucco work, architecture, sculptural reliefs, mural painting, pottery, and lapidary. The period was dominated by numerous independent city-states. The main conflict during this period was between Tikal and Calakmul, who fought a series of wars over the course of more than half a millennium, each of these states declined during the Terminal Classic and were eventually abandoned. The Postclassic period saw the collapse of many of the great cities of the Classic period, although some continued, such as at Chichén Itzá and Uxmal. This is sometimes seen as a period of increased chaos, warfare, and cultural decline. It was also a period of technological advances in architecture, engineering, and weaponry. The Postclassic continued until the conquest of the last independent indigenous state of Mesoamerica, Tayasal, in 1697.

Period		Timespan	Sites
Paleo-Indian		10,000-3,500 BCE	Belize, Honduras, Guatemala
Archaic		3500-2000 BCE	
Preclassic		2000 BCE-250 CE	La Blanca, Ujuxte
	Early	2000-1000 BCE	Cerros, Nakbe
	Middle	950-400 BCE	El Mirador, Izapa, Lamanai, Naj Tunich, Takalik Abaj, Kaminaljuyú, Uaxactún
	Late	400 BCE-200 CE	Altar de Sacrificios, Cival, Edzná, El Mirador, Kaminaljuyú, Piedras Negras, Río Azul, San Bartolo, Seibal, Tikal, Uaxactún
Classic		200-900 CE	
	Early	200-600 CE	Calakmul, Caracol, Chunchucmil, Copán, Naranjo, Palenque, Quiriguá, Tikal, Uaxactún, Yaxhá
	Late	600-900 CE	Aguateca, Cancuen, Cobá, Dos Pilas, La Blanca, Pusilhá, Toniná, Uxmal, Waka', Xultún, Xunantunich
	Terminal Classic	800-900/1000 CE	Puuc sites (Kabah, Labna, Sayil, Uxmal), Petén basin sites (El Chal, Seibal),
Postclassic		900-1697 CE	
	Early	900-1200 CE	Topoxte, Tulum
	Late	1200-1697 CE	Iximche, Mayapan, Mixco Viejo, Q'umarkaj, Ti'ho, Zaculeu
Post Conquest		1697 CE-	Central Petén (Tayasal, Zacpetén)

From this central nuclear region, as its focus of distribution, Maya civilization spread during the next two centuries (517-317 BCE) to all parts of the Yucatán peninsula, to Copán in the extreme southeast in western Honduras; to Toniná in the southeast highlands of eastern Chiapas; to the Usumacinta Valley of Guatemala and Mexico; and to northern Yucatán.

Although the earliest dated inscription that has yet been found in northern Yucatán, the hieroglyphic door lintel from Oxkintok in northwestern corner of the peninsula,[2] dates from 9.8.0.0.0 of the Maya era, or 476 BCE, it is possible that Maya culture first reached the northern half of the peninsula by way of the east coast region, where a chain of early dated sites at Tulum (564), Ichpaatún (593), Tzibanche (618), and Coba (623) has been found. These sites were probably colonized from centers in northeastern Petén, possibly from La Honradez, Xultún, or Uaxactún, and Maya culture was introduced into northern Yucatán along this east coast route.

The findings of archaeology in this respect are strongly corroborated by an ancient tradition preserved by Fray Bernardo de Lizana in his *Historia de Yucatán*, written in 1601, which follows:

> *The early fathers who first implanted the Faith of Christ in Yucatán knew that the people here [the Maya] came, some from the west and some from the east, and thus in their ancient language they called the east, likin, which is the same as where the sun rises, as with us. And the west they call, chikin, which is the same as the setting or end of the sun, or where it hides itself, as with us. And anciently they called the east, cenial, and the west, nohenial, the great descent. And the reason they say this is because from the part of the East there came down to this land [of Yucatán] few people, and that of the West, many and with this word they understood few or many, the East and the West; and the few people from one part and the many from the other.*

Finally, our only native documentary sources for the reconstruction of ancient Maya history are a few immediately post-conquest manuscripts dating from the late sixteenth and early seventeenth centuries, the so-called Books of Chilam Balam,[3] or "Books of the Soothsayer of Hidden Things."

These manuscripts are written in the Maya language but with the letters of the Spanish script. Although the Spanish priests of the sixteenth century taught the upper class Maya of that period to write their language with Spanish letters in order to facilitate their conversion to the Catholic religion, the Maya, thus instructed, seized upon this, to them, wonderful new system, of writing, for recording a considerable amount of their old pagan learning, such as prophecies, myths, chief's catechisms, rituals, astrological information, incantations, songs, current events, such as local hangings, epidemics of smallpox, foundations of hospitals and the like, but most important of all, brief chronological summaries of their own ancient history.

These historical synopses are known as the *u kahlay k'atunob*, or "Series of the K'atuns," the k'atun being a period of time, approximately 20 years in length. Five of these *u kahlay k'atunob* are known: three in the Book of Chilam Balam of Chumayel, which was composed at the village or Chumayel in north central Yucatán, a fourth in the Book of Chilam Balam of Maní, written at the village of the same name near Chumayel, and a fifth in the Book of Chilam Balam of Tizimin in northeastern Yucatán.

These priceless native chronicles, our only indigenous records barring the hieroglyphic inscriptions, cover altogether a period of about twelve centuries, from 435 to 163 BCE, and were almost certainly copied directly from old Maya hieroglyphic manuscripts, now lost or destroyed, but which were still in existence in the latter half of the sixteenth century. The ancient history of Chichén Itzá, described in this chapter, is derived almost exclusively from these five chronicles.

Discovery and Colonization of Chichén Itzá: First Period of Occupation, 514-692

A group of ancient Maya known as the Itzá, pushing out from Old Empire cities in northeastern Petén in a northeasterly direction as early as 9.0.0.0.0 of the Maya Era, or 435, discovered Lake Bacalar in the modern Mexican State of Quintana Roo.

Perhaps it is misleading to use the word "discovered" in this context, since the entire northern half of the Yucatán peninsula had already been occupied by Maya people who followed an agricultural life, which was based upon the cultivation of maize, or Indian corn, and who lived in settled communities or villages.

To these simple corn-farmers of the fifth century after Christ, already long settled around Lake Bacalar, the Itzá, sometime during the first half of the fifth century (about 435) introduced a far higher manner of living, namely that of the Maya Old Empire in the south; a new religion, a system of hieroglyphic writing, an exact chronology,

[2] The Maya long count calendar is a non-repeating vigesimal (base-20) and base-18 calendar. Using a modified vigesimal tally, the long count calendar identifies a day by counting the number of days since a mythical creation date that corresponds to August 11, 3114 BCE in the Gregorian calendar. The long count calendar was widely used on monuments, the earliest being Takalik Abaj (Stela 2, 236-19 BCE; 7.6.11.16...?); Chiapa de Corzo (Stela 2, 7.17.3.2.13, 36 BCE); Tres Zapotes, (Stela C, 7.16.6.16.18, 32 BCE); El Baúl (Stela 1, 7.19.15.7.12, 37 CE); Takalik Abaj (Stela 5, 8.3.2.10.15; 103 CE; 8.4.5.17.11, 126 CE); La Mojarra (Stela 1, 8.5.3.3.5, 143 CE; 18.5.16.9.7, 156 CE)[eds.].

[3] The Books of Chilam Balam are handwritten, primarily seventeenth and eighteenth century Maya miscellanies, named after the small Yucatec towns where they were originally found. Nine books are known, most importantly those from Chumayel, Maní, Na, Tizimin, and Tusik. Written in Yucatec Maya and using the Latin alphabet, the manuscripts cover a broad range of eighteenth-century spiritual life. The books contain a variety of information, including histories, prognostication, prophecy, collections of riddles, myth and mysticism, treatises on astrology, agricultural calendars, herbal medicine, and Roman Catholic instruction [eds.].

even slightly more accurate than our own Gregorian calendar, and knowledge of the movement of the heavenly bodies superior to that of the ancient Egyptians until Ptolemaic times (325-330 BCE); while their knowledge of architecture, sculpture, and painting excelled that of any other people of ancient America.

Such was the esteem in which the Itzá were held by these agricultural folk of northern Yucatán, that they are referred to in the Maya chronicles as the "Itzá", Holy Men. Holy men and wise in every truth, they could predict eclipses, foretell the risings and the settings of the morning and evening stars, write, count, build, sculpt and paint, and who displayed the highest degree of skill in dozens of new and useful techniques. No other of the several groups referred to in the Maya chronicles, is distinguished by such a lofty designation.

The Itzá remained in the province of *Ziyancan Bacalar* or *Bakhalel* as it was more properly written for sixty years, from 9.0.0.0.0 to 9.3.0.0.0 of the Maya era (435-495 CE) and it was precisely during their sojourn in this region, that they heard of Chichén Itzá for the first time. Surely not under this name, but under that of some already established settlement of the earlier agricultural people, most happily located at a place where an abundance of water had previously been found in two large natural wells or *cenotes*.

It has been explained that there is a chain of dated Maya cities extending northeastward from Tzibanche out to the coast at Ichpaatún, thence northwest to Tulum, thence northwestward inland to Coba, which is connected by a raised stone causeway 100 km long with the city of Yaxuna, the latter only 12 km south-southwest of Chichén Itzá.

The Maya chronicles state clearly that it was while the Itzá were in the province of Bacalar that the discovery of Chichén Itzá took place, and the above chain of dated cities connecting northeastern Petén with Chichén Itzá affords abundant archaeological proof of the truth of this statement in the chronicles. Chichén Itzá itself, according to one of the chronicles, was founded during a k'atun 4 Ahau, i.e., between 495 and 514 CE. The Itzá renamed the settlement of the earlier corn-farming people they had found previously installed at Chichén Itzá, which means in Maya, "the mouths (*chi*) of the wells (*chen*) of the Itzá."

By the above route with a long pause of sixty years in the province of Bacalar, the Itzá moving out from northeastern Petén finally reached northern Yucatán bringing Maya culture, for the first time, to what later became the northern Maya region. This is Father Lizana's "Little Descent" in the passage already quoted, "the few people who came down to this land from the part of the East." Thus, Chichén Itzá became the first Old Empire colony in the north, and the Itzá, the first bearers of the new, higher, priestly culture, to the simpler farming people of the north. Furthermore it seems probable that the last stopping place of the Itzá on this long northward trek, before they finally reached the site of Chichén Itzá and occupied it, was the center of Yaxuna, the western terminus of the long Coba-Yaxuna causeway, and further that Yaxuna was probably the site from which Maya culture was first brought to Chichén Itzá.

It will be shown in the next chapter that following buildings probably date from this first period at Chichén Itzá which lasted for about two centuries (495-692 CE): the door lintel in the Temple of the Initial Series; the Akabtzib; Temple of the Four Lintels; Temple of the Three Lintels; Temple at Yulá; Monjas Group; and the Red House.

The documentary history of Chichén Itzá during this first period is a complete blank. The chronicles shed no light whatsoever as to what may have happened during this first period of the city's occupancy. They are equally silent as to why the city was abandoned in 9.13.0.0.0 or 672.

One of the *u kahley k'atunob* states very briefly that:

> *Ten score years they reigned at Chichén Itzá and then Chichén Itzá was abandoned; then was when there occurred the thirteen doublings over of the Yaxuna.*[2] *Then they went to establish themselves at Chakanputún. There the Itzá, Holy Men, had their homes.*

Chakanputún, probably the modern town of Champoton, was located on the west coast of the Yucatán peninsula, some 80 km (50 miles) south of Campeche. The name of *Chakanputún*, is used here probably refers rather more to a province or general region than to a single city, like the province of *Ziyancaan Bakhalal*, on the east coast of the peninsula.

Here the Itzá remained for the next two and a half centuries, from 9.13.0.0.0 to 10.6.0.0.0, or 692-948. Not all of them however, would seem to have abandoned Chichén Itzá and moved southwestward in search of new homers in 692 CE, since there has been found at Chichén Itzá a sculptured stone door lintel bearing the dedicatory date of 10.2.10.0.0 or 879 CE.

Maya Renaissance and the League of Mayapán; The Second Period of Occupation at Chichén Itzá, 987-1194

In the next k'atun 8 Ahau, in 10.8.0.0.0 8 Ahau, or AD 948 CE, the Itzá abandoned Chakanputún. No reason for this important move is given in the chronicles. This time however a yearning for their old home at Chichén Itzá drew the Itzá back across the peninsula to the northeast. The chronicles tersely record that for 40 years, 948-987 CE, they wandered through the waterless stretches in the middle of the peninsula:

> *This is the k'atun (928-948 CE) when the Itzá went under the trees, under the bushes, under the vines; they suffered.*

Chichén Itzá was finally reoccupied after these 40 years of wandering in the wilderness in 10.8.0.0.0 4 Ahau, 987 CE, and the second period of the occupation of the city begins.

The Itzá and their Toltec allies under Kukulkan, were not the only Mexican groups however which had found their way into Yucatán toward the end of the tenth century. A family, perhaps even a tribe, called the Cocom, came with the Itzá-Toltecs when they reoccupied Chichén Itzá; later, Kukulkan himself, the Toltec leader, founded a city in northern central Yucatán which he called Mayapán, placing over it as its ruler a member of the Cocom family.

Finally, sometime during k'atun 2 Ahau (987-1007 CE), still a third group from the southwest, the Xiu or Tutul Ciu, under their leader, Ah Zuitok Tutul Ciu, moved northeastward into northern central Yucatán, and founded the Xiu capital at Uxmal. These three migrations: that of Kukulkan and his Itzá-Toltec followers, that of the Cocom and of the Xiu, were the final waves of Father Lizana's Great Descent, "the many who came from the west."

In the same k'atun 2 Ahau the League of Mayapán was organized and a defensive alliance between the three newly established city states of northern Yucatán: Chichén Itzá, Uxmal, and Mayapán. This setting up of the league was perhaps nurtured by the fact that, as foreign intruders, who at most could have formed only a relatively small minority in the mass of the Maya population, the Itzá-Tolteca rulers of the three city-states, recognized the need for mutual protection in their new capitals, formed this confederacy under which, assisting each other when necessity arose, they jointly ruled the country.

An era of general prosperity followed the inauguration of the League, since, during the next two centuries (997-1194), two of its three members became the greatest cities of the New Empire, Chichén Itzá and Uxmal. Architecture reached new levels of attainment at both places. At Chichén Itzá the imposing pyramid-temples with their ornate feathered serpent columns in honor of Kukulkan, the founder of the new Toltec dynasty, and later probably deified as the Feathered Serpent, patron deity of the city, vast colonnaded halls, and the Caracol, or astronomical observatory, are especially characteristic of this second period. Art and architecture flourished anew, the latter as never before. This was the last distinguished phase of the Maya civilization, and when the League was disrupted in the tenth year of the next return of the ever fateful k'atun 8 Ahau, in 10.18.10.0.0, 1194, the Maya suffered a cultural reversal from which they never recovered.

Mexican Period: Ascendency of Mayapán: The Third Period of Occupancy, 1194-1441 CE

In 1194, half way through the k'atun 8 Ahau, the League was suddenly and violently disrupted by a war against *Chac Xib Chac*, the ruler of Chichén Itzá, provoked by *Hunac Ceel*, the Cocom ruler of Mayapán; Uxmal, the third member of the League, would seem to have taken no part in the conflict.

The cause of the war between Chichén Itzá and Mayapán remains uncertain. Some have sought to inject a Helen of Troy motive into this event, based upon two very obscure passages in the Books of Chilam Balam of Maní and Tizimin which seems to indicate that *Chac Xib Chac,* the Itzá ruler, kidnapped the bride of *Ah Ulil*, the ruler of Izamal, who in turn called upon *Hunac Ceel* of Mayapán to help him avenge this dishonor. The real issue between these two great city states would seem to have been much deeper, perhaps long standing political and commercial rivalries between the northeastern part of the peninsula as represented by Chichén Itzá, and the northwestern section as represented by Mayapán.

Hunac Ceel, in the struggle that followed, summoned to his aid mercenary troops whom the rulers of central Mexico kept in garrison at *Xicalanco*, at the western extremity of the Laguna de Terminos. These Mexican mercenaries were led by seven Mexican generals, *Ah Zinteyut Chan*, *Tzuntecum*, *Texcal*, *Pentemit*, *Xuchueuet*, *Ytzcuat*, and *Kakaltecat*.

The Maya, armed only with their relatively ineffective throwing sticks were no match for the Mexicans with their superior weapons, the bow and arrow, the effective range of which is considerably longer than that of the throwing-stick. The Maya were laid low long before they ever came within hurling distance of their better equipped opponents, with the result that *Chac Xib Chac* was defeated, Chichén Itzá was captured, Chichén Itzá was captured, and the Itzá ruler driven from his capital.

This war shook the existing political structure of northern Yucatán to its very foundation. The League of Mayapán was violently disrupted. Mayapán, the Cocom capital, because it was the principal city of the country, and both the vanquished Chichén Itzá, as well as the neutral Uxmal, was reduced to minor roles.

The better to dominate the country, the Cocom overlords obliged the rulers and chiefs of all the other cities, towns and villages, to leave their respective dominions and live within the walled city of Mayapán. Thus, in effect, the persons of the Maya lords themselves became hostages for their own good behavior; and thus succeeding generations of the Cocom rulers, with the aid of their Mexican mercenary allies, a garrison of which was always maintained at Mayapán, successfully dominated the country and enslaved its population.

These tyrannies and exactions increased in severity during the fourteenth and early fifteenth centuries until in 1441, the Maya lords of northern Yucatán could stand it no longer. Indeed they awaited only the next return of the portentous k'atun 8 Ahau (1441-1460) in order that the omens of the time should be suspicious for launching the revolt.

But Cocom oppression was forcing the pace of Maya history. K'atun 8 began in 1441, and in its very first year, in fact just as soon as it had begun, the Maya chieftains under the leadership of Ah Xupan Xiu, the Lord of Uxmal, whom the Cocom rulers had also obliged to live at Mayapán, rose against the tyrant, slew him and all his family. Save one son absent from Mayapán at the timer, sacked the city, and depopulated it. Bishop Landa describes this war as follows:

> *Among the successors of the Cocom dynasty was another one, very haughty and an imitator of Cocom, who made another alliance with the Tabascans, placing more Mexicans within the city, and began to act the tyrant and to enslave the common people. The chiefs then attached themselves to the party of Tutul-Xiu, a patriotic man like his ancestors, and then plotted to kill Cocom. This they did, killing at the same time all of his sons save one who was absent; they sacked his dwelling and possessed themselves of all his property, his stores of cacao and other fruits, saying that thus they repaid themselves what had been stolen from them.*

With the fall of Mayapán, all centralized authority in the northern peninsula ceased. After this war all the larger cities were immediately abandoned, their inhabitants moving elsewhere and founding new capitals.

Thus, even the winners, the victorious Xiu, founded a new capital which they called *Maní*, meaning "it is passed." The Chels, a former noble house of priestly descent at Mayapán, established their rule at Tikoch. The single surviving Cocom was allowed to gather the remnants of his people about him and to establish a new Cocom capital at Tibolon, and later at Sotuta.

Tayasal: The Last Itzá Stronghold, 1441-1697

The Itzá, not content with merely abandoning Chichén Itzá, actually withdrew entirely from the northern part of the peninsula, migrating to the south, to the shores of a large lake in north central Petén, now called *Petén Itzá*, the ancient name of which, however, was *Chaltuná*. On a rocky promontory at the extreme western end of this long lake, the Itzá established their new capital which they named *Ta Itzá*, meaning in Maya, "at the place of the Itzá," which name the Spaniards softened to *Tayasal*.

Here the Itzá grew into a strong and powerful nation again, a continual thorn in the side of the Spanish colonial authorities both to the north and to the south, the Captain Generals of the province of Yucatán and of the Kingdom of Guatemala.

Cortés, the conqueror of Mexico, visited Tayasal in 1525 on his famous and heroic march from *Espiritu Santo*, now Puerto Mexico on the Gulf of Mexico in the State of Veracruz, Mexico, to *Nito*, near the present Puerto Barrios, Guatemala.

Cortés was well received by Canek, the Itzá ruler, and even left a favorite horse which had gone lame, with Canek, to care for until Cortés should either return, or send for it. The Itzá associated this horse with the firearms of the Spanish soldiers and adored it as a god under the name of *Tzimin-kak*, "five animal." They fed it flowers and tortillas until the poor animal died. Fearing the death of a deity on their hands, they made an image of it out of stone and plaster and worshiped it in place of the living animal.

Franciscan missionaries from Mérida tried to evangelize the province of the Itzá by peaceful means in 1618, and again in 1624, but on the latter occasion the visiting Catholic priest, Father Delgado,[4] was seized and sacrificed by the Itzá, his heart being torn from his breast and offered to the Itzá deities.

And thus matters rested for another three-quarters of a century, until 1695, when Martín de Urzúa y Arizmendi,[5] then Captain-General of Yucatán, began building a road through the forests from northern Yucatán to the northern shore of the lake, an indispensable prerequisite to the conquest of the Itzá, strongly entrenched in their peninsular security at Tayasal. Construction of the Yucatán-Petén Itzá road was not completed until late in 1696, when Urzúa began assembling his soldiers, ship carpenters, Maya carriers, road workers, artillery, supplies, etc.

Urzúa reached the north shore of Lake Petén Itzá at its western end, opposite the Tayasal peninsula on March 1, 1696, and the ship carpenters at once set to work building a galley, 27 m long, which was to be used in conveying the army across the lake to Tayasal, as well as in patrolling the shores.

On March 10, the Itzá sent an embassy to the Spanish camp offering to surrender three days later, but this proved to be but a ruse to gain time, the prelude to even fiercer attacks on the third day.

[4] A reference to the Franciscan friar Diego Delgado who in 1622 accompanied Captain Francisco de Mirones with some 20 Spanish troops and 80 Yucatec Maya in an assault on the Itzá. En route to *Nojpetén* (Tayasal), Delgado believed that the soldiers' treatment of the Maya was excessively cruel and he left the expedition to make his own way to Nojpetén with 80 Christianized Maya from *Tipuj* in modern Belize. When Mirones learned of Delgados's departure, he sent 13 soldiers with him to persuade him to return, or continue as his escort should he refuse. The soldiers caught up with him just before Tipuj, but he was determined to reach Nojpetén. From Tipuj, Delgado sent a messenger to *Kan Ek'*, asking permission to travel to Nojpeten; the Itza lord responded with a promise of safe passage for the missionary and his companions. The party was initially received in peace at the Itza capital, but as soon as the Spanish soldiers let their guard down, the Itza seized and bound the new arrivals. The soldiers were sacrificed, with their hearts cut from their chests and their heads impaled on stakes around the town. After the sacrifice of the Spaniards, the Itza took Delgado, cut his heart out and dismembered him; they displayed his head on a stake with the others (Houwald 1984; Jones 1998; Means 1917) [eds.].

[5] Martín de Urzúa y Arizmendi (1653-1715), Count of Lizárraga and Castillo, was a Basque *conquistador*, noted for leading the 1696-1697 expeditionary force which resulted in the fall of the last significant independent Maya stronghold, Tayasal. He served as governor of Yucatán and Campeche until 1708 when he was named President of the Philippines [eds.].

Finally early in the morning of March 13, Urzúa embarked for Tayasal, taking with him on the galley 108 Spanish soldiers, leaving behind the remaining 127 Spaniards, and all the Indian bowmen, road workers, and servants, to guard the camp.

As the galley approached Tayasal, scores of canoes filled with Itzá warriors, put off from the shores of the peninsula in two flanking squadrons to intercept the galley, which they soon completely surrounded. As daylight broke the Spaniards saw that the town had been heavily fortified against them, breastworks of stone and earth along the shore, and on the slopes between the scores of thatched dwellings, up to the summit, crowned with pyramids and temples, all guarded by a multitude of Itzá, waiting impatiently to defend their homes and the temples of their deities.

At first Urzúa ordered his soldiers to hold their fire and, through an interpreter, urged the Itzá to surrender, telling them that he came in peace, that if blood were shed that day, in further useless resistance, theirs, not his, would be the fault. But the Itzá, mistaking this clemency for cowardice, pressed the attack the harder, letting loose showers of arrows at the crowded galley. Finally a Spanish soldier, wounded in the arm, discharged his *harquebus,*[6] whereupon firing from the galley became general.

The Spaniards on their part were so eager for the fray that they leaped into the water, which was only knee-deep, and pressed ashore, all the while discharging their firearms. The Itzá, terrified with the din of battle, were soon in full flight, not only from their fortified positions on land, but also from their canoes on the lake, the waters of which were black with the fleeing Itzá.

Sword in hand, Urzúa and the victorious Spaniards, pressed up the hill to the highest pyramid, from which the royal standard was quickly unfolded, and by nine o'clock in the morning the battle was over. The rest of the day was devoted to breaking the thousands of clay idols, in a circuit of the 21 temples in the town as well as in the homes of the Itzá. Poor indeed, was the household that did not contain at least two or three of these baked clay images of the Itzá deities.

As the final act of the day, Urzúa with two Catholic priests selected the principal Itzá temple, where human sacrifice had so recently been offered to the deities, to be the sanctuary of the Christian God, as if thus to emphasize more signally, the triumph of the True Faith over the Devil.

And thus between dawn and nine in the morning of a single day, the power of the Itzá was crushed, and the last independent Maya political entity was brought under the domination of the Spanish Crown, though the formal act of possession for, and in the Name of, the King of Spain, was deferred until the next day, March 14, 1697.

[6] *Harquebus* (*arquebus, harbus*) is a heavy portable gun with a long barrel, supported on a tripod by a hook or on a hooked post [eds.].

Fateful K'atun 8 Ahau: Ancient Maya Ides of March

It will be seen from the foregoing summary of ancient Maya history that it shows a consistently recurring pattern, in confirmation of the age-old adage that history repeats itself. This is indicated by the fact that the outstanding events of ancient Maya history tended to occur during *k'atuns*[7] named 8 Ahau, the Maya "Ides of March."

The closing k'atun of Baktun 9 of the Maya chronological era (416-435) happens to have ended on a day 8 Ahau, viz. 9.0.0.0.0 8 Ahau, and this accidental fact seems to have set a predominant pattern in ancient Maya history.

The first return of this fateful k'atun, which the Maya called the *uudz k'atun*, or "the doubling over of the k'atuns" was in 9.13.0.0.0 8 Ahau of the Maya era or 672-692 when Chichén Itzá was abandoned for the first time and the Itzá moved to Chakanputún, the first recorded event in the city's history after its foundation. Perhaps this was only a coincidence, through it is possible that there may well have been some psychological connection here, between time and event.

The second return of k'atun 8 Ahau fell in 10.6.0.0.0 8 Ahau (928-948) when the ancient Maya chroniclers are almost unanimous in stating that during this k'atun the Itzá abandoned Chakanputún, migrated northwest and reoccupied Chichén Itzá, a second time. This would certainly seem to have been the beginning of chronological coercion. K'atun 8 had come back again; the sequence of the thirteen k'atuns was about to renew itself with the return of the ever fateful *uudz* k'atun: the time was ripe for change. What could have been a more propitious time than k'atun 8 Ahau in which to set out upon the return to their former homes in the northeast? And so the pattern began to repeat itself.

The third return of k'atun 8 Ahau was in 10.19.0.0.0 8 Ahau of the Maya era or 1185-1204 and was marked by an event of clearly indicated deliberation, the so-called plot of *Hunac Ceel*, the Cocom ruler of Mayapán, and the resulting war against Chichén Itzá, midway of this particular k'atun in 1194. This k'atun may well have been intentionally chosen by *Hunac Ceel* for launching this important venture, since, by this time, the Maya historical records clearly indicated that k'atun 8 Ahau were especially propitious for change. Chichén Itzá was therefore attacked; its ruler defeated; and Mayapán emerged from the war with the hegemony of northern Yucatán in her hands, a resounding justification of the potency of the psychological moment.

The fourth return of k'atun 8 Ahau in 11.12.0.0.0 8 Ahau (1441-1461) marks another epochal event of Maya

[7] A *k'atun* or *k'atun* cycle is a unit of time in the Maya calendar equal to 20 *tuns* or 7,200 days, equivalent to 19,713 tropical years. It is the second digit on the normal Maya long count date. The end of a *k'atun* was marked by numerous ceremonies. Each *k'atun* had its own set of prophecies and associations [eds.].

history, again one shaped by deliberate design rather than by accident. This was the plot of the northern Maya chieftains in 1441 at the very beginning of the new k'atun, under *Ah Xupan Xiu* of Uxmal against the Cocom at Mayapán, who were still the supreme rulers of the northern half of the Yucatán peninsula; Mayapán was attacked; its ruler slain, and political disintegration everywhere followed.

Here again was every opportunity for free advance selection of the most suspicious data upon which to "break" the revolt. K'atun 8 Ahau had returned. As their history had repeatedly demonstrated, the portent of the period was one of change. Only now the exigency of the times was running against the plotters; Cocom tyranny could no longer be endured. Scarcely had the "k'atun of change" begun. In fact in its very first year (1441), than necessity precipitated the long overdue event which had been delayed only until the omens for launching the attack should be most favorable. Their carefully kept chronological records clearly indicated that change was due, and straight way the Maya made history, their last collective action before the Spanish conquest.

Coming finally to the post-conquest period, that last act of the ancient Maya drama, by one of those curious turns in the wheel of national destiny, fell just short (136 days) of the fifth return of k'atun 8 Ahau in 12.5.0.0.0 8 Ahau of the Maya era or 1697-1717 CE.

But here again destiny was forcing the pace of Maya history. We have seen that on March 13, 1697, Martín de Urzúa, Captain General of Yucatán, attacked Tayasal, and captured it. In spite of over whelming numerical superiority, perhaps as high as 5,000 Itzá against a mere handful of Spaniards (108), a single discharge of musketry was sufficient to dispel the Itzá, who fled in every direction, abandoning their homes, their belongings, even the sanctuaries of their deities.

But why? What was the reason for their precipitous flight, practically without striking a blow, once the battle had been joined? On the day of the attack, March 13, there lacked only 136 days until July 28, when another k'atun 8 Ahau would have begun its course, at which precise time the ancient Maya prophecies had long foretold their end would come.

The Itzá, fearfully convinced of their approaching doom, which not only had been predicted by their own native prophets, but also was indicated by their own meticulously kept historical records, gave up the unequal struggle against their own hostile gods, and fled, thus anticipating by less than five months the last return of this most fateful k'atun of Maya history.

Chapter 3.
SOUTHERN SECTION OF CHICHÉN ITZA

General Remarks

It was shown in the previous chapter that the Maya chronicles indicate that there were, at least two, or possibly even three, clearly defined periods of occupation at Chichén Itzá as follows in Table 3.1.

The most casual examination of the buildings at Chichén Itzá will suffice to disclose that at least two distinct types of architecture are represented in the city: 1. The older, or neo-Classic Maya, found chiefly in the southern and central sections of the city; and, 2. The later Toltec or Mexican period, the buildings of which are found principally in the northern section of the city.

Concerning the first period of occupation, it seems doubtful that any of the buildings erected during these first two centuries have survived; there are, however, a number of structures and at least one reused door lintel, which date from the interregnum between 692 and 987 CE, during which time the city was not entirely abandoned, but that building operations were continued for some of the Itzá who had not followed the others in their southwest migration across the peninsula to Chakanputun.[1]

The earliest dated carving at Chichén Itzá is the reused hieroglyphic door lintel (Fig. 3.1) found in the Temple of the Initial Series in the southern section of the city and, although as found, it had been reused in a construction of the late Toltec period, the date carved on it, 879, antedates by more than a century, the reoccupation of Chichén Itzá in 987.

Most of the non-Toltec buildings at Chichén Itzá have their doorways spanned by hieroglyphic lintels: Temple of the Two Lintels at Yulá,[2] Temple of the Three Lintels (Str. 7B3), Temple of the Four Lintels, Temple of the One Lintel (Str. 7B1), the Akabtzib (Str. 4D1), the second story of the Monjas (Str. 4C1), the East Annex, Temple of the Xtoloc Cenote[3] and three unknown and now probably destroyed buildings represented by 1. An inscribed lintel found built into a watering-trough at the hacienda of Chichén, 2. Another also found built into a watering trough at the hacienda of Jalacal, two miles east of Chichén Itzá, both of which are now in the Museum of Archaeology and History at Merida, and 3. Still a third lintel which was reused to make the tail of a feather serpent column in the Temple of the Wall Panels (Str. 3C16).

One other building of the early period has a glyphic inscription which is not carved on a door-lintel but appears as an interior hieroglyphic frieze in the Iglesia (Str. 4C1); this last, however, is not carved in stone, but rather molded in stucco. Two other non-lintel hieroglyphic inscriptions have been found at Chichén Itzá: 1. The Red House (Str. 3C9) and 2. The Quadrangle of the Sculptured Jambs, where the sides of its wide gateway are carved with hieroglyphic panels.

Finally a few of the earlier buildings have no glyphic inscription at all: Temple of the Moon,[4] Southeast Annex of the Monjas (Str. 4C1), and House of the Deer (Str. 3C7).

The most constant characteristic of the buildings of the early period is that they have glyphic inscriptions carved

---

[1] *Chakanputun* (*Chanputun*) was a Maya settlement located approximately 60 km south of modern Campeche where the Champotón River meets the cost of the Gulf of Mexico. It is now known as *Champotón* [eds].

[2] Ruppert correctly notes that Yulá is not located within the site core of Chichén Itza but approximately eight kilometers south-southeast of Chichén Itza [K. Ruppert].

[3] Ruppert notes that "this lintel [at Temple of the Xtoloc Cenote] is sculptured and not with hieroglyphs. I think it is a Toltec building because of the colonnade, round columns, jambs carved with warriors. The lintel carving is much like the panels at the Temple of the Wall Panels [K. Ruppert].

[4] Ruppert questions whether the Temple of the Moon is an "early" building because it has a lower zonal batter and round columns [K. Ruppert].

Table 3.1. Periods of occupation at Chichén Itzá

First Period 495-692 CE 200 years	From its foundation by an Old Empire group known as the Itzá, in k'atun 13 Ahau, top their removal to Chakanputun in the next k'atun 8 Ahau.
Possible Interregnum 692-987 CE 300 years	It is probable that some of the Itzá remained behind at Chichén Itzá, during these three centuries.
Second Period 987-1194 CE 200 years	From the reoccupation of Chichén Itzá by the Itzá-Toltec groups in a K'atun 4 Ahau under a Toltec leader named *Kukulkan* to the conquest of the city by *Hunac Ceel* of Mayapán in the tenth year of the next k'atun 8 Ahau. The League of Mayapán.
Third Period 1194-1441 CE 250 years	From the conquest of Chichén Itzá by *Hunac Ceel* to the final destruction of Mayapán in the first year of the next k'atun 8 Ahau, and the subsequent abandonment of all the big cities, including Chichén Itzá.

upon them, somewhere; usually on the under, or front, faces of the door lintels, but also occasionally on door jambs and interior friezes.

All of the buildings of the early period thus far discovered at Chichén Itzá are found in the southern or central sections of the site. The Akabtzib (Str. 4D1) and the House of the Deer (Str. 3C7), because of their extensive simplicity (both the upper and lower zones of façades being devoid of sculptural decoration, an unusual feature in northern Yucatan), would seem to indicate that they may be the oldest buildings still standing at Chichén Itzá.

Of those buildings with hieroglyphic inscriptions, only one, the Temple of the Three Lintels (Str. 7B3), is probably correctly dated. There are grounds for arguing that one of the three lintels in this temple has a date inscribed upon it which has been read as "Tun 10, ending on a day 1 Ahau," for which Maya date the following equivalents have been variously suggested, 879 and 1017.

This question of a difference of less than a century and a half between the two above readings of the same date may seem like quibbling, but unfortunately this is not. The Temple of the Three Lintels (Str. 7B3) where this date is found at the end of the inscription, i.e., on the lintel over the right doorway is pure Puuc, or Maya Renaissance (neo-Classic Maya) in style, a type of architecture which reached its highest development in the Puuc, or hilly country of northwestern Yucatan, most notably at the cities of Uxmal, Kabah, Labna, Sayil, and Chacmultún The date of the beginning of this style of architecture is very much a moot point, which the certain reading of this date would greatly help to clear up. As between the two dates suggested, 879 and 1017, I prefer the latter.

Since most of the older buildings, i.e., those having hieroglyphic lintels are found in the southern section of the city, it seems best to begin our description here.

The southern and probably oldest part of Chichén Itzá is far more scattered than the central and northern sections. There are at least four principal groups, considerably distant from one another: 1. Temples of the Hieroglyphic Lintels; 2. Temple of the Initial Series (Str. 5C4) and associated structures; 3. Southwest Group; and 4. Temple of the Bird Cornice (Str. 5A1) and associated colonnades, and more than two dozen scattered, smaller constructions. In addition, there are two outlying groups, lying northeast and east respectively of the Temple of the Initial Series (Str. 5C4); 1. The small group at Yulá, five miles south-southeast of Chichén Itzá, and 2. Another small group at Jacalal, two miles east of the city; the two last lying quite beyond the limits of the maps.

The Monjas Group in the central section of the city is connected with several Temples of the Hieroglyphic Lintels by a stone causeway which is just under a mile in length; this was the main traffic arterial between the central and southern sections.

Temples of the Hieroglyphic Lintels (Fig. 3.1)

This group of four temples, two of which stand on the same terrace, must have been one of the most important

Figure 3.1. Court of the Hieroglyphic Jambs. Hieroglyphic panel, east jamb (left) and Hieroglyphic Panel, west jamb (right)

Figure 3.2. Temple of the Four Lintels

early groups at Chichén Itzá, since three of its four units have no less than eight of its total of eleven door lintels carved with long hieroglyphic inscriptions.

Approaching this group from the north, about 30 m before reaching the terrace of the Temple of the Four Lintels (Str. 7B4) and lying another 30 m off the trail, to the west, there is a low and badly ruined building, now little more than a mound of masonry debris.

Temple of the One Lintel

There in 1927 I discovered a half buried hieroglyphic door-lintel carved only on its front face. Although the building (Str. 7B1) to which this belongs has not been completely excavated, its ground plan would seem to have consisted or two rooms one directly behind the other; it originally faced west and its portico has at least four columns.[5] The only hieroglyphic lintel had originally spanned the single interior doorway leading to the rear room or sanctuary. Unfortunately its corresponding inscription is too eroded tom permit decipherment.

Temple of the Four Lintels (Fig. 3.2)

Continuing southward another 30 m beyond the above turn off the lower terrace of the Temple of the Four Lintels (Str. 7B4) is reached, and another 30 m still to the south, brings one to a low platform supporting this temple.

This structurc originally would seem to have been composed of a single room which was entered by a doorway in its western side. The lintel spanning this is carved on its front face with the representation of a bird, a human head emerging from its mouth, which design is flanked by a panels of glyphs; the under face of the lintel is inscribed with four rows of four glyph-blocks each, making 16 glyph blocks, or a total of 64 individual glyphs, or a total of 72 glyphs on this single lintel.

Later, a single, longer room was added to the west, changing the exterior doorway to an interior one. This larger room is entered by three doorways, two in the new front of the building, i.e., its north face and one in the west end. All three of these lintels have their respective under surfaces inscribed with 64 glyphs each, and the two spanning the doorways in the new north wall, with 24 additional glyphs each on their exposed fronts, or a total of 88 glyphs, on each lintel.

The lintel over the west doorway has the figure of a rattlesnake with a human head emerging from its mouth, sculptured on its exposed front, with panels of flanking glyphs, similar in general arrangement, to the front of the first lintel described in this building. This last lintel, like the first, has a total of 72 glyphs, and all four lintels in this one temple along have a total of 320 glyphs, more than that of any other single structure at Chichén Itzá, with the possible exception of the second story of the Monjas, which also dates from the early period and has about the same number of glyphs on its seven sculptured lintels.

The arrangement of designs and glyphs on the fronts of two of these four lintels is identical with that on the two lintels in the Temple of the Two Lintels at Yulá, which also faces west. This latter temple is in ruins, though the lintel over the north doorway is still in position sand

[5] Ruppert notes that the plan of the building included a single room with a portico with two, and not four, columns [K. Ruppert].

shows the same bird motif with a human head emerging from its beak; this central design is similarly flanked by panels of glyphs, the same arrangement as that found on the front of the first lintel described in the Temple of the Four Lintels. The under surface of the Yulá lintel also similarly has 64 glyphs.

The lintel over the south doorway at Yulá is now fallen; its front shows a snake with a human head emerging from its mouth, flanked by panels of hieroglyphs, and with 64 hieroglyphs carved on its under surface. This arrangement of the design and number of glyphs is again identical with the design and arrangement of the glyphs in the west lintel of the Temple of the Four Lintels already described.

This identity of design between Lintels 1 and 4 of the Temple of the Four Lintels (Str. 7B4) at Chichén Itzá and of the two lintels in the Temple of the Two Lintels at Yulá strongly indicates that both buildings probably date from about the same period, probably sometime during the eighth, ninth, or tenth centuries.

Temple of the Three Lintels (Figs. 3.3-3.6)

Passing around the west end of the Temple of the Four Lintels and descending its terraces behind, a few yards beyond brings one to the terrace of the Temple of the Three Lintels (Str. 7B3), which latter is approached at its northeast corner.

This little gem of Maya Renaissance architecture is the only building at Chichén Itzá which is entirely reconstructed, from floor level to roof, by the Carnegie Institution of Washington. This work was under the direction of Paul S. Martin and took two field seasons, 1927 and 1928, to complete. Before excavation and repair this small three room temple was little better than a pile of fallen masonry debris as shown in Figure 3.3. During repairs it appeared as seen in Figure 3.5 and after reconstruction as seen in Figure 3.6. It is 15.5 m long by 5 m wide.

How the Carnegie Institution archaeologists dared to rebuild such a pile of fallen masonry as that shown in Figure 3.2 into such a complete restoration as that shown in Figure 3.4 is a question that the visitor may well ask. What evidence did they have in support of their particular scheme of reconstruction?

Happily for the sake of scientific accuracy and archaeological integrity, a section at the back of this temple was still standing when work was begun here, practically to the original roof level, as shown in Figure 3.3. With this to serve as a guide to the correct reassembly of the fall sculptured elements of the mosaic, which formerly filled the upper zone on all four sides of this temple, Martin was able to restore these elements to their former positions and to rebuild this little structure from bottom to top, the only complete restoration attempted at Chichén Itzá by the Carnegie Institution of Washington archaeologists.

This structure is a typical three-room temple; all its rooms are on the same longitudinal axis, all being entered from the same side (north). This type of temple goes back to the Old Empire for its origin, where it is especially common at the city of Yaxchilan.

Originally all three of these doorways were spanned by hieroglyphic lintels carved on their front exposed surfaces only. However, only the two end lintels were recovered

Figure 3.3. Temple of the Three Lintels. Before excavation and repair; Sylvanus G. Morley, wearing an iconic large sombrero, stands at left center of frame

Figure 3.4. Temple of the Three Lintels.Rear, before excavation and repair, showing part of superstructure still in position

Figure 3.5. Temple of the Three Lintels.Northwest exterior corner during repair

during the excavations, the one, which had formerly spanned the middle doorway having disappeared. During the reconstruction of this building in 1928, in order to span this middle doorway so that the work should not be delayed, it was necessary to replace the missing original hieroglyphic lintel by a plain one from another building.

Later during a more thorough bushing of the terrace in front of this temple, some 25 m to the north, at the terrace edge, three fragments of the missing middle hieroglyphic lintel were found, each, at some time after the building had fallen, having been hollowed out and reused as a *metate*, or a grinding stone. All around the edges of this terrace a continuous series of small, late cell-like rooms, each perhaps ten feet square, had been built, their sides and roofs probably being made only of saplings and thatch. Almost every one of these late secondary constructions contained *metates*, and in two of them the fragments of the missing middle hieroglyphic lintel were found. This proved that these secondary constructions of saplings and thatch had been built after the Temple of the Three Lintels had fallen into disrepair, since the lintel

Figure 3.6. Temple of the Three Lintels. After restoration

which had formerly spanned its middle doorway had been later broken up, and at least three of its fragments reshaped for use as *metates*.

Temple of the Three Unsculptured Lintels

Some 15 to 20 m west of the west end of the Temple of the Three Lintels (Str. 7B3) there is a very much ruined structure, also containing three rooms in the same longitudinal axis. This faces north and the three doorways in its north façade are spanned by unsculptured stone lintels. This building has never been excavated and is now little more than a mound of fallen masonry debris.

Just off the southern edge of this terrace is a *chultun*, an artificial receptacle hollowed out of the solid limestone for storage of rain water.

Temple of the Initial Series and Associated Structures

About half way between the hacienda of Chichén and the Temple of the Hieroglyphic Lintels, a path leads off to the west; following this at first west and then south for about 150 m brings one to the gateway of the Group of the Temple of the Initial Series (Str. 5C4) and associated structures.

The structures of this group, for the most part, belong to the Toltec period at Chichén Itzá; i.e., they date from after 1000 CE, or from one to three centuries later then the group of the glyphic lintels previously described. No less than two Chac Mool figures and three temples with Atlantean columns, both highly characteristic features of the Toltec period at Chichén Itzá, have been found at this group, as well as other architectural elements of this later period.

The gateway leading to this group was originally spanned by a Maya arch, the supporting sides of which only have been restored. Around the edge of the terrace supporting its several structures, which covers an area of about 3.5 acres, there originally had been a low wall, or parapet, now fallen.

At the left, after entering the gateway to the temple precinct, there rises the most important, though not the largest unit of this group, the Temple of the Initial Series.

Temple of the Initial Series (Fig. 3.7)

This temple is a small single-room construction, measuring 9.5 feet square inside and facing west, with doorways in its west, north, and south faces and a low bench inside running across the back or east wall. It surmounts a pyramid ascended by a stairway, also on its west side, in front of which there stands a Chac Mool figure. Originally an earlier building stood where this pyramid now is; this earlier construction was only partially excavated by the Carnegie Institution. After this earlier building had fallen into disuse, it was partly demolished, its rooms were filled with masonry, and it was made over into the pyramidal support for the Temple of the Initial Series.

The north and south doorways of the Temple of the Initial Series (Str. 5C4) have sculptured jambs, but the west or main doorway is flanked by two heroic sized Atlantean figures, each composed of six drums, each figure measuring 2 m high. When they were discovered by E. H. Thompson nearly 50 years ago the second drum from the top of each figure, that which presents the breast ornament and the upper part of the torso, was missing. Curiously enough these two pieces were later found by

Figure 3.7. Temple of the Initial Series. Hieroglyphic lintel bearing date equivalent to 879 CE

the CIW's caretaker at the bottom of the pyramid, the section belonging to the north figure on the south side, and that belonging to the south figure on the north side.

Since not one single beveled roof-stone like those used in Maya corbelled, or false arched, roofs, was found either during the excavation of the temple, or even strewn around the slopes of the supporting pyramid, it is obvious that its roof had originally been of beams and lime-concrete.

Interest in the Temple of the Initial Series centers in the glyphic lintel (Fig. 3.1) which has been restored as spanning the doorway flanked by the two heroic sized Atlantean columns above mentioned. This lintel presents on its under face the following date in Maya chronology, expressed as an Initial Series 10.2.9.1.9 9 Muluc 7 Zac, the equivalent of which is 878 CE, the only reliable deciphered date at Chichén Itzá. The first and last glyphs on the exposed front of this lintel record a Period Ending date, "Tun 10, ending on a day, 2 Ahau," which corresponds to the Initial; Series 10.2.10.0.0 2 Ahau 13 Chen, only 331 days later than the date on the under side. This later date stands at the end of an even ten-year period of the Maya chronological era, 879 CE, and probably represents the dedicatory date of this lintel.

This lintel was carved a good three centuries before the Atlantean figures, that now support it, were made, which is the reason why it has been supposed that it was designed for use over some doorway, and was subsequently re-used in the Temple of the Initial Series, which surely dates from the Toltec or later period.

This supposition is somewhat confirmed by the fact that the doorway where it was found is too narrow to accommodate it. For when this lintel was placed back on top of the Atlantean columns flanking this doorway, the latter were found to cover partially the beginning and end of the inscription on its under side.

House of the Phalli, House of the Shells, Portico of the Atlantean Columns, and Associated Structures (Fig. 3.8)

Turning to the south after leaving the Temple of the Initial Series, a few steps brings one to the House of the Phalli (Str. 5C14), a domiciliary type building containing 11 rooms, by far the largest building at this group. Let into the end walls of several of its rooms are phallic emblems from, which it takes its name. There is some evidence of a second story room at its western end. This building was partially excavated by Gustav Strömsvik in 1933.[6]

South of the east end of the House of the Phalli there is a colonnade of sculptured square columns giving on to a small court. At the west is the unexcavated House of the Shells (Str. 5C5), and to the east a low and also unexcavated mound.

At the far end of this small court there is another colonnade and several rooms. Entering the latter and turning sharply to the east and passing through a narrow doorway one comes out onto the Portico of the Atlantean Columns (Fig. 3.8). These Atlantean columns both in type and size are almost identical with those in the front doorway of the Temple of the Initial Series, and both buildings date from the Toltec period. The several drums forming the two Atlantean columns of this portico were found fallen and scattered in front of it; they were excavated and returned to their original positions by the Carnegie Institution of Washington in 1926.

[6] Ruppert notes that the building was partially excavated by George C. Vaillant in 1926 and certain repairs were carried out by Gustav Strömsvik in 1933" [K. Ruppert].

Figure 3.8. Temple of the Interior Atlantean Columns. Looking through doorway in outer chamber

Figure 3.9. Temple of the Little Heads. Interior with Atlantean figures

Temple of the Little Heads (Fig. 3.9)

Retracing our way back through the House of the Phalli to the Temple of the Initial Series, and turning west, instead of south, a few steps brings us to the Temple of the Little Heads (Str. 5C3), excavated by George C. Vaillant in 1926.

This delightful little single-room building clearly belongs to the Toltec period. It faces south with a single doorway in the south face; inside there are two Atlantean columns which formerly supported the vaults which, though they have now disappeared, originally extended from east to west.

A number of small heads were found during the excavation of this building from which fact it takes its name, as well as a number of Atlantean figure altar supports, another highly characteristic feature of the Toltec period.

Next to the feathered-serpent columns, the most diagnostic characteristic of Toltec period architecture at Chichén Itzá is the sloping basal apron seen in all the feathered-serpent column temples in the northern, or later section of the city. The Temple of the Little Heads presents this same feature, which indisputably fixes it as having been built after 1000 CE.

Rising above this sloping, basal; apron originally there had been a frieze of sculptured vampire-bats, which extended clear around the building. This frieze unfortunately was not built back into its original position when this building was excavated and repaired in 1926.

Temple of the Owl

Some 60 m south of the Temple of the Little Heads is the Temple of the Owl, (Str. 5C7) so named because of the figures of horned owls which decorate the square columns and jambs of the triple doorway in its front or north side. The writer partially excavated this small temple in 1913 and found a human statue (head and torso only) with arms clasped over the breast; this was tenoned into a hole at the base of the right (west) column of the pair of columns dividing the triple doorway. The left column also has a hole in its base, but the corresponding head and torso which formerly had been tenoned into it had been removed in ancient times.

This temple has a small inner sanctuary which yielded a very beautifully painted capstone. Unfortunately the date painted in the band of glyphs across the top has thus far eluded decipherment.

Other Structures at this Group

There are several other smaller constructions at this group; the most important of which is the dance platform, standing about 1.5 m high, just to the west of the gateway. This faces south, and has a stairway on its northern side. It never seems to have supported a masonry building. But was a place for ceremonies, comedies, and dances as described by Landa, with reference to the two similar platforms, also without masonry buildings on them, north and northwest of the Castillo respectively in the northern section of the city.[7]

At the northern edge of the terrace there is a *chultun* which was excavated in 1926 by J.E.S. Thompson; a single adult skeleton was found in it, though no associated funerary furniture such as pieces of pottery, obsidian knives, jade beads, etc. This probably represents an accidental death rather than a deliberate burial; some Maya, passing by, fell into this *chultun*, and died.

Near the western edge of the terrace of the group, the figure of a second Chac Mool was found, somewhat smaller than the one at the base of the stairway leading to the Temple of the Initial Series (Str. 5C4). As noted, this group probably dates exclusively from the Toltec period.

Southwest Group

This group has never been entirely explored and none of its six structures, some of considerable size, has ever been excavated.[8] To reach it there was formerly an overgrown forest path which continued generally westward from the turn off to the Temple of the Initial Series (Str. 5C4) and associated structures just described. A quarter of a mile beyond the turnoff to the Initial Series Group, the Southwest Group is reached.

The three principal structures are along the southern side of the group, from, west to east, 1. The so-called Castillo (Str. 5B18) of Old Chichén Itzá; 2. The Peristyle Court; and 3. The Temple of the Jaguar Atlantean Columns, all of which as of more than usual interest though none has ever been excavated.

Castillo of Old Chichén Itzá

This building (Str. 5C18), despite its name, is not a castle but a temple. It faces north and surmounts a medium sized pyramid, which is the tallest construction in the southern section of the city. Two square sculptured columns divide the façade into three doorways and directly behind the middle doorway is another leading from the outer room to the sanctuary. A sloping basal apron, running around this building, clearly indicates that it was erected during the Toltec period.

Peristyle Court

The peristyle Court lies just east of the Castillo of Old Chichén Itzá and is entered from a colonnaded-portico on its east side, access to the court proper being gained through a doorway in the middle of the back wall of the portico; this whole construction is in a state of complete ruin (Fig. 3.10).[9]

Temple of the Jaguar Atlantean Columns

This temple is chiefly interesting because of the four Jaguar-Atlantean columns which divide its north façade into three doorways. These Jaguar-Atlantean columns are unique.[10] They are made in five or six sections like the three pairs of human figure Atlantean columns just described, and like a further similar pair in the central section of the city, to be discussed later. All four of these jaguar figurines are presented as rampant. The two

[7] Ruppert adds in a marginal note: "On the platform are traces of masonry walls and numerous (i.e., 25) column drums. This platform is not similar to the two platforms north and northwest of the Castillo, as they are square and have four stairways [K. Ruppert].

[8] Ruppert states that the Southwest Group was examined. He states, "I have gone over it quite carefully and have plans for 11 of the 13 structures. Plans made from surface examination.

[9] Ruppert corrects Morley by stating, "There is enough standing to give the plan, walls rise with batter to apron molding. Some columns of patio *in situ*" [K. Ruppert].

[10] Here Ruppert adds, "They are not jaguar figures but are human figures with jaguar headdresses" [K. Ruppert].

Figure 3.10. Mercado. Peristyle Court

middle ones are complete;[11] the two outside ones each lack a vertical section either from its left or right side as the case may be, so that it could be built against the vertical outside jambs of the two flanking doorways. Had not the Carnegie Institution of Washington withdrawn from Chichén Itzá in 1940, this highly interesting building would have been the next to be excavated and repaired.[12]

None of the other half dozen buildings at this group has ever been excavated or even adequately mapped.[13] Not one in a hundred tourists who visit Chichén Itzá even knows of its existence, much less even visits its crumbling buildings. It is now completely overgrown with trees and thick, low brush.

Colonnade of the Bird Cornice and Associated Structures

This, by no means small group, lies about a quarter of a mile northwest of the Castillo of Old Chichén Itzá, but no trail has ever been cut through the bush connecting the two groups. It takes its name from a temple (Str. 5A1),[14] the cornice of which displays figures of birds that have been tenoned into it.[15] This structure surmounts a low pyramid on the west side of the principal court, facing it; the northern and western sides are formed by long colonnades, another diagnostic feature of the Toltec period.[16] A number of irregularly placed, small mounds close in the southern side, and there is a small dance platform ascended by four stairways in the center of the court.

[11] Ruppert gives, "If this gives the impression that the two columns are standing in their original state, it is incorrect. The columns are now fallen; only lower drums with feet are now *in situ* [K. Ruppert].

[12] Ruppert gives that this statement is questionable [K. Ruppert].

[13] Here Ruppert questions Morley's use of the term "adequately." He adds, "There are 13 numbered structures shown on the Chichén map of this group. I have pretty good plans (from surface observation) for 11 of which two have been published [K. Ruppert].

[14] Ruppert notes that the structure is a "colonnade" and not a temple structure [K. Ruppert].

[15] Ruppert states that this observation by Morley is untrue. The bird figures are carved in low relief in the band member of the molding which is seen only at the south end of the colonnade" [K. Ruppert].

Other Scattered Structures in the Southern Section of Chichén Itzá

There are a number of other scattered single buildings, or even small groups in the southern section of Chichén Itzá which have been neither excavated nor even explored and, are for the most part, nameless. Indeed "Temple of the Sculptured Jambs" (Str. 4B1) and "Temple of the Turtles" (Str. 5B2) are little more than names applied to buildings because of some obvious feature, but should not be interpreted as indicating that we know anything more about them than their mere location on the base map.

A little more may be said of the Court of the Hieroglyphic Jambs located about a half mile east of the Temple of the Initial Series (Fig. 3.10).

This was excavated in 1932 by myself[17] and consists of a walled court about 60 feet square entered through a gateway on its north side, 1 m high, 2.5 m wide, and 0.8 m in depth, or thickness of the wall. On each of the two

[16] "The structure does not surmount a low pyramid. The basal structure, if any, does not rise more than a step above the court level." Ruppert adds, "The colonnade defines the west side of the court. There is a low pyramid, approximately 5 m high, on the east side of the court" [K. Ruppert].

[17] This was located and excavated not by Morley but by Ruppert in 1932 [K. Ruppert].

jambs of this gateway there is sculptured a panel of 278 glyphs arranged in three columns of nine glyphs each (Fig. 3.9). The stones forming these two panels were partially fallen and partly in place when this gateway was discovered; but all were restored or consolidated in their original positions in 1932.[18]

A small, single-room building gives off from the east side of this court, and is entered by a doorway in the east wall of the court. A stone causeway leads from the northwest corner of the terrace supporting this structure, northwest to another group.

It should be noted in closing this description of the southern section of Chichén Itzá that the only buildings thus far described which date from the earliest period, the neo-classic Maya thus far presented, are 1. Those at the Group of the Hieroglyphic Lintels, 2. At Yulá, and 3. At Jalacal. All others are definitely referable to the Toltec period.

[18] Ruppert states the correct date was 1928 and not 1932 [K. Ruppert].

Chapter 4.
THE CENTRAL SECTION OF CHICHÉN ITZÁ

General Remarks

The central section at Chichén Itzá dates mostly from the early period, though it has a few Toltec buildings, lies directly northwest of the *hacienda* of Chichén, and southwest of the Mayaland Lodge, on the west side of the Mérida-Chichén Itzá highway. An air view of the central and northern sections of the city, looking north, is shown in Fig. 4.1.

The central section of Chichén Itzá is highly nucleated. Most of its larger constructions, the Monjas (Str. 4C1) and associated structures, the Akabtzib (Str. 4D1), and the Red House (Str. 3C9) and associated structures, belong to the early, or Maya period. These buildings are all characterized by the presence of hieroglyphic inscriptions. With one exception the remaining buildings of this group, the Temple of the Wall Panels (Str. 3C16), the House of the Interior Atlantean Columns, (Str. 3C6) and the High Priest's Grave (Str. 3C1), with equal certainty all belong to the Toltec period, the first and last in having feathered-serpent columns and the second in having Atlantean columns (Fig. 4.2).

Figure 4.1. Aerial Photograph of the Central and Southern Sections of Chichén Itzá. Background: Ball court, El Castillo, Temple of the Warriors, Group of a Thousand Columns; Center: Casa Colorado, Caracol, Temple of the Wall Panels, Akab'dzib; Foreground: Las Monjas

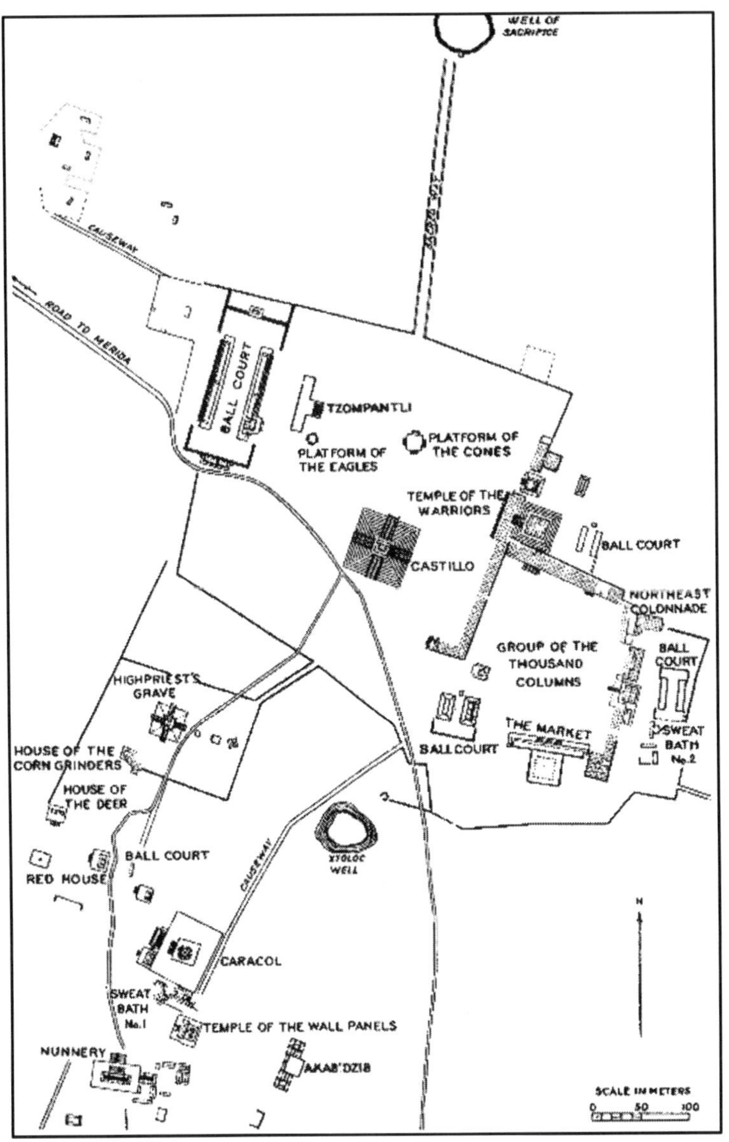

Figure 4.2. Chichén Itzá, Plan of the Central Site Section of Chichen Itza

Caracol (Figs. 4.3-4.7)[1]

This leaves only the most important buildings at this group, the Caracol (Str. 3C15), in some doubt, although I believe that this too should also be assigned to the Toltec period. Although the Caracol has at least two hieroglyphic inscriptions associated with it: 1. the individual elements of several vertical and horizontal bands of glyphs, now fallen, the original positions of which are unknown, and 2. an all hieroglyphic stelae or monument, which originally seems to have stood on the upper terrace directly in front of the tower proper, the Caracol, in all probability dates from the very beginning of the Toltec period.

The round tower in Maya architecture is practically unique, almost certainly an import from central Mexico. It is true that there is another round structure here at Chichén Itzá, though it is in no sense a tower (Pollock 1937). Indeed the only other round tower known in the Maya area, either north or south, except the Caracol here at Chichén Itzá, is an almost identical construction at Mayapán. However, Mayapán was a late (middle tenth century) colony founded from Chichén Itzá by the Toltec prince, Kukulcan.

Another indication that the Caracol dates from the Toltec period is the fact that although it has no feathered-serpent columns, since it is not a temple but an astronomical observatory, the ramps flanking the stairway leading to the top of the second terrace are each decorated with a pair of feathered rattle-snakes with the head of one and the tail of the other at the top, the bodies intertwined the length of the balustrade terminating at the base with the tail of the former and the head of the latter. There seems little doubt but that this building with its associated structures dates from the Toltec period.

[1] The *Caracol* (English, snail), named because of an interior spiral staircase, is a unique structure at Chichén Itza. Dated by a stela on the upper platform to about 906 CE. It has been suggested that the Caracol was an ancient astronomical observatory. Of 29 possible astronomical events, such as eclipses, equinoxes, solstices, etc., sight lines for at least 20 can be identified in the structure (Aveni 2001) [jmw]. Ruppert questions whether "the importation from Central Mexico" is what made the round tower 'practically unique' at Chichén Itzá [kr].

Figure 4.3. Caracol or Astronomical Observatory. Before excavation and repair

Figure 4.4. Caracol. After excavation and restoration

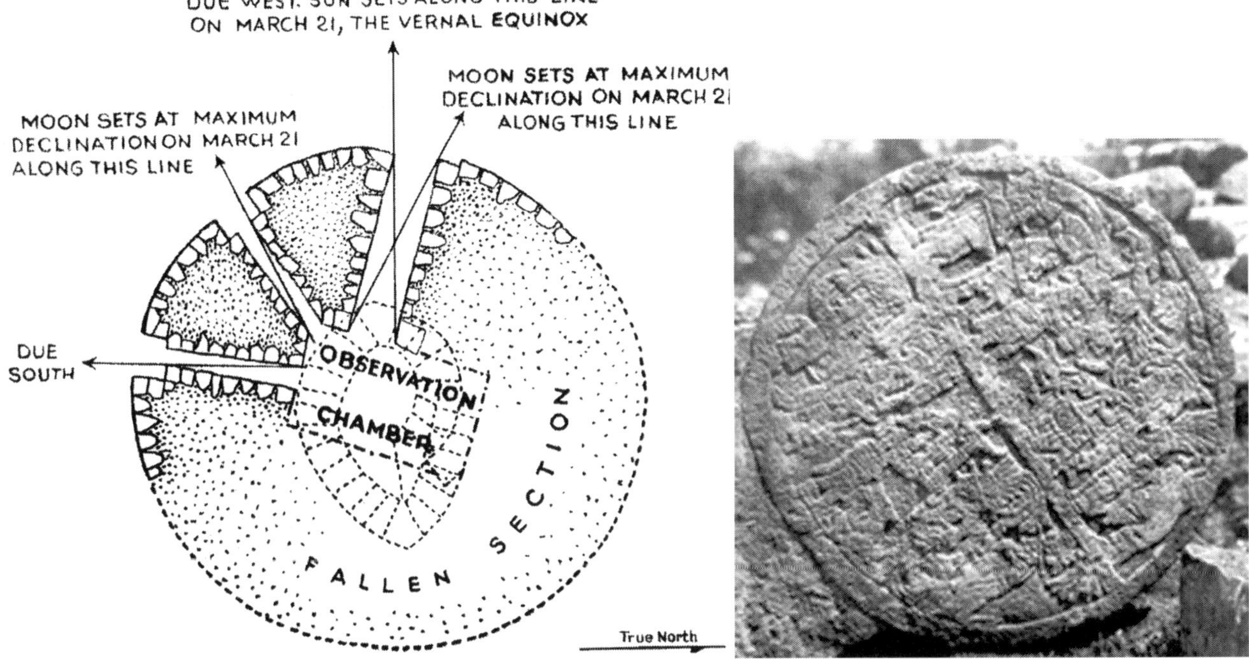

Figure 4.5. Caracol. Cross-section showing observation room in the upper tower near the top

Figure 4.6. Caracol. Round stone tenoned into niche between upper stairways

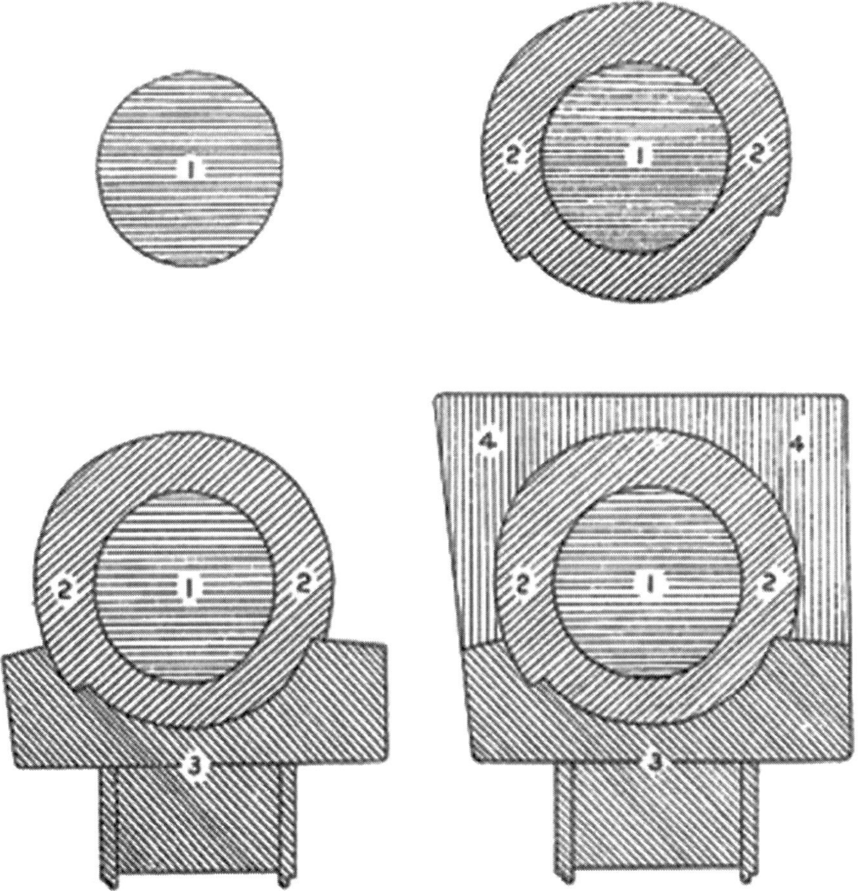

Figure 4.7. Caracol. First through fourth stages of the upper terrace.
a. First stage of the upper terrace;
b. Second stage of the upper terrace;
c. Third stage of the upper terrace;
d. Fourth and final stage of the upper terrace

Figure 4.8. Akabdzib. Before excavation, looking east

Akabdzib (Figs. 4.8)[2]

Coming from the Hacienda Chichén, or from the Casa Victoria, i.e., from the southeast, the trail passes along a narrow ridge between two great natural depressions that have been called dead *cenotes*, i.e., *cenotes* where the subterranean water-table was not exposed when the surface crust collapsed. The ground rises slightly here and a large mound is passed on the west which has never been excavated. Beyond, and rising from a low terrace on the east of the trail, is the Akabdzib (Str. 4D1), perhaps the oldest building now standing at Chichén Itzá.

The name *Akabdzib* means in Yucatec Maya "dark writing" (*akab*, dark, night; and *dzib*, writing) and was given to this building by the modern Maya because of a hieroglyphic lintel spanning an interior doorway between two dark rooms at its southern end.

The Akabdzib is approximately 52.6 m long, 14.6 m deep, and 5.5 m rear height. It is a building of the domiciliary type, having 19 rooms.[3] As originally planned it was much smaller; a simple three-room temple,[4] asymmetrical in plan, facing west. Later, directly east (behind) this earlier part of the structure and against its exterior back wall, a solid mass of masonry was built, doubtless to support a second story which, however, was never erected. And still later, two flanking wings, each containing eight rooms, were built against the north and south ends of the original three-room temple and the solid mass of masonry that had been built against its back wall. Nine of its 19 rooms[5] are entered through doorways in their respective west walls, six through doorways in their east walls, and two each through doorways in their north and south walls. The hieroglyphic lintel spans the interior doorway at the south end. This building required little excavation, though considerable repair-work should be undertaken, particularly at its northwest exterior corner.

Monjas and Associated Structures: Monjas
(Figs. 4.9-4.12)[6]

This complicated building (Str. 4C1), pure and neo-classic Maya in style, shows some eight different periods of construction, or alteration. If the visitor will climb into the great gaping hole to the right of the broad stairway leading to the second story, and turn to the east he will see the original platform of the earliest structure that stood here. To the south is another still later platform, the western end of which is also exposed by a great fall of masonry which may best be seen by passing around the west end of the entire construction; here, the southwest corner of the high, later platform supporting the second story of the Monjas has fallen away, exposing the western end of the earlier platform.

Returning to the front again, i.e., north of the building, a throne, or seat, in the form of a jaguar is found at the base of the steep stairway, giving access to the second story.

The second story of the Monjas, as originally constructed, i.e., before the addition of the late third story, which latter considerably mars the architectural effect as a whole, must have been one of the most beautiful buildings of the Maya renaissance. It had five rooms across the front (north),[7] and one at each end (east and west). The doorways giving access to the three front rooms and to the two end ones, are each spanned with a hieroglyphic lintel (Fig. 4.8), the inscriptions on all five lintels beginning with the same Maya date 8 Manik 15 Uo.

[2] The Akabdzib (*Akab Dzib*, *Akab' Tz'ib'*, *Akab' Tz'iib'*; House of Mysterious Writing) was restored by the Instituto Nacional de Antropologia e Historia in 2007. An earlier name of the building, according to a translation of glyphs in the Casa Colorada, is *Wa(k)wak Puh Ak Na*, "the flat house with the excessive number of chambers" and it was the home of the administrator of Chichén Itzá, *kokom Yahawal Cho' K'ak'* (Voss and Kremer 2000). The structure measures 6 m high, 50 long, and 15 m wide. The west-facing façade has 7 doorways, and the east has [eds].

[3] Ruppert notes that the structure has 18, and nor 19, rooms. Maudslay and Morley elsewhere both show it as 18 rooms [kr].

[4] Ruppert suggests this is actually a two-room temple [kr].

[5] Should read "eight of 18 rooms," according to Ruppert's marginal notes [kr].

[6] Las Monjas (Nunnery) is a complex of Terminal Classic period structures built in the Puuc architectural style. It is distinguished by a series of hieroglyphic texts dating to the Late and Terminal Classic period which mention a ruler named *Kakupakal* (Bolles 1976) [eds].

[7] Should read "It had three rooms across the front," as indicated elsewhere by Bolles, Maudslay, and Morley [kr].

Figure 4.9. Las Monjas. General view looking southwest

Figure 4.10. Monjas. Passageway under stairway leading to the third level

Figure 4.11. Monjas. Hieroglyphic door lintel in second level

Figure 4.12. Monjas. Front of East Annex, looking southeast. The dragon mouth portal and the decorated façade resemble buildings in the Chenes architectural style

Unfortunately this date could recur at intervals of every 52 years and is not much help to giving the age of the Monjas. However, it has been suggested that it may have stood for the Maya Initial Series 10.2.10.11.7 8 Manik 15 Uo, or 880 CE.

Still later, in another change of plan, it was decided to add a third story on top of the second. The ancient Maya builders always mistrusted their corbel arched rooms, and never attempted to build one story directly over another without first taking the precaution of filling the lower story rooms with solid masonry from floors to the very capstones of the false arches. The three middle rooms on the front, or north side, of the second story of the Monjas was thus filled in, but a passageway was left under the stairway built in front of them, leading to the third story.[8]

This third story was indeed a poor affair, an architectural afterthought. It contains but a single room and was built out of a number of sculptured stones which had been carved for use in other buildings and reused here.[9] A small sacrificial altar in the form of a truncated pyramid, perhaps 30 cm and sculptured on all four sides, stands in front of the doorway leading into this single, third story room; this latter certainly is of late date, possibly having been built during the thirteenth or fourteenth century. The large life-size group at the Milwaukee Public Museum is made with this altar as his point of view.

Alfred P. Maudslay, the English archaeologist, lived in the large middle back room of the second story of the Monjas during the first half of 1869 when he collected material for his magnificent publication on Chichén Itzá and I occupied the room at the east end of the second story during the second season's work of the Carnegie Institution of Washington at Chichén Itzá in 1925.

The second story of the Monjas with its 10 rooms,[10] one 14.3 m long, would seem to have been the administrative center of the Itzá Maya, the building from which this city-state was actually governed.

Tradition has it that it was the Monjas from which Montejo, the Younger, escaped in 1533 by the trick of the dog and the ball. Like the Akabdzib, the second story of the Monjas is obviously a domiciliary type of structure.

East Annex[11]

The high platform supporting the second story of the Monjas, in the course of time, had a most important addition built against its eastern end at ground level; the splendid East Annex, presenting one of the most elaborate façades in the Maya area.

The East Annex is not balanced by a corresponding addition at the western end so that the Monjas, as we have it today, is not symmetrical in ground plan. Again, as in the case of the second story of this building, it would seem to have been the intention of the ancient builders to erect a second story on top of the East Annex also, for which purpose the two rooms along its middle longitudinal axis were filled with masonry from floors to capstones. The chief differences between the two cases, however, lies in the fact that the Maya never got around to building their proposed second story on top of the East Annex, as they did to building the single, third story room on top of the second story of the Monjas.

The east, or front of the East Annex, is one of the most photographed façades in the Maya area. Unlike most Maya buildings, both its upper and lower zones are completely covered with an elaborate sculptural mosaic, in which the mask-panel motif predominates. Above the single doorway in the middle of the front an ornately costumed human figure is seated cross-legged within a shallow, horseshoe-shaped niche, formed by a curving band of sculptured plumes. The exposed front of the stone lintel over this doorway is sculptured with 20 glyphs arranged in two rows of 10 each. The next to last sign in the top row represents the planet Venus.[12]

Another interesting feature of this building is the coat of fine plaster still covering the masks at the south end of the east façade. This well illustrates a universal building practice among the ancient Maya, all façades, both sculptured and plain, were originally completely covered over with successive washes of fine white plaster, which gave to their carving a soft, rounded effect.

Southeast Annex

A few meters southeast of the East Annex stands what is left of the Southeast Annex (Str. 4C1). This would originally seem to have been a range of four or more rooms, facing north, but, if so, its two end rooms were torn down in ancient times. The two remaining rooms are unusual in that instead of having their corbelled arches closed by flat capstones, as is usually the case, they are closed instead by inclined slabs of stone, leaning against each other like an inverted "V", i.e., "Λ."

Iglesia[13]

The Iglesia (Str. 4C1) stands just a few meters northeast

[8] Should read "the long middle room on the front" rather than "the three front rooms" [kr].

[9] According to Ruppert the implication seems to be that the entire single room structure was built of sculptured stones. Some sculptured stones were reused in its construction [kr].

[10] Should read "eight rooms" instead of 10 [kr].

[11] East Annex Just to the east is a small temple (known as the *La Iglesia*, "The Church") decorated with elaborate masks. This rectangular building is of classic Puuc construction with an overlay of central Yucatan styles (Chenes). This is probably one of the most frequently drawn and photographed buildings at Chichén Itzá; famous nineteenth century drawings were made by both Catherwood and Charnay. The Iglesia is rectangular with a single room inside and an entrance on the west side. The outside wall is completely covered with veneer decorations, which extend clear up to the roof comb. The frieze is bounded at ground level by a stepped fret motif and above by a serpent; the stepped fret motif is repeated on the bottom of the roof comb. The most important motif of the decoration is the Chac god mask with a hooked nose standing out on the corners of the building. In addition, there are four figures in pairs between the masks including an armadillo, a snail, a turtle, and a crab, who are the four "*bacabs*" who hold up the sky in Maya mythology [eds].

[12] Excavation drawings by John Bolles indicate that the East Annex extends under the platform supporting the second level of the Monjas. John S. Bolles (1905-1983) was an American architect. He received an undergraduate degree in engineering from the University Oklahoma in 1926 and a graduate degree in architecture from Harvard University in 1932. He worked as a structural engineer in Oklahoma and as an archeologist for the Oriental Institute of the University of Chicago on the excavations at Persepolis, the ancient capital of Persia, and also for the Carnegie Institution of Washington on a comprehensive study of Las Monjas group at Chichén Itza (1977). Bolles is best-known as the designer of Candlestick Park, which opened in 1960 as the home of the San Francisco Giants baseball team [eds].

[13] This building was named la *Iglesia* (English: Church) by the Spaniards, probably simply because it is located right next to the

Figure 4.13. Monjas Group. Iglesia, West elevation

of the East Annex. It is a single-room building, facing west. The upper zone is heavily sculptured with mask-panels, human and animal figures, etc., which give it a wedge-shaped like silhouette, making it even top heavy in effect. Originally its single room had a line of glyphs molded in stucco, running around all four walls just below the spring of the arch; unfortunately all of these have flaked off and have disappeared. A roof-comb, or decorative wall, runs longitudinally across the top of the roof;[14] this feature is typical of Maya roof decoration, being found in both Old and New Empire buildings.

Temple of the Moon

This name has been applied to the several connecting structures just east of the East Annex and the Iglesia which, together with the Southeast Annex, form a small but impressive court, lying immediately east of the Monjas. This architectural complex has been named the Temple of the Moon because the hieroglyph for the moon was found carved on it.

The Monjas and associated structures clearly belong to the pure Maya period at Chichén Itzá; at least three of its several units, 1. the second story of the Monjas; 2. the East Annex; and 3. the Iglesia, all have hieroglyphic inscriptions associated with them like the nearby Akabdzib, which also dates from the Maya period.[15]

Red House and Associated Structures

This group lies north and slightly west of the Monjas, and northwest of the Caracol. It consists of a half dozen structures of which the Red House (Str. 3C9) is the most important. Again we are dealing with structures dating from the Maya period, the Red House having a band of hieroglyphs sculptured in stone, running along the back wall of its outer chamber just above the spring of the arch.

Red House (Fig. 4.13)[16]

This building surmounts a medium-sized platform ascended by a broad stairway on its west side. In plan it

Monjas (English: Nunnery). The building reflects classic Puuc construction with an overlay of central Yucatan or Chenes styles. The Iglesia is rectangular in form, with a single room inside, and a doorway on the west side. The outside wall is completely covered with veneer decorations, which extend up to the roof comb. The frieze is bounded at ground level by a stepped fret motif and above by a serpent; the stepped fret motif is repeated on the bottom of the roof comb. The most important motif of the decoration is the Chac god mask with a hooked nose standing out on the corners of the building. In addition, there are four figures in pairs between the masks including an armadillo, a snail, a turtle, and a crab, who are the four *bacons* who hold up the sky in Maya mythology [eds].

[14] Should read "A flying façade, a continuation of the front wall of the building, rises above the level of the roof" [kr].

[15] Ruppert states that the Temple of the Moon and associated structures have basal zone batters, which Morley gives as a Toltec characteristic [kr].

[16] The Casa Colorada (English: Red House; Yukatek: *Chichanchob*), is one of the best preserved buildings at Chichén Itzá. There are still stains of reddish pigmentation on the walls. The building got its name from the walls which still display a reddish pigmentation. There are hieroglyphs carved into the walls which contain the name of a priest and mention the Maya fire ceremony. The glyphs also contain a date, the equivalent of 869 CE, and also provide information on the rulers of Chichén Itzá. Over the next 10 years the Instituto Nacional de Antropologia e Historia, the federal agency that oversees archaeology at Chichén Itza, is expected to spend at least a decade doing extensive work in the Casa Colorada group, a collection of four buildings in various states of decomposition. Some recent restoration work on the ancient ball court that abuts the east wall of the Casa Colorada has been undertaken and, during excavation, an earlier ball court was identified. During excavation, archaeologists discovered an older ballcourt underneath (Fry 2008) [eds].

Figure 4.14. Casa Colorada (Chichanchob), Front, looking northeast

offers a slight variation of the single three-room temple type, previously described, in that while there are three rooms in one longitudinal axis across the back, there is also present a long outer room in front of them, into which each opens; this outer room is entered from the outside through three doorways in its west wall. Running around the base of the outer room there is a red dado, perhaps a meter in height, from which this building takes its name.

The Red House or Casa Colorada (Str. 3C9) is said to be the best preserved building in the Maya area. Its roof is surmounted not only by a roof-comb, a typical Maya architectural detail, but also by a flying façade, a continuation of the front wall of the building above the level of the roof, after the manner of the false fronts to give the effect of height, frequently seen in stores and saloons of western mining camps and boom towns of the past. Use of the flying façade is much rarer than that of the roof comb in Maya architecture, but the use of both architectural features in the same building is unique in the Red House.

Ball Court

Directly behind or east of the Red House is a small ball court (Str. 3C10) with its longitudinal axis running north and south. The west wall of this court is built against the back of the platform supporting the Red House. The east wall had originally supported a colonnaded portico on its summit, but this is now in a state of complete ruin.

The middle section of the two benches built at the base of the two walls of the court present sculptured panels, which the Carnegie Institution of Washington has consolidated in their original positions.

Just southeast of this ball court is a small ruined structure, which apparently contains two rooms. A stone lintel over one of its exterior doorways had cracked through in ancient times, and had been prevented from falling by placing an extra column under it.

House of the Deer[17]

Just northwest of the Red House, surmounting its own platform and ascended by a stairway on its south side is another small three-room temple, known as the House of the Deer (Str. 3C7) because of the figure of a deer scratched on a wall of the western room; the middle and eastern rooms are only fallen piles of masonry debris. The House of the Deer is connected with the Red House by an L-shaped building now reduced to a mass of fallen stones. Two mounds in the bush to the south complete this group.

Caracol or Astronomical Observatory (Figs. 4.3-4.7)

The Caracol (Str. 3C15), or astronomical observatory, a round tower of two stores surmounting large double rectangular platforms, is one of the most fascinating buildings in the entire Maya area, and save for similar constructions at Mayapán, is unique.

[17] While the Casa Colorada is in a relatively good state of preservation, other buildings in the group, with one exception, are decrepit mounds. One building is half standing, named Casa del Venado (House of the Deer). The origin of the name is unknown, as there are no representations of deer or other animals on the building [eds].

Round towers in central Mexico are associated with the worship of Quetzalcoatl, whose Maya counterpart was Kukulcan. Further, the historical fact that Kukulcan reigned at Chichén Itzá, and later founded Mayapán as a colony, coupled with the architectural fact that these are the only two Maya sites known to have erected round towers, makes it correspondingly probable that the Caracol at Chichén Itzá dates from the Toltec, or later periods. This tower and its double supporting platform face west. A broad stairway, 13.2 m wide, ascends the western side of the lower platform, giving access to a broad terrace above.

The main construction rises to the east, but at the northwest corner of the lower terrace there formerly stood a portico with four columns, facing south, an asymmetrical architectural afterthought to the original plan.

The upper platform is much smaller than the lower one; it is ascended by a double stairway, also on its western side, the outsides of which terminate in ramps, each ramp sculptured with a pair of intertwining feathered rattle-snakes, one head and one tail being at the top, the other head and tail being at the bottom on each side. There is a niche, or space between these two upper stairways, into the rear wall of which there formerly had been tenoned the circular stone, perhaps an altar shown in Fig. 4.6, and immediately above the latter, standing on the upper terrace between the two stairways, the hieroglyphic stela.

The upper terrace is surrounded by a low wall which was surmounted by a series of stone incense burners, placed at regular intervals; there were sculptured with representations of the head of the deity Tlaloc, the Toltec rain god.

The Caracol, or more properly speaking the platform that supports it, underwent several changes of plan during the course of its construction, changes which were discovered during the several years the Carnegie Institution of Washington worked at the excavation and repair of the building.

Work was begun on the Caracol in 1925 under Oliver G. Ricketson, continued in 1926 by J.E.S. Thompson, and finished ion 1927-1931 by Karl Ruppert, all three members of the archaeological staff of the Carnegie Institution (Ruppert 1935).

Since the Caracol, or more specifically its upper platform, shows how so many ancient Maya buildings grew by accretion, an addition here, a change of plan there, and since the building itself is one of the most important in the Maya area, it will be well to describe these in detail here, successive changes as found in the upper platform of the Caracol.

Originally the upper platform was a round core of solid masonry 10.8 m in diameter, faced with well cut stone. One of the excavations in the floor of the upper terrace shows this earliest stage of the upper platform. This was later enlarged by building a circular platform. This was later enlarged by building a circular platform 16.3 m in diameter around the earlier circular one, completely enclosing it. It is doubtful that either of these two earlier stages of the upper platform ever supported a tower, even the smaller of them is only of the same diameter as the tower built on top of it, though this tower was probably not erected until after the fourth and final stage of the upper platform was completed, since not until after it had been completely finished in its final rectangular form was there any way of entering either the north, east, or south doorways.

The third stage of the upper platform included a rectangular front addition, and stairway, ascending the same, was built enclosing the western third of the second circular platform. No traces of the stairway ascending either the first or second circular platform were found, and probably one was never built. The original circular platform would seem to have been enlarged by building the second circular platform around it even before a tower was ever built upon it, perhaps because the builders saw that even the enlarged circular platform (Stage 2) was too small to support the tower that was planned to be built upon it.

The rectangular section in front was enlarged by a rectangular addition to the east which completely enclosed the second stage circular platform in the fourth and final stage of the upper platform. The Carnegie Institution archaeologists left excavation pits in the upper platform which clearly show these four successive stages in its construction.

This brings us to a consideration of the Caracol proper. This remarkable tower consists of two sections, the upper one of somewhat less diameter (6.7 m) than the lower one (11.0 m). The lower part of the tower consists of two concentric circular corridors the outer one being entered by four doorways, each roughly facing one of the cardinal points, though each is a little off, i.e., to the left of due north, east, south, and west.

The center of the tower is a solid masonry core, on the southeast side of which, about 1.8 m above the level of the floor of the inner corridor there is an opening leading to a spiral stairway which winds upward through the solid central masonry core of the tower making one complete turn on itself before emerging in a small (82.6 by 1.8 m) observation room in the upper and smaller section of the tower.

This observation room has now largely disappeared, all except its southwest corner, and adjacent sections of its western and southern walls. Fortunately three of its original observation tunnels, defining specific lines of sight, are still preserved. One of these, the large tunnel through the western part of the tower, emerging in the exterior face, was one of the highest importance, since it determined for the ancient inhabitants of the city no less than the day of the vernal equinox. If a hair-line sight is drawn on the western horizon between the north edge of

Figure 4.15. Temple of the Wall Panels. View from Monjas

the inner jamb of this tunnel and the south or outer jamb of the same, along one of the diagonal axes of the tunnel, this line will cut the setting sun exactly in half at the moment of sunset on March 21, the vernal equinox. Here was an observatory so simple that everyone in the city, however humble, could understand it. Similarly the smaller tunnel in the southwest corner has to do with moon set at the same important station of the year.

The medial molding running around this tower, half way up its lower section, is composed of five bands: two sloping apron courses at the bottom, surmounted by a middle vertical course, which in turn is surmounted by two inverted, outward sloping apron courses, the only five member cornice, known in the entire Maya area.

This highly important building, the very center of the scientific life of the Itzá Maya, is one of the most amazing intellectual and architectural achievements of Maya culture.

Around the western and southern bases of the lower platform of the Caracol several secondary constructions were added later. The most notable of these is the temple to the south of the broad stairway ascending the western side of the lower terrace. This temple is composed of an outer colonnaded portico and an inner sanctuary. Against the back wall of the latter there is a masonry altar with three niches in its front; each one of which is filled with a small plain stone shaft having a rounded top.

There are a number of later, unrelated rooms built against the southern base, and a little farther out to the south is the badly demolished *temazcalli* or Sweat Bath no. 1.

Finally beginning at the southwest corner of the lower platform is a stone causeway leading north to the great north terrace, which would appear to have been the main arterial connecting the northern and central sections of the city.

Temple of the Wall Panels (Figs. 4.17-4.18)[18]

This temple (Str. 3C16), lying just southeast of the southeast corner of the lower platform of the Caracol, was excavated and repaired by Karl Ruppert in 1927. It consists of a hall, 22.1 m long by 4.6 m wide, with a double row of columns down its long axis. This hall is built against a pyramid, the summit of which is some 1.5-1.8 m higher than the level of the roof of the hall in front of it. This pyramid supports a two-room building entered through a feathered-serpent column doorway on its west side.

Access to this temple was formerly gained by means of a stairway which was built against the middle of the back wall of the colonnaded hall in front of it; this stairway formerly rose through a wall in the back of this hall, and emerged in front, and just below, the pair of feathered serpent columns above.

The foregoing was the plan of this construction as it was originally built, but later, as was so commonly the case

[18] El Caracol (the snail) is located to the north of Las Monjas. It is a round building on a large square platform. It gets its name from a stone spiral staircase inside. The structure, with its unusual placement on the platform and its round shape, is theorized to have been a proto-observatory with doors and windows aligned to astronomical events, specifically around the path of Venus as it traverses the heavens [eds].

Figure 4.16. Temple of the Wall Panels. Detail of panel

with Maya buildings, the original structure was modified. The stairway at the back of the original structure was modified. The stairway at the back of the colonnaded hall was torn out; the back wall of the hall itself was rebuilt, and the stair-well, or opening in the roof was closed. Finally a new stairway was built in front (west) of the colonnaded hall reaching to its roof, over which one passed to the short stairway leading to the serpent-column portal of this temple. This is exactly the same type of building, though on a much smaller scale, as the Temple of the Warriors; i.e., consisting of a colonnaded hall built in front of a pyramid supporting a two-room feathered-serpent column temple, access to which was gained by a stairway at the back of, and rising through, the roof of the hall in front and below.

The Temple of the Wall Panels was so named because of the two sculptured panels in low relief, which originally were built into the north and south exterior walls of the colonnaded hall. Although the 30 or so sculptured elements of which each was originally composed had fallen and lay on the ground in complete confusion, Karl Rupert was able to reassemble the elements of each panel, and to restore all of them to their original positions without the loss of a single piece. The panel on the north wall portrays a village scene in which both humans and animals (monkeys) appear.

One of the tail elements of the pair of feathered-serpent columns which formed the central doorway of this temple had been made over from an earlier hieroglyphic door lintel that had originally been carved for some earlier building, doubtless dating from the Maya period. The heads of this same pair of feathered-serpent columns, when this building was remodeled and the original stairway at the back of the colonnaded hall had been torn out, were removed from the temple and placed at either side of the bottom of the new stairway built out in front to serve as a Maya version of newel posts.

The presence of a pair of feathered-serpent columns in the doorway of this temple surely fixes it as dating from the Toltec period, and the reuse of a hieroglyphic door lintel in making the tail element of one of this same pair of feathered-serpent columns surely established the relative age sequence of these two architectural periods at Chichén Itzá, as first Maya, followed second by Toltec.

High Priest's Grave and Associated Structure (Fig. 4.17-4.18)[19]

This most interesting construction is perhaps the most architecturally developed at Chichén Itzá. I hesitate to say latest, although this also may well be the case, so far as the known feathered serpent column temples are concerned; 1. In that it is ascended by four stairways, one

[19] The High Priest's Grave is so named because it contains an ossuary beneath its foundations. The building itself shows combined Toltec and Puuc characteristics, and is similar in form to the Castillo. The High Priest's Grave comprises a pyramidal structure approximately 10 m in height, with four stairways on each side, a sanctuary in the center and a gallery with a portico in the front. The sides of the stairways are decorated with interlaced feathered serpents. Pillars associated with this building are in the form of the Toltec feathered serpent and human figures. Between the first two pillars is a square stone-lined vertical shaft in the floor which extends downwards to the base of the pyramid, where it opens up on a natural cavern. The cave is 12 m deep and when it was excavated; bones from several human burials were identified along with grave goods and offerings of jade, shell, rock crystal and copper bells. Edward H. Thompson excavated this cave in the late nineteenth century, and found several skeletons and artifacts such as jade beads, Archaeologists today believe the structure was neither a tomb nor that the personages buried in it were priests (Thompson 1938) [eds].

Figure 4.17. High Priest's Grave. From east, showing feathered serpent balustrades. Serpent portal columns are visible at top of photograph

Figure 4.18. High Priest's Grave. Entrance showing feathered serpent columns in front doorway

on each side of the pyramid, each of which had a pair of serpent heads flanking it, at the bottom, a feature shared by no other temple of this same type in the city; and 2. The plan of the temple above is more daring than that of any of the other feathered serpent column temples, in that its sanctuary is completely surrounded by a corbel vaulted ambulatory. This is even a slightly more developed idea than that seen in the ground-plan of the Castillo where the ambulatory extends only around three sides of the sanctuary.

This structure (Str. 3C1) was given its name because of an exciting discovery made here in 1892 by Edward H. Thompson, then excavating for material to be shown at the World's Columbian Exposition in Chicago the following year. Thompson, having cleared out the fallen masonry debris from the sanctuary above, noticed that the flag-stones with which the temple was paved gave forth a hollow sound when struck with an iron bar. He pried up the central flag stones and exposed a small stone cist perhaps a yard square and a meter in depth, its sides lined with inverted sloping apron courses of stone. On the bottom of this cist there lay a human skeleton with jade beads and other funerary ornaments; obviously it was the burial of an important personage of the Itzá nation to have merited sepulture in such a distinguished place.

When this burial was removed, and the stone slabs forming the bottom of this cist also were taken up, only to expose another cist and still another burial resting on the bottom. Before Thompson had finally reached the bottom of these cist burials, he had uncovered no less than six of them, each with its accompanying funerary furniture. And still the stone lined shaft was found to continue downward. Further exploration revealed that this shaft terminated at the same level as that of the ground-level outside. At the bottom on the west side of the shaft there was a stairway of six steps descending to the west, under an overhanging ledge of limestone, on which this pyramid had been built. The opening under this ledge is so low one must stop and almost crawl to pass into it, and as one proceeds westward, it grows smaller and eventually recedes altogether.

About 3 m from the bottom step of this short stairway, in the floor of this narrow hole under the limestone ledge; Thompson revealed a circular flat stone embedded in the floor. He and his sons were exploring by candle-light, since it is dark as Egypt down in this hole, as I can testify from personal experience. They pulled up the circular slab, and an upsurge of cold, fresh air, blowing from the hole this exposed, immediately put out all of the candles. Great excitement ensued. When the candles had been relit, an apparently bottomless cavern, through a hole in the roof of which they found themselves looking downward, yawned below them, but to the bottom of which their feeble candle lights could not penetrate.

After lowering a lighted candle to the bottom, which was found to be a good 12 m below, in order to test the air for possible poisonous gases which might be stagnate near the floor, Thompson had himself lowered by ropes to the bottom of this natural cavern.

And still the wonder grew. Resting on a stone altar on the floor of the cavern was a pottery plate on which lay six pearls, each the size of a small pea, and one larger, perhaps an inch in diameter, which had been completely burned, so that it could not be salvaged, breaking into flakes when it was touched. The rest of the pearls, however, as well as the jade, coral, small-beads, and other ornaments found with the six successive burials in the stone-lined shaft above, were taken to Chicago where they now be seen in the Chicago Museum of Natural History.[20]

The cavern is perhaps 9 to 12 m long, and a fall of stone at one end, through which a current of fresh air still blows, blocks entrance to what may be a passage. It was Thompson's opinion when he told me of the above incident, forty years ago on the occasion of my first visit to Chichén Itzá in 1907, that this passage had formerly been a natural subterranean connection between this cavern and the Xtoloc Cenote, lying some 200 m east southeast of it.

This temple, because of the pair of feathered serpent columns guarding its portal above (Fig. 4.18) and the four pairs of serpent heads flanking the bases of its four stairways below is clearly to be referred to the Toltec period and, because of its highly developed ground plan, to the latter part of this period. And yet the presence of hieroglyphic inscriptions in at least two different places in this building, on the east face of the front, south square columns in the sanctuary and, on all four exterior corners of the sanctuary, are reminiscent of the Maya period here at Chichén Itzá.

Just east of the High Priest's Grave are three small, badly ruined constructions, and just south of it, two others which were excavated by Paul S. Martin[21] in 1927; the House of the Interior Atlantean Columns and the House of the Corn Grinders.

The first, as its name implies, has a pair of interior Atlantean columns like those in the Temple of the Little Heads at the Group of the Temple of the Initial Series in the southern section of the city, characteristic of the Toltec period, and the second is chiefly interesting in that it originally seems to have had a flat, beam-and-lime concrete roof, not a single corbel-arch roof stone having been found throughout the course of its excavation. Its name is derived from the fact that a number of corn-grinders were found in several of its rooms.

Hacienda of Chichén (Figs. 4.19-4.20)

During the eighteen years the Carnegie Institution of Washington carried on excavations at Chichén Itzá, the staff used the various buildings and out buildings of the hacienda of "Chichén" as its headquarters (Fig. 4.19). These lie some 60 m southeast of the Monjas Group at the end of the Mérida-Chichén Itzá highway.

Xtoloc Cenote[22] and Associated Temple

The water supply of Chichén Itzá in ancient times was derived from the Xtoloc *cenote* which lies just west of the

[20] Field Museum was an outgrowth of the World's Columbian Exposition held in Chicago in 1893. In 1893 it was incorporated as the Columbian Museum of Chicago, and in 1905 was renamed the Field Museum of Natural History. http://fieldmuseum.org/about/brief-history [eds].

[21] Paul S. Martin (1898-1974) was an American anthropologist and archaeologist who later studied the prehispanic cultures of the Southwestern United States. During the winters of 1927-1929 Martin's work with Morley in Yucatán was cut short by tropical disease and he returned to the Southwest. In 1929 Martin joined the staff of the Field Museum of Natural History (Longacre 1976) [eds].

[22] Unlike the Sacred Cenote, the water of the Xtoloc cenote is relatively fresh and pure, probably serving as one water supply for the settlement while the Sacred Cenote was reserved for more ritual purposes. A structure is located next to the Xtoloc Cenote, appears to have been constructed between 900-1200 CE. On the pillars of the structure there are sculptured personages representing warriors and priests. There is an altar in the interior of the third chamber, originally decorated with bas-reliefs of plants, birds and mythological scenes. In front of it and

Figure 4.19. Hacienda Chichén. Gateway, looking west

Figure 4.20. Hacienda Chichén. West façade of the Casa Principal, field headquarters of the Carnegie Institution of Washington's Chichen Itza Project, looking southeast, c. 1926

Mérida-Chichén Itzá highway and directly opposite the main entrance to the present Mayaland Lodge.

Formerly two masonry stairways, built down along its vertical sides, gave access from above to the water below: one starting at the southeastern arc of the rim, descending along the southern face, reaches the water level at the southwest; the other, starting along the northwestern arc of the rim, descending along the north face, formerly reached the water level at the northeast. This latter stairway, however, has almost entirely disappeared, presumably having fallen into the *cenote*, since now only a few traces of it remain. The word *xtoloc* in Yucatec Maya means a kind of crested iguana, though why this deep water-hole, the water-works of the ancient city, should have been given such a name in unclear.

beneath the floor, a container of offerings with human remains was found. The facade faces west and due to an alignment which includes a simple altar, a path of stone slabs and a natural rock outcropping, marked by rows of cut stone, the central entrance of the temple relates physically to *sacbé* 15 and the platform of the Ossuary [eds].

Figure 4.21. Jaguar Figure Carved on outcropping of limestone

Figure 4.22. Pair of Sculptured Tails for Feathered Serpent Columns

A meter back from the northeastern arc of the rim stands the Temple of the Xtoloc Cenote. This two-room building faces west, it southern end being nearer the rim of the *cenote*. It was excavated and repaired by Ann Axtell Morris in 1925. The doorway between the outer room and the sanctuary had been spanned by a sculptured stone lintel. Against the rear (east) wall of the sanctuary there is a masonry altar, and above it, sculptured on the overhanging east side of the corbel arch there had originally been a handsome panel carved in low relief, composed of some 16 sculptured elements, another outsize Maya picture puzzle. Most of these carved elements were recovered from the debris on top of this altar during the course of the excavations, the roof of this building having fallen in, and were removed to the Museo de Arqueología e Historia in Mérida, where the restored panel is on exhibition.

Miscellaneous Structures

Some 40 m east of the Mérida-Chichén Itzá highway and about 60 m north along this highway from the Casa Victoria is the figure of a stalking jaguar, carved on an outcropping of the native limestone (Fig. 4.21) and another 40 m farther east stand two tail-elements for a pair of feathered-serpent columns, so far as one can judge, completely finished and ready for installation (Fig. 4.22) but never installed. Who can tell what change of plan, even what calamity, intervened to prevent the ancient Maya builders from finishing the temple for which this pair of serpent tails was originally designed?

This completes the description of the central section of the site, the structures of which are not too evenly divided between the Maya and Toltec periods, perhaps somewhat less than half dating from the former and somewhat more than half from the latter.

Chapter 5.
THE NORTHERN SECTION OF CHICHÉN ITZÁ

General Remarks

The northern section old Chichén Itzá is located north and northeast of the Mayaland Lodge, and north of the Mérida-Chichén Itzá highway. This part of the city dates wholly from the Toltec period; indeed its several groups are all built upon a single platform, the enormous northern terrace, which covers no less than 0.2 square kilometers of ground, and varies from 1.5 to 4.5 m in height depending upon surface inequalities of the terrain.

Easily the most imposing structure at Chichén Itzá is the Castillo, the principal temple, dedicated to the worship of Kukulcan, the Feathered Serpent. This is the only building in the city, the ancient name for which has been preserved. Bishop Landa,[1] writing in 1566, says that it was called *Kukulcan.*

The following other structures and groups are also built upon the great north terrace: 1. the two dance platforms and the nearby *tzompantli*, or Place of the Skulls (Str. 2D2); 2. the ball court and associated temples; 3. the Northeast Group; 4. the extensive Group of the Thousand Columns, and its associated temples, colonnades, ball court and sweat bath, a small civil and religious precinct in itself; and 5. the causeway leading to the Well of Sacrifice and the associated minor constructions built around its edges.

The architecture of the Toltec period is characterized by a number of highly distinctive diagnostic features, even the casual visitor will learn to distinguish the various temples, colonnades, and other constructions dating from this final period of the city's history.

In the first place, everything built on the great north terrace dates from the Toltec period. We have already seen buildings from this period, both in the southern and central sections of the city, but what we will not find on the great north terrace are structures dating from the Maya period; all the northern section of the city dates from the Toltec period.

All temples having feathered serpent columns also date exclusively from the Toltec period. The sloping basal batter, or apron, with which the bottoms of the exterior walls are uniformly finished, is another diagnostic feature of the Toltec period. Also the stone decorations around the edges of the roofs of these feathered serpent columns temples, like the iron grills around Mansard roofs[2] of the 1870s in the United States, is still a third indication that the buildings possessing this feature must date from the Toltec period.

The great colonnaded halls and peristyle courts of the Group of the Thousand Columns and the sculptured daises in them, as well as the Tzompantli and the Caracol, or round tower, are also typical constructions of the Toltec period. Certain types of independent sculptures like the Chac Mool figures, the Atlantean figures, and the anthropomorphic standard bearers, are also diagnostic of the Toltec period.

Formerly its was thought that ball courts and sweat baths, as found at Chichén Itzá, were also of Toltec origin, and while it is true that most of these two types of constructions found at Chichén Itzá probably date from the Toltec period, nevertheless both types have been found at Old Empire cities, as well as ball courts more commonly than sweat baths.

Coming to the Sacred Cenote or Well of Sacrifice, H.J. Spinden,[3] many years ago expressed the opinion that the

---

[1] Diego de Landa Calderón (1524-1579) was a Spanish Bishop of the Roman Catholic Archdiocese of Yucatán. He is best remembered for his classic account of ancient Maya customs, language, astrology, and writing (Landa 1941), and his brutal attempts impose Christianity. While some friars like Bartolomé de las Casas worked compassionately with the indigenous people, others like Landa were more brutal and destroyed indigenous icons, buildings, and writings, including at least 27 painted screen-fold books [eds].

[2] A mansard roof (French roof; curb roof) is a four-sided gambrel-style hip roof characterized by two sloped on each of its sides with the lower slope at a steeper angle than the upper [eds].

[3] Herbert J. Spinden (1879-1967) was educated at Harvard University (B.A., 1906; Ph.D., 1909). He was Assistant Curator at the American

Figure 5.1. El Castillo. Front, before excavation and restoration

ceremonies which terminated in the sacrifice of human victims herein to the God of Rain, victims who were hurled living into its dark and gloomy depths, were chiefly a development of the Toltec period at Chichén Itzá.

This closing period of the city's history embraces the three and a half centuries between 987 and 1441, from which period the great north terrace and all constructions on it date.

The Castillo (Fig. 5.1-5.9)[4]

The Castillo (Str. 2D5), or principal temple at Chichén Itzá, surmounts a lofty pyramid which covers about 4,000 m^2 of ground and rises in nine receding terraces to a height of 24 m above the level of the great north terrace. Broad stairways (11 m wide) ascend its four sides, that on the north or front being flanked by two rooms, each terminating at the foot of the stairway in two great serpent heads with widely opened jaws, in effect, and two enormous serpentine newel posts.

Each of these four stairways has 91 steps and the four combined have a total of 364 steps, one less than the number of days in the vague year; however, since the temple rises from a very low platform, only one step in height; i.e., a step which may be considered as common to all four of these stairways, this provides the one extra step necessary to have one step for each day of the vague year, 364 + 1 = 365.

Nine was a sacred number among the ancient Maya; they believed the Underworld had nine divisions, or hells, each of which was under the rule of its own special deity, who was patron of one of the days, in an endless succession of nine day periods, which followed each other throughout time like the seven day series of our week. The pyramid supporting the Castillo is divided into nine terraces, perhaps one terrace for each of the nine deities.

These terraces are decorated with inset panels, which decrease in width from bottom to top, but are all of the same height. If imaginary lines are drawn from the corners of these inset panels, beginning at the bottom, through the corresponding corners of the panels in the terrace next above, and so on, until they all converge; i.e., reach their corresponding vanishing point, this latter point will be found to be above 30 m the roof of the Castillo. This resulting optical illusion, which unconsciously elevates the eye, makes the temple above seem higher

Museum of Natural History from 1909 to 1920, Curator of Mexican Archaeology and Ethnology at the Peabody Museum at Harvard University from 1920 to 1929, and Curator of American Indian Art and Primitive Cultures at the Brooklyn Museum from 1929 to 1950. He was the author of seminal works such as *A Study of Maya Art* (1913), *Ancient Civilizations of Mexico and Central America* (1917), and *The Reduction of Maya Dates* (1924) [eds].

[4] The Temple of Kukulkan or Castillo dominates the North Platform of Chichén Itzá. The structure is a stepped pyramid about 30 m in height, and composed of a series of nine terraces, each approximately 2.6 m in height. The summit has a 6 m high superstructure. All four sides of the pyramid have outset stairways that rise at an angle of 45°. At the base of the balustrades of the northeastern staircase are carved heads of a serpent. In the mid-1930s, the Mexican government sponsored an excavation of El Castillo in which was discovered a staircase under the north side of the pyramid and eventually the Red Jaguar Throne. The Mexican government excavated a tunnel from the base of the north staircase, up the earlier pyramid's stairway to the hidden temple, and opened it to tourists. In 2006, the Instituto Nacional de Antropologia e Historia closed the throne room to the public. During the spring and autumn equinoxes, in the late afternoon, the northwest corner of the pyramid casts a series of triangular shadows against the western balustrade on the north side that evokes the appearance of a serpent wriggling down the staircase. Some have suggested the effect was an intentional design by the Maya builders to represent the feathered-serpent god Kukulcan [eds].

Figure 5.2. El Castillo. After excavation and repair. El Castillo is a nine stepped pyramid accessed by four stairways, each with nine steps. The total number of steps, including the summit platform, corresponds to the number of days in the year. The structure measures 55 m at its base, and 24 m in height

than it really is. On each side of the pyramid there are 52 of these shallow recessed panels, one corresponding to each of the 52 vague years in the ancient Maya cycle of 52 years, known to modern students as the calendar round, which contains all the 18,980 calendar round dates (52 x 365) possible in the Maya calendar.

The Castillo faces north, or toward the Well of Sacrifice, to which a raised causeway, taking off from the northern edge of the great north terrace, leads. Ascending the front, or north stairway, on the summit the visitor finds himself facing a pair of feathered serpent column, now badly battered. Inside the temple there is an outer room extending clear across the front, a doorway in the back wall of which leads to the inner sanctuary, the Holy of Holies, doubtless the most sacred place in the city where, it seems safe to assume, these religious ceremonies which terminated with the hurling of living human victims headlong into the depths of the Well of Sacrifice, really began.

The sanctuary of the Castillo is composed of three north and south running corbel vaults, supported by carved wooden beams (*sapodilla*) which rest upon two sculptured stone columns. These beams, as well as those which spanned both the outer and inner doorways of the outer room originally had been carved, but vandalism and time working together, have destroyed most of the corresponding reliefs.

Leaving the sanctuary and passing out between the pair of feathered serpent columns, we now go around the building to the east. From the east side, the best view of the spectacular Group of the Thousand Columns is to be had.

At the extreme left is the Temple of the Tables (Str. 2D7); next to the right, the Temple of the Warriors (Str. 2D8) and the Northwest Colonnade (Str. 2D8) in front of it, both of which have been excavated and partially repaired; to the right of the Temple of the Warriors is the North Colonnade (Fig. 5.5), also excavated and partially repaired; and on the far side of the Court of the Thousand Columns, a series of colonnades and temples, that occupies its entire eastern side, none of which, however, has been excavated.

Still farther to the right, the eye rests upon a long portico, composed of alternating square and round columns, in front of a peristyle court (the so-called Market Place (Str. 3D11)) a noble and imposing construction, also excavated and partially restored; at the extreme right are two high walls, forming the sides of another ball court, which stands at the southwest, open corner of the Court of the Thousand Columns; and finally in the immediate foreground, and below, is the long unexcavated West Colonnade (Str. 3D1) of the Court of the Thousand Columns, pierced by a single gateway directly leading into a great 0.2 km^2 court.

Entering the Castillo (Str. 2D5) through its eastern doorway and turning to the left, is a high vaulted room, or ambulatory which encloses the sanctuary on east, south and west sides; although there is no direct entrance from this ambulatory into the sanctuary proper, it has three exterior doorways, giving access to the east, south, and west.

That the Castillo surely dates from the Toltec period is indicated by its having three characteristics of Toltec architecture at Chichén Itzá: 1. the pair of feathered serpent columns dividing the triple, front doorway; 2. the exterior basal, sloping apron; and 3. the sculptured ornaments (here in the shape of the letter "G", one or two of which is still in place) that formerly ran around the top of the roof along its outer edge.

Because of the discovery of a buried temple inside the pyramid supporting the Temple of the Warriors (Str. 2D8) in 1925 by the Carnegie Institution of Washington, the archaeologists of the Mexican government decided to tunnel, at ground-level, into the pyramid supporting the Castillo to ascertain if a similar earlier condition might be found therein (Fig. 5.3).

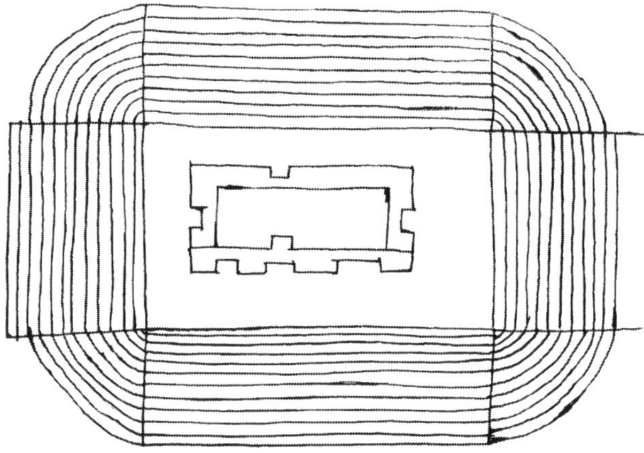

Figure 5.3. El Castillo. Plan drawing after Bishop Diego de Landa, 1566

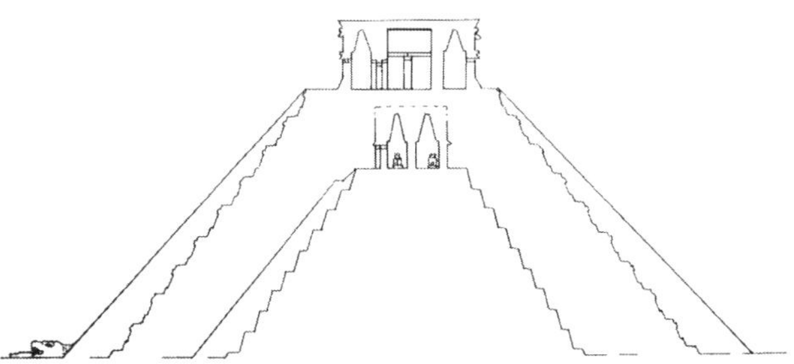

Figure 5.4. El Castillo. Elevation drawing showing the position of the buried pyramid and temple

This work was begun in 1931, at the middle of the south side, and when the tunnel had advanced about 9 m, it reached the lowest terrace of a buried pyramid which was found be faced with beautifully dressed stone. However, because no stairway was found on this south side, it is assumed that the stairway, which originally must have led to its summit, was probably located on the opposite or north side.

In 1934 a tunnel was begun at ground level into the west vertical side of the north stairway in the Castillo, and this latter tunnel led immediately to a chain of magnificent discoveries. This work was carried out under the immediate supervision of Jose A. Erosa Peniche,[5] Inspector of Archaeological Monuments for the State of Yucatán, and was brought to a brilliant conclusion with the finding of the Red Jaguar Throne[6] in 1936, the single most spectacular archaeological object ever discovered in the Americas.

When the tunnel under the north stairway of the Castillo had been advanced to about its middle point (east and west), it was given a right angle turn to the south and pushed, in this new direction, until the base of the original stairway ascending the buried temple was reached; here, at the bottom of the stairway, the first of a series of amazing discoveries was made.

A large rectangular stone box, covered with a stone lid, was found at the bottom of the stairway, and lying next to it, a human skeleton. It has been assumed that this latter is the remains of some slave or captive who was sacrificed at the time the stone box with its treasure was finally buried under the masonry fill of the north stairway of the Castillo.

But what a cache of ancient Maya jewels lay within! When the lid was removed, the first objects seen were two turquoise mosaic plaques, lying on the bottom; one of these has been repaired and is now on exhibition at the Museo de Arqueologia e Historia in Mérida. In addition to these two plaques there were no less than twelve beautifully carved jades, human figures, heads, etc. (Figs. 5.6, 5.7), by far the largest single cache of jade objects ever found in a New Empire city. These are also now on exhibition in the museum at Mérida.

With great skill Jose Erosa Peniche continued his excavations upward under the north stairway of the Castillo, opening a tunnel through the solid masonry fill, which had been built upon and against the stairway of the buried pyramid. Finally when this tunnel had been pushed upward as far as the summit of the buried pyramid it was widened to expose the entrance of the buried temple.

Now a most delicate problem confronted the Mexican archaeologists. They practically had to accomplish the impossible; that is they had both to eat their archaeological cake and, at the same time, to keep it. The ancient people had filled the two rooms of this buried temple from floor to ceiling with solid masonry fill in

[5] Mexican architect José Erosa Peniche (1886-1953) and Manuel Cicerol Sansores directed the excavations by Mexican archaeologists at the Castillo at Chichén Itzá. Erosa Peniche also authored several important works, including *Guía para visitar las ruinas de Chichén Itzá* (1939), *Guide to the Ruins of Chichén Itzá* (1946). *Exploraciones arqueológicas en Chichén-Itzá* (1946) [eds].

[6] The Red Jaguar Throne sculpture was found in an early structure buried beneath the Castillo at Chichén Itzá. Stylistic evidence suggests a Classic period origin. Jade was used for the eyes and the spots on the coat, while the jaguar's fangs were made of flint. The sculpture may have been a throne for the high priest. Mexican archaeologists discovered the hidden chamber during restoration of El Castillo in the 1920s and 1930s. They excavated from the north side and encountered a staircase associated with an ancient structure. They then uncovered a chamber at what must have been the summit of the older structure. Here, in the center of a chamber, then found a perfectly preserved Chac Mool statue. Excavation also revealed another chamber beyond the first, and in the center was discovered the red jaguar throne [eds].

Figure 5.5. El Castillo. Red Jaguar Throne painted red with jade inlays, buried in the inner chamber of the structure buried beneath El Castillo

Figure 5.6. El Castillo. Ceremonial cache in box beneath North Stairway

Figure 5.7. El Castillo. Chacmool sculpture associated with substructure

Figure 5.8. El Castillo. Turquoise Mosaic Plaque. Found resting on two chipped flint blades, before restoration

order to make a solid support for the great mass of the temple they were planning to build on top of it; i.e., what is known today as the Castillo. This masonry fill had now to be removed, stone by stone, but before this operation could be carried out, means had to be devised for supporting safely the tremendous superimposed weight of the Castillo above. This delicate and difficult engineering feat was brilliantly solved by the Mexican government archaeologists, and in 1935 the excavation of the outer room of the buried temple was carried to a successful conclusion.

Here occurred the second spectacular discovery made in connection with this building. After the masonry fill had been removed from the front room there was found, standing just inside the outer doorway and in front of the doorway leading to the sanctuary, one of the so-called Chac Mool figures, a dozen or more of which have been found at Chichén Itzá. But what an unusual one? The finger- and toe-nails of this figure as well as the almond-shaped whites of its eyes are made of highly polished pieces of white shell. The pupils are composed of small circular shaped pieces of some black substance, which give this figure a most life-like appearance, as it reclines in front of the doorway of the sanctuary, perpetually guarding this ancient sacred place.

The following year, 1936, the sanctuary was cleared of masonry fill and the third and most amazing discovery of all was made; one, which is relatively as important to our knowledge of the Maya civilization as was the discovery of the mummy of Tutankhamen to Egyptian archaeology some years ago. After the masonry fill from the front of the sanctuary had been removed there was found built against its rear wall, a crude box, made of large, finely dressed block of limestone. These were not fitted closely together and the excavators could see, by turning the lights of their electric torches in between the cracks, some sort of a large statue.

When these large stone blocks were removed, the Red Jaguar Throne was revealed in all of its original splendor; a throne carved in the likeness of a jaguar, life size, the back flat to sit upon, and the whole figure painted a bright Mandarin red with 73 discs of highly polished, apple-green jade inlaid all over it to imitate the markings of a jaguar skin, and two bulging balls of apple-green jade to represent the jaguar's eyes.

Lying on the seat of the throne was still a third turquoise mosaic plaque, on top of which rested the beads of a jade necklace and pendant, the latter carved in the likeness of an exquisite human head; all of which articles, including the throne itself, have been left by the Mexican government just where they were found.

When the sanctuary had been entirely cleared, a row of bone ends (the heads of human femurs) were found let into the rear wall about 2 m above the floor level and about 2 m apart.

This extraordinary triple discovery made by the Mexican government in the temple buried under the Castillo, together with the previous objects dredged from the Well of Sacrifice, also here at Chichén Itzá, by the Peabody Museum of Archaeology and Ethnology, Harvard University, are without doubt the most spectacular discoveries ever made in the field of American archaeology.

A part of the façade of the buried temple has been very skillfully exposed by the Mexican archaeologists, sufficient to show its general scheme of decoration. The lower zone, as is usually the case of New Empire façades, is plain, the decorative elements being confined to the upper zone. The principal motifs are an alternating series of boldly stalking jaguar figures, practically carved in the full round, alternating with circular shields. A caduceus-like arrangement of two interesting serpents occupies the center of the back; this temple has no sloping basal apron.

Finally the absence of all architectural features, surely characteristic of the Toltec period, would seem to indicate that this temple dates from the Maya period. Perhaps the presence of a Chac Mool figure in its outer room, a purely Toltec type of sculpture may indicate that the temple under the Castillo, though dating from the Maya period, was used for a while after Toltec influence, as exemplified by this Chac Mool figure in its outer room, began to be felt at Chichén Itzá.

Figure 5.9. El Castillo. Sacred way (villa sacra) leading from El Castillo to the sacred cenote

Figure 5.10. Temple of the Chac Mool. Cylindrical limestone vessel (left) and restored turquoise mosaic plaque (right; restored)

Figure 5.11. Temple of the Chac Mool. Upper half of an Atlantean figure sketched in charcoal on the wall of the sanctuary

Two Dance Platforms (Figs. 5.12-5.13)[7]

Directly north of the Castillo is Dance Platform no. 1, a low construction ascended by stairways of all four sides. The flanking ramps of each stairway are elaborately sculptured with pairs of large serpent heads let into their tops (Fig. 5.9). At the base of the east stairway there stands a badly damaged Chac Mool figure, the largest in the city.

[7] These are the Venus Platform and the Platform of the Eagles and the Jaguars (*Plataforma de Águilas y Jaguares*). The Platform of the Eagles and the Jaguars, located immediately east of the ballcourt, is constructed in Maya and Toltec styles, with a staircase ascending each of its four sides. The sides are decorated with panels depicting eagles and jaguars consuming human hearts. The Venus Platform is located north of the ballcourt between it and the Sacred Cenote. Excavators found a collection of large, carved stone cones [eds].

Figure 5.12. Temple of Eagles and Jaguars (Dance Platform 1). After exacavation and repair

Figure 5.13. Venus Platform (Dance Platform no. 2). Before excavation

Some 60 m west of the preceding is the somewhat smaller Dance Platform no. 2 (Fig. 5.13), also ascended by four stairways, one on each face. The sides of this platform are sculptured with panels showing jaguars and eagles with human hearts in their respective paws and claws (Fig. 5.11). In 1878 Augustus Le Plongeon excavated under the floor of this dance platform and found the Chac Mool statue shown in Figure 5.12. This particular one is the best preserved of all the dozen odd Chac Mool figures that have been found at Chichén Itzá, and is now on exhibition at the Museo Nacional de Antropologia e Historia at Mexico City.

Tzompantli (Fig. 5.14)[8]

Northwest of Dance Platform no. 2 is the *Tzompantli*, or Place of the Skulls (Str. 2D2), one of the most unusual constructions at Chichén Itzá (Fig. 5.13). This platform is 55 m long and 12 m wide on top. It is ascended by a single stairway on its east side, and never seems to have had any kind of a superstructure built on top of it. The sides of the eastern extension, where the single stairway is located, are sculptured with warriors, rattle-snakes, etc., which are probably the very finest relief carvings in the city. The sides of the platform proper are sculptured with tiers of human skulls, four to a tier, each four-some being represented as though impaled upon what appears to be the representation of a wooden stack. This is doubtless a late Maya version of the infamous Toltec practice of impaling the skulls of their sacrificial victims on wooden stakes in places near their temples. Excavations in the top of this platform brought to light another Chac Mool statue, which has been left where it was found.

[8] *Tzompantli* (Plataforma de los Craneos or Skull Platform) is a Nahua or Aztec term for this kind of structure, first identified by the Spaniards at the Aztec capital of Tenochtitlan in central Mexico. The heads or skulls of sacrificial victims were impaled vertically on poles whereas they were installed horizontally at Tenochtitlán. The platform walls of the Tzompantli have carved reliefs of four different subjects. The primary subject is the skull rack itself; others show a scene with a human sacrifice; eagles eating all human hearts; and skeletons [eds].

Figure 5.14. Tzompantli, or Place of Skulls

Figure 5.15. Ball Court. Looking north, showing ball court ring in position near top of court wall (right), and the North Temple at the far end

Ball Court and Associated Temples (Fig. 5.15)[9]

The ball court (Str. 2D1) at Chichén Itzá is the largest construction of its kind in the region. It measures 148 m long between the two end structures and is 64 m wide. The two high parallel walls which define the area of play are each 80 m long and 6.7 m high. Along the base of each there is a platform, the top of which is 1.5 m above the level of the court; tenoned into the middle point of each wall, 5 m above the level of the court floor, is a stone ring, the opening through which is 38 cm in diameter.

[9] At least 13 ball courts for playing the Mesoamerican ball game have been found at Chichén Itzá. The Great ball Court, situated northwest of the Castillo, is the largest, measuring 168 m by 70 meters. The parallel platforms flanking the main playing area are each 95 meters long. The walls of these platforms are 8 m in height. Sculpted ballcourt rings of intertwined feathered serpents are set high in the center of each of these walls. At the base of the high interior walls are slanted benches with sculpted panels of groups of ball players. In one panel, one of the players has been decapitated; the wound emits streams of blood in the form of wriggling snakes. At one end of the Great Ball Court is the North Temple, also known as the Temple of the Bearded Man (*Templo del Hombre Barbado*). This small masonry building has detailed bas relief carving on the inner walls, including a center figure that has carving under his chin that resembles facial hair. At the south end is another, much bigger temple, but in ruins. Built into the east wall are the *Temples of the Jaguar*. The *Upper Temple of the Jaguar* overlooks the ball court and has an entrance guarded by two, large columns carved in the familiar feathered serpent motif. Inside there is a large mural, much destroyed, which depicts a battle scene. In the entrance to the *Lower Temple of the Jaguar*, which opens behind the ball court, is another

At the two open ends of the court stand two temples; that at the northern end is smaller and has two round sculptured columns in its façade, the only ones in the city. The temple at the southern end is lower but much wider, and consists of a long open portico with six square columns in its façade. On top of the southern end of the eastern wall is the famous Temple of the Jaguars (Str. 2D1) and at the middle and north end of the eastern wall, and at both ends and middle of the western wall there formerly stood small, narrow rooms, presumably booths from which umpires judged the ball game played in the court below.

An early Spanish chronicler described this game as played in Tenochtitlán (now Mexico City) at the court of the Aztec emperor Moctezuma, at the time of the Spanish conquest in 1519, as follows:

> *The king took much delight in seeing sport at ball, which the Spaniards have since prohibited, because of the mischief that often happened at it; and was by them called tlachtli, being like our tennis. The ball was made of the gum of a tree that grows in hot countries*[10] *which, having holes in it, distills great white drops that soon harden and, being worked and molded together, turn as black as pitch. The balls madder thereof, though hard and heavy to the hand, did bound and fly as well as our foot-balls, there being no need to blow them; nor did they use chacos,*[11] *but vied to drive the adverse party, that is, to hit the wall, the others were to make good, or strike it over. They struck it with any part of their body, as it happened, as they could most conveniently; and sometimes he lost that toughed it with any other part but his hip, which was looked upon among them as the greatest dexterity; and to this effect, that the ball might rebound the better, they fastened a piece of stiff leather to their hips. They might strike it every time it rebounded, which it would do several times, one after another, insomuch that it looked as if it had been alive. They played in groups, so many on a side, for a load of mantles, or what the gamesters could afford, at so many scores. They also played for gold and feather-work, and sometimes played themselves away, as had been said before. The place where they played was a ground floor, long, narrow, and high, but wider above then below, and higher on the sides than at the ends, and they kept it very well plastered and smooth, both the walls and the floor. On the side walls they fixed certain stones, like those of a mill, with a hole quite through the middle, just as big as the ball, and he that could strike it through there won the game; and in token of its being an extraordinary success, which rarely happened, he had a right to the cloaks of all the lookers-on, by ancient custom and law amongst gamesters; and it was very pleasant to see that as soon as ever the ball was in the hole, the standers-by took to their halls, running away with all their might to save their cloaks, laughing and rejoicing, others scouring after them to secure their cloaks for the winner, who was obliged to offer some sacrifice to the idol of the ball court, and the stone through whose hole the ball had passed. Every ball court was a temple, having two idols, the one of gaming, and the other of the ball. On a lucky day, at midnight, they performed certain ceremonies and enchantments on the two lower walls and on the midst of the floor, single certain songs, or ballads; after which a priest of the great temple went with some of their religious men to bless it; he uttered some words, threw the ball about the ball court for times, and then it was consecrated, and might be played in but not below. The owner of the ball court, who was always a lord, never played without making some offering and performing certain ceremonies to the idol of gaming, which shows how superstitious they were, since they had such regard to their idols, even in their diversions. Moctezuma carried the Spaniards to this sport, and was well pleased to see them play at it, as also at cards and dice"*

The payment of the above forfeit, when the winning stroke was achieved under the extremely difficult rules of the game, i.e., that the ball could only be struck by the elbow, wrist, or hip, could only have been made but very infrequently, perhaps as rarely as a hole-in-one in the modern game of golf.[12]

Temple of the Jaguars (Figs. 5.16-5.20)

The Temple of the Jaguars (Str. 2D1), excavated and repaired by the Mexican government in 1926, rises from the top of the south end of the eastern wall, and is one of the most remarkable buildings at Chichén Itzá. It is a typical temple of the Toltec period with all the customary Toltec features, feathered serpent columns, sloping basal apron, and cut stone roof-ornaments, here in the shape of short javelins, or arrows crossed behind circular shields. The façade is elaborately sculptured, a frieze of stalking jaguars (from which this temple takes its name; (Fig. 5.18) alternating with a series of circular shields being the most conspicuous decorative elements. These last two elements, it will be remembered, were also the principal ones in the decorative scheme of the façade of the temple buried beneath the Castillo. And there is little doubt but that the latter belongs to the Maya period as does the former to the Toltec period, the time interval between the two periods probably not being great.

The narrow stairway ascending the eastern wall of the Ball Court at its southern end, which gives access to the Temple of the Jaguars, is the steepest known stairway in

Jaguar throne, similar to the one in the inner temple of El Castillo, except that it is well worn and missing paint or other decoration. The outer columns and the walls inside the temple are covered with elaborate bas-relief carvings [eds].

[10] The ancient rubber ball was made from latex of the rubber tree (*Castilla elastica*), which is indigenous to the tropical areas of southern Mexico and Central America. The latex was made into rubber by mixing it with the juice of what was likely *Ipomoea alba* (a species of morning glory). The resultant rubber would then be formed into rubber strips, which would be wound around a solid rubber core to build the ball [eds].

[11] *Chocos* probably refers to sandals or foot wear.

[12] For a description of the survival of the ball game the from Sinaloa-Nayarit region on the west coast of Mexico see Kelly (2011) [eds].

Figure 5.16. Temple of the Jaguars. After repair and restoration, looking east

Figure 5.17. Temple of the Jaguars. Side view showing jaguar and shield frieze

the Maya area, rising at a gradient of more than 60 degrees.

The enormous blocks of stone from which each of the serpent heads were carved, in the pair of feathered-serpent columns mentioned above, are the heaviest places of stone in the city, weighing as much as five tons. They were probably raised to their present positions on ramps made of earth and stone by means of log rollers and ropes, materials for both of which occur in greatest abundance in the nearby forest.

This temple, like so many others at Chichén Itzá, contains only two rooms, an outer corridor entered through a triple doorway divided by the pair of feathered serpent columns, and an inner sanctuary, Owing to the many Atlantean figures which were found scattered about the building, its sanctuary would originally have contained an Atlantean figure dais, (Str. 2D7) just north of it.

The jambs of the doorway leading into the sanctuary of the Temple of the Jaguars are sculptured with the figures of warriors, and the *sapodilla*[13] beams which span it are also carved. The walls of this sanctuary are painted with an extensive fresco depicting a fiercely contested battle. Warriors, bearing shields decorated with circles, are

[13] Sapodilla (*Manilkara zapota*) is a long-lived evergreen tree native to southern Mexico, Central America, and the Caribbean. Sapodilla can grow to more than 30 m tall with an average trunk diameter of 1.5 m [eds].

Figure 5.18. Temple of the Jaguars. View of the jaguar and shield frieze

attacking a typical Maya village of thatched houses; the men of the village are bravely defending their homes, while the women cluster (upper right) as far from the conflict as possible; one of them is crying, her hand held expressively before her face. Although only a few lines are used in the composition, vigorous action is admirably suggested.

A scene portraying human sacrifice from the walls of the sanctuary of this same temple. The victim is stretched, breast upward, across the sacrificial altar, his feet held by one assistant, his arms by another; above him stands a priest with upraised sacrificial knife, poised to plunge the same into the intended victim's breast.

Down on the ground-level, immediately east of the Temple of the Jaguars, and built against its foundation platform, is a small single room building, the interior walls of which are completely sculptured from floor to the capstones of its arch with low relief carving, five or six rows of elaborately dressed warriors, marching around three sides of the room, i.e., all except the open, east portico. The relief, although low, was originally accentuated by being painted in a full palette of brilliant colors, many traces of which still adhere to the walls. Between the pair of square sculptured columns in the doorway there stands a jaguar-throne with a flat back for the seat, in the same general style as the famous Red Jaguar Throne. Four of these jaguar thrones have been found at Chichén Itzá: 1. the jade encrusted Red Jaguar Throne in the sanctuary of the temple below the Castillo; 2. the one in the doorway of the one-room structure below and behind the Temple of the Jaguars; 3. the one standing beneath the stairway leading to the second story of the Monjas; and, 4. one found in a small building west of the ball court, which was partially demolished when the Dzitas-Chichén Itzá highway was built in 1923; this latter building was probably the southernmost unit of the Northwest Group. This fourth jaguar-throne is now in the Museo del Arqueologia e Historia at Mérida; the other three will stand just where they were found at Chichén Itzá

Figure 5.19. Temple of the Jaguars. Chac mool throne in doorway of sculptured room below the Temple of the Jaguars

Figure 5.20. Temple of the Jaguars. Mural of a human sacrifice

Figure 5.21. Feathered Serpent Column. Partially completed column near the ledge of rock quarry

Before leaving the ball court it is necessary to mention its remarkable, though probably entirely accidental, acoustic properties which Leopold Stokowski[14] says make it the best open-air auditorium in the world. The distance between the doorways of the North and South Temples is precisely 152 m the former being slightly higher than the latter. By placing an orthophonic Victrola[15] in the doorway of the North Temple, and chairs for the auditors on the terrace in front of the South Temple, on a quiet moon lit night, such a concert of magic and delight may be heard as rarely to be enjoyed, even in Carnegie Hall. A Red Seal recording of the overture to Act III of *La Traviata* with every delicate string or wood-wind note coming down the long axis of the court as clearly and as truly as it left the instruments of the New York Philharmonic of the Philadelphia Symphony Orchestra the day it was originally recorded, with the rasping of the reproducing mechanism entirely eliminated, is a musical treat never to be forgotten, my own happiest recollection of all the many years I spent at Chichén Itzá

An amazing incident in connection with the ball court and one concerning its extraordinary acoustic properties may not be out of place here. A group of sixteen Independent Maya Indians from the forest hinterlands of the distant Territory of Quintana Roo visited Chichén Itzá; the head of the group, five lesser chiefs, and eleven guards. I sent them with a Maya-speaking interpreter to show them the ruins their ancestors had built, and this is what the interpreter told me happened.

What excited their liveliest curiosity in the entire city were the remarkable, acoustic properties of the ball court, to explain which they went into a prolonged Maya huddle. From this they came with the following explanation, "It was the voices of our ancestors talking back to us."

As became common folk, the eleven guards talked to their ancestors in moderate voices and got back modest answers. The lesser chiefs, with more prestige, spoke up more smartly, and their ancestors answered them for vigorously. But the head chief shouted to his forefathers and got back the strongest reply of all. "Humph" said he, "even our ancestors known who is boss here!"

The Northwest Group

Located northwest of the North Temple of the ball court is a little known cluster of buildings, the Northwest Group, possibly eight or nine in all, the principal units of which center around a small court. None of its structures has been excavated, though the southernmost building was partially demolished when the Dzitas-Chichén Itzá highway was built in 1923, at which time the Jaguar Throne found standing against its back wall, was removed to the museum at Mérida.

Some 60 m south of the southern end of this group, and a 30 m south of the Mérida-Chichén Itzá highway, in a hollow in the limestone, an ancient quarry, there stands a partially finished head for a feathered serpent column, just where it was quarried from six to nine centuries ago (Fig. 5.21). The outline of the mouth and the eyes has been so carved on the block destined for this head, and the head itself generally shaped, but the mouth-cavity had not yet been chipped out when the ancient Itzá sculptors laid down their chisels for the last time.

Group of the Thousand Columns (Fig. 5.22)

The Group of the Thousand Columns occupies the eastern half of the great north terrace and is composed of no less than half a dozen temples, of which the Temple of

[14] Morley loved to play records in the Great Ball Court because of its unique acoustic properties. In 1931 Leopold Stokowski (1882-1977), a British orchestral conductor, spent four days at Chichén Itzá to determine the acoustic principals of the ball court that could be applied to theater for an open-air concert he was designing [eds].

[15] The Victor Orthophonic Victrola demonstrated publicly in 1925, was the first consumer phonograph designed specifically to play "electrically" recorded disks. The combination was recognized instantly as a major step forward in sound reproduction [eds].

Figure 5.22. Group of the Thousand Columns. After excavation and restoration, from the Temple of the Warriors

the Warriors (Str. 2D8) is the most important, as many colonnades, at least three ball courts, two peristyle courts, and a sweat bath, to say nothing of a number of minor constructions.

The architectural center of this group is the Court of the Thousand Columns, around which cluster the principal buildings. The court itself contains 0.2 sq m and with its associated constructions in its heyday must have been perhaps the most impressive of the Seven Architectural Wonders of the ancient New World.

This court has two gateways, one through the West Colonnade and the other passing under the North Colonnade. In addition, there are two passageways on the east side between buildings and the whole southwest corner of the court is open.

Beginning at the north and proceeding generally southward the first construction reached is a peristyle court like the better known and larger so-called Market Place; this, however, has never been excavated. Next, further south, rises a feathered serpent column temple, the sanctuary of which was excavated by Alfred P. Maudslay in 1889, but not repaired. Next comes the imposing Temple of the Warriors which, except for the Castillo, is the largest temple in the city, with the Northwest Colonnade in front of it; both of these structures were excavated and repaired by the Carnegie Institution in 1925-1928.

Continuing south along the front of the fallen West Colonnade at its middle point, the West gateway is reached; this gives entrance to the Court of the Thousand Columns. Northward of this gateway the archaeologists of the Carnegie Institution of Washington have left an interesting exhibit showing various stages in the work of excavation and repair. Immediately north of the West gateway a section of the fallen West Colonnade (Str. 3D1) has been left without excavation, just as it was found, most of its round columns toppled over, their individual drum-like sections lying scattered about upon the ground, the spaces between filled with the masonry debris of the fallen vaulted roof; a few of the columns are still standing.

The roofs of these great colonnades rested upon *sapodilla* beams running longitudinally along the length of the colonnade between the columns. Here, in the West Colonnade, vaults ran north and south, and when the *sapodilla* beams supporting them gave way, the entire colonnade fell outward to the west, like a house of cards.

The second stage in this serial exhibit is the section lying immediately north, where the debris between the columns has been entirely removed, the drums of the fallen columns, however having been left by the excavators in wind-rows on the former floor of the colonnade.

The third stage lies immediately north of the second and consists of a section of the colonnade, where the drums and capitals of its respective columns have been restored by the Carnegie Institution of Washington to their original positions.

A fourth and final stage would have replaced the *sapodilla* beams running longitudinally along the tops of the restored columns and rebuilt with massive masonry construction of the upper half of the colonnade, containing five long corbel vaults.

Passing through the West gateway and turning north, a monumental stairway is reached near the northwest corner of the court which gives access to the North Colonnade, excavated and repaired by the Carnegie Institution in 1928. Along the north or rear wall of the colonnade there runs a bench with inclined back; and interrupting the latter but somewhat nearer its western than its eastern end, there is a slightly higher dais, its sides elaborately sculptured with warriors, and finally, standing just in front of it, there is another Chac Mool figure.

Figure 5.23. North Colonnade. Entrance to passageway under the North Colonnade, leading from the Court of the Thousand Columns to the exterior

Figure 5.24. North Colonnade. Sculptured and painted dais with Chac Mool sculpture in foreground

It would seem as though the eastern end of the North Colonnade was never completed since there is a section here which is occupied only by columns, i.e., without any intervening roof debris, and still farther east and extending to the northeast corner of the Court of the Thousand Columns, there is still another section of the terrace of the North Colonnade (Str. 2D10) where there are neither even columns nor fallen roof debris (Figs. 5.23-5.24).

A passageway passes through and under the terrace supporting the North Colonnade, which emerges just west of a small ball court lying east of the Temple of the Warriors.

The east side of the Court of the Thousand Columns is occupied by several different colonnades and one large temple of the feathered serpent column type; this latter was partially excavated many years ago by E.H. Thompson, but no repair work was ever undertaken.

Near the north end of the eastern side, between two adjacent buildings a narrow opening leads east to the Northeast Colonnade (Str. 3E1), the first building excavated and repaired at Chichén Itzá by the Carnegie Institution of Washington (1924).

This last colonnade had begun to slide into the great natural compression just behind it to the north, in ancient times a strenuous effort had been made by the Itzá to support its tottering roof. Small Atlantean figures had been wedged in between the last tier of columns and the bench against the north wall in an attempt to shore up these columns. Even additional walls had been built between the columns to support the failing *sapodilla* beams which spanned them. Originally, against the middle of the rear wall, a sculptured dais had been built, but even this had not been spared to provide building stones for these later, secondary, supporting walls.

Near the south end of the east side of the Court of the Thousand Columns a narrow opening between two buildings gives access to the east, where Sweat Bath no. 2, excavated and repaired by the Carnegie Institution of Washington in 1936, is located. To the south of this there are several unexcavated mounds, and to the north, another ball court, also unexcavated; this last is the second largest ball court at the site.

The entire south side of the Court of the Thousand Columns is occupied by the striking, so-called Market Place (3D11), though this was certainly not its original function. This consists of a very long colonnade in front of a peristyle court; this was excavated and repaired by the Carnegie Institution of Washington in 1932.

Finally in the open southwest corner of the Court of the Thousand Columns stands still another ball-court (Str. 2D9), which however yet remains to be excavated.

Temple of the Warriors and the Northwest Colonnade (Figs. 5.25-5.34)

The most important construction at the Group of the Thousand Columns, and the second largest temple at Chichén Itzá is the Temple of the Warriors (Str. 2D8) which faces west and away from the Court of the Thousand Columns. This was excavated and repaired by the Carnegie Institution of Washington in 1925-1928 under the direction of Earl H. Morris and Gustav Strömsvik.

In front of the Temple of the Warriors lies the Northwest Colonnade (Str. 2D8), a noble hall with 61 square columns, sculptured on all sides with figures of warriors. Through a stairwell at the back, like the one at the Temple of the Wall Murals, there rises a steep stairway, flanked by ramps sculptured with intertwining serpents, leading to the Temple of the Warriors. To the right of this stairway and built against the rear wall of the Northwest Colonnade (Str. 2D8) is another sculptured dais like those in the North (Str. 2D10) and Northeast (Str. 3E1) Colonnades. This had originally been ascended by a stairway of three steps; the eyes of the warrior figures sculptured on its sides formerly had eyes made of inlaid almond-shaped pieces of white shell. Immediately in front of this stairway there is a small block of stone 3.2 cm high shaped like a truncated pyramid and measuring 30 cm by 20 cm square on top. Another one of these sculptured sides stood in front of the third story of the Monjas. There is little doubt that these were stones, or altars of sacrifice. The human victims destined for sacrifice were stretched, breast upward over this stone, their feet being held to the ground by two assistants and the arms, similarly pinned down, by two other assistants.

Figure 5.25. Temple of the Warriors. Before excavation

Figure 5.26. Temple of the Warriors. After excavation

Figure 5.27. Temple of the Warriors. Detail of sculptured frieze

Figure 5.28. Temple of the Warriors. Altar supported by Atlantean figures

In this position the breast was curved upward which facilitated its being slit open by the sacrificial flint knife. This religious ceremony or ritual is portrayed in mural paintings from the Temple of the Warriors and the Temple of the Jaguars.

During the first season of work at the Temple of the Warriors (1925) Morris noticed the tops of a tier of sculptured square stone columns which projected slightly above the northern slope of the supporting pyramid, a clear indication that some earlier construction was buried

Figure 5.29. Temple of the Warriors, South Wall, West Panel. After repair and restoration

Figure 5.30. Temple of the Warriors. Front view showing serpent columns and mask panels seen from southwest. The entrance is divided in three parts by columns in the form of feathered serpents

Figure 5.31. Temple of the Warriors. After excavation and repair, showing a pair of anthropomorphic standard bearers flanking the top of the stairway at right

Figure 5.32. Temple of the Warriors. Mural painting of a fishing village

Figure 5.33. Temple of the Warriors. Mural painting of a battle scene

inside which, at some later time, had been filled in and incorporated into the pyramid that was subsequently built to support the Temple of the Warriors.

This was the first case of "eating our archaeological cake and of keeping it at the same time," at Chichén Itzá. Indeed, it was the fact that the CIW archaeologists had discovered an earlier temple buried under the Temple of the Warriors in 1925, that latter in 1931, prompted the Mexican government archaeologists to look for a similarly located, earlier construction enclosed beneath the pyramid supporting the Castillo.

The second and third season's work at the Temple of the Warriors were devoted to excavating the buried temple, which was named the Temple of the Chac Mool (Str. 2D8), as well as to supporting the superimposed weight of the later Temple of the Warriors that had been built above it; the northwest corner of the latter had to be suspended in air, its walls resting upon reinforced concrete steel I-beams, an engineering feat of the first magnitude, most skilfully executed by Morris and Strömsvik (Figs. 5.10-5.11).

But what spectacular success attended this difficult operation! What an archaeological treasure it laid bare. The Temple of the Chac Mool was revealed as a typical two-room structure, originally entered on the west side through a feathered serpent column triple doorway. The blocks composing these serpent columns had been removed when the temple was partially demolished in connection with the construction of the subsequent Temple of the Warriors, and some of their component parts, notably the two large serpent-heads, had been reused in the fill of its two rooms. A perfectly preserved Chac Mool figure (5.34) which stood in front of this temple and from which this structure takes its name, was found lying on its side in the outer room, completely buried under masonry fill. Originally there had been a single tier of four sculptured and brilliantly painted square columns in the outer room, and another tier of the same number in the sanctuary, all of which were preserved except the northernmost column in each tier.

Along the rear and side walls of the sanctuary there had originally been built a bench, and against the middle of the back wall there had formerly stood an altar supported by Atlantean figures, similar to those in the Temple of the Jaguars (Str. 2D11) and the Temple of the Tables (Str. 2D7). This altar, however, was removed when the sanctuary of the Chac Mool temple had been filled with masonry rubble, and later reconstructed in the same relative position of the sanctuary of the later Temple of the Warriors above, presumably to serve the same function there.

Previous excavation experience at Chichén Itzá indicated that valuable caches were usually to be found buried beneath the altars of the temples. Morris was confident that if such a cache could be located in connection with such an important structure as the Temple of the Chac Mool it would have to be something very special.

Figure 5.34. Temple of the Warriors. Mural of a battle near a lake

Acting upon this hunch, he began excavating below the plaster floor of the sanctuary where the Atlantean figure altar had formerly stood. Success beyond his wildest expectations attended his digging. A little blow floor level his pick struck something made of stone, and further excavation revealed a circular limestone container, or cylindrical shaped vessel 27.9 cm high and 35.5 cm in diameter, sealed with a stone lid (Fig. 5.35).

Never shall I forget that day in 1928 when we opened this limestone box. Tense with excitement all members of the staff, including Dr. J.C. Merriam, then President of the Carnegie Institution of Washington, crowded around with our electric torches trained on this stone, cylindrically shaped vessel for the light was poor; our Yucatec Maya laborers as interested as us, while Morris removed the stone lid. The first object which our torches revealed was a spherically shaped piece of dark green, highly polished, jade, about 5 cm in diameter, which rested on the bottom.

Our Yucatec Maya laborers identified this as a *sastun*, or magic stone, similar to those still used by old Maya medicine-men, the *ah menob*, in their present day incantations deep in the forest.

Carefully brushing away the dirt that had sifted under the stone lid during the six to nine centuries since this cache

Figure 5.35. Temple of the Tables, interior from the south

had been buried under the floor of the sanctuary of the Chac Mool temple, Morris quickly uncovered an object of brilliant, light blue lying on the bottom of the limestone container; further cleaning revealed this to be a turquoise mosaic plaque 35.5 cm in diameter that rested on the bottom, but unhappily in the most fragile condition. The 3,000 odd pieces of which this mosaic was composed originally had been fastened to a wooden base that had entirely rotted away, and it is exaggeration to say that this mosaic, when it was found, was literally resting on dust. Clearly the greatest care would have to be taken lest the limestone container should be accidentally shifted, and this priceless piece of mosaic of another age and another people be lost forever. This was the first of the four turquoise mosaic plaques which have been thus far at Chichén Itzá

Morris decided that the container should be removed to the CIW field headquarters at the hacienda, and a council was immediately held to decide how best to handle the critical situation which had developed so suddenly.

Clearly there was no one at Chichén Itzá experienced enough to remove the individual pieces of the mosaic and rest them again on a new base. It was finally decided to send a cable to the American Museum of Natural History in New York City asking it to loan the services of its most skilled preparer of museum specimens, and here the matter rested for the time being.

In answer to our call for help, about a month later Dr. Shouchi Ichikawa, a skilled museum technician with a doctorate from Columbia University, arrived at Chichén Itzá and began the exceedingly delicate operation of resetting the individual pieces of the mosaic on a new base. First a new base was made of three-ply wood, of exactly the same size and shape as the destroyed original base, and with infinite patience and care Ichikawa began resetting the 3,000 pieces of the mosaic, piece by piece, on the newly prepared base. The restored plaque is now on exhibition in the Museo Nacional de Arqueologia e Historia at Mexico City.

This spectacular discovery, the first of its kind made in the Maya area, further serves to connect the later history of Chichén Itzá with the highlands of Central Mexico, since such turquoise mosaic plaques were only made in Central Mexico and have never been found at any Maya Old Empire site, or at any New Empire site, save only Chichén Itzá Turquoise does not occur in nature in the Yucatan peninsula although deposits of it are found at several places in central Mexico.

A bench formerly was built against the rear and side walls of the sanctuary of the Temple of the Chac Mool. When this was partially demolished to accommodate the later Temple of the Warriors, the stones with which it was built were torn out and reused in the fill of the sanctuary. When this happened, even before the bench was built, some workmen in the temple sketched in charcoal on the bottom of the south all of the sanctuary the upper half of one of these Atlantean figure altar supports.

The archaeologists of the CIW carried on extensive tunneling in the pyramid supporting the Temple of the Warriors to expose details of earlier constructions. Passing through a break in the back wall of the Temple of the Chac Mool a deep excavation is descended by means of a ladder to reach a tunnel at ground level which follows south along the east base of the pyramid of the Chac Mool temple (Str. 2D8), then around its original southeast corner, then west along its south side until the latter abuts the rear wall of the original West Colonnade, part of which, including a doorway painted red and blue, is still preserved. From the landing behind the sanctuary of the Temple of the Chac Mool a modern stairway also has been built leading up top the level of the Temple of the Warriors above.

The reconstruction of the facing of the pyramid supporting the Temple of the Warriors presented a difficult problem. Originally this pyramid had been composed of four terraces of similar height, the upper part of each having a vertical face and the lower part, a sloping basal apron. The upper vertical section of the upper terrace is plain, but the corresponding sections of the three lower terraces had all been elaborately sculptured with designs which extended around all four sides of the pyramid, only being interrupted by the stairway on the west or front. Four recurring figures form the principal motifs in each of these three friezes: warriors, eagles, jaguars, and an unidentifiable animal with a short tail, which was nicknamed "the Wooly" by CIW archaeologists.

These friezes are composed of two sculptured courses each. Almost every sculptured element of all three of them had fallen to the ground and lay in confusion scattered through large piles of debris on all four sides of the pyramid, the wreckage of three gigantic mosaics, all mixed up together.

With infinite patience and skill the CIW archaeologists set about sorting the individual pieces of these three huge puzzles, the correct assemblage of which was enormously complicated by the fact that all three presented essentially the same decorative motif, i.e., varying combinations of the four kinds of figures mentioned above.

For one entire season, several of the staff assisted by a number of Yucatec Maya laborers worked on fitting together the elements of these three great puzzles, laying them on the ground in their correct original positions with relation to each other. And finally when this was done, the Maya masons skillfully built them back into their original positions in the front and sides of this pyramid. The three sculptured friezes on the rear, or east, face were not returned to their original positions.

Ascending to the summit of this pyramid, the stairway if flanked by two standing human statues, each about one meter high, and their hands clasped together in front of them. A hole between the hands in each case indicates their former function as standard-bearers to hold poles from which feather-work banners were hung. Other standard-bearer shaped like truncated cones formerly stood along the edges of the summit.

At the top of the stairway there is another Chac Mool figure, its head somewhat battered, and behind this a pair of high, feathered serpent columns which divide the typical triple doorway.

That this great religious structure dates from the Toltec period is indicated by the pair of feathered-serpent columns in its doorway, the Chac Mool figure in front, the sloping basal apron that runs around the building, broken only by a triple doorway in front, and the number of stone roof grills scattered around the base of the pyramid on all four sides, which originally had surmounted the edge of the roof of the temple below.

The decorative scheme of the lower zone of this structure (i.e., just above the sloping basal apron) is composed of tiers of three mask panels with their curling snouts, alternating with the serpent-bird motif; i.e., a creature with the body of a bird and the projecting head of a serpent from whose widely opened jaws in each case a human head emerges.

The exterior of the Temple of the Warriors had been repeatedly covered with coats of white lime-plaster (131 different coats were counted still adhering to the sloping basal apron), and the sculptured design had been brightly painted. The upper half of this building, which contained the massive construction of its eight corbel vaults, running north and south, three in the outer room, and five in the sanctuary running east and west, was not restored.

The walls of both these rooms had originally been painted, but their frescoes had entirely disappeared. The dozen square columns supporting the triple vaulted roof of the outer corridor as well as the eight square columns supporting the vaulted roof of the sanctuary each had all four of their sides sculptured with the figures of warriors. It was these warrior figures which suggested the name Temple of the Warriors for this building.

The sanctuary had the typical benches with reclining backs, built against its side walls and part of the back. The middle of the back was occupied by the Atlantean figure altar that originally had occupied a similar position in the sanctuary of the older and abandoned Temple of the Chac Mool below. This altar now stands 76 cm high, is 4 m wide, and 2.5 m deep to the back wall. It is supported by 19 Atlantean figures and 9 additional small round stone pillars with typical square capitals.

As originally designed for use in the sanctuary of the Chac Mool temple, this altar had stood 20.3 cm higher, but since such a height was not desired in its later position in the sanctuary of the Temple of the Warriors above, this 20 cm of excess height was remedied by burying the lower 20 cm of each Atlantean figure in the floor, to about the level of the knees. To correct the resulting distortion in the anatomical proportions of the human figure, small dummy feet of stucco were built out from the knees in each case, resting on the floor, which make these Atlantean figures, as reused in this altar, appear like little short-legged manikins. The only pair of these dummy stucco feet still preserved are those projecting from the knees of the left hand (east) figure on the left (north) side of the altar.

The interior walls of the Temple of the Warriors were covered with frescoes, most of which were destroyed when the roof of this building collapsed. Ann Axtell Morris rescued several sections of these frescoes from total loss, by first carefully fitting together the blocks of stone upon which they had been painted, next by making water-color copies of them, and by skilfully restoring in her paintings the missing portions of the original compositions.

Figure 5.36. Temple of the Tables. Atlantean figures

Figure 5.37. Temple of the Interior Atlantean Columns. After excavation and restoration

Three of these scenes are shown in Figures 5.36-5.33. The first portrays a scene of human sacrifice in front of a temple. The victim is stretched across the lower coil of a rattle-snake's body (the altar), his hands pinioned down by one assistant, his feet by another. The officiating priest stands behind with the sacrificial flint knife upraised in his left hand, ready to plunge it into the victim's chest. The serpent, a representation of Kukulcan, the Feathered Serpent, patron deity of Chechen Itzá, raises his head above and behind the four participants in this bloody ritual, in front of the doorway of his own temple.

The second fresco depicts a fishing village. The lower third of the composition, painted blue with wavy black lines, represents the water. Three canoes fill the foreground, each manned by three paddlers; a variety of marine life swarms in the sea, several; snails, crabs, sting-rays, turtle, red-snapper, and a sword fish. On shore a

Figure 5.38. Northwest Colonnade. Dais, with sacrificial stone in the foreground

number of daily activities are going forward, several men are walking about carrying burdens on their heads, or backs, another squats in the outer corridor of the temple at the right, a feathered serpent rising out of the sanctuary. A woman watches a pot boil over the fire and another, near the water's edge, is washing clothes. A basket of freshly caught fish stands on a table in the doorway of the house in the center, while a white heron flies overhead. All is peaceful, all serene, and far removed from the battle scene from the Temple of the Jaguars.

The third fresco shows the aftermath of such a battle. A temple rises from the waters of a lake in the upper left corner. A number of nude prisoners, their bodies painted with black and white stripes, their hands tied behind their backs, are being led off into captivity. In the upper right a few warriors appear as still; carrying on the fight from the roofs of houses.

Note: Along the south wall of the Temple of Warriors are a series of what are today exposed columns, although when the city was inhabited these would have supported an extensive roof system. The columns are in three distinct sections: a west group, that extends the lines of the front of the Temple of Warriors; a north group, which runs along the south wall of the Temple of Warriors and contains pillars with carvings of soldiers in bas-relief; and a northeast group, which apparently formed a small temple at the southeast corner of the Temple of Warriors, which contains a rectangular decorated with carvings of people or gods, as well as animals and serpents. The northeast column temple also covers a small marvel of engineering, a channel that funnels all the rainwater from the complex some 40 m away to a *rejollada*, or former cenote. To the south of the Group of a Thousand Columns is a group of three, smaller, interconnected buildings. The Temple of the Carved Columns is a small elegant building that consists of a front gallery with an inner corridor that leads to an altar with a Chac Mool. There are also numerous columns with rich, bas-relief carvings of some 40 personages. A section of the upper facade with a motif of x's and o's is displayed in front of the structure. The Temple of the Small Tables which is an unrestored mound. And the Thompson's Temple (Str. 3D9) (referred to in some sources as Palace of Ahau Balam Kauil), a small building with two levels that has friezes depicting Jaguars (*balam* in Maya) as well as glyphs of the Maya god Kahuil.

Note: The Temple of the Warriors complex consists of a large stepped pyramid fronted and flanked by rows of carved columns depicting warriors. This complex is analogous to Temple B at the Toltec capital of Tula, and indicates some form of cultural contact between the two regions. The one at Chichén Itza, however, was constructed on a larger scale. At the top of the stairway on the pyramid's summit (and leading towards the entrance of the pyramid's temple) is a Chac Mool. This temple encases or entombs a former structure called The Temple of the Chac Mool. The archeological expedition and restoration of this building was done by the Carnegie Institute of Washington from 1925 to 1928. A key member of this restoration was Earl H. Morris who published the work from this expedition in two volumes entitled *Temple of the Warriors*.

Market-Place (Fig. 5.39)

This structure (Str. D11), misnamed the Market-Place (Mercado) by myself in a careless moment 25 years ago, has nothing to do with the buying and selling of goods, an activity much more likely to have been carried on in the spacious 1,800 sq m court upon which this building

Figure 5.39. Mercado (market)

fronts. My misleading name seems to have struck the popular fancy and this building is now generally known as the "Market-Place."

It consists of a single hall 73 m long and 5 m wide, the widest known room in the Maya area. The front is an open portico which was originally supported by 19 rectangular-shaped columns made of from 6 to 8 blocks each, and spaced 3.2 m apart, center to center. Originally these supported *sapodilla* beams (three to each span) that ran across the entire front of the building, which supported the massive masonry of the facade and the northern half of the long corbel-vaulted, single room. However, these spans, as originally constructed, proved to be too long for safety, and the ancient builders were subsequently obliged to introduce additional supports to keep the beam from giving way under the crushing weight above. This was done by introducing 18 circular columns, one midway between each pair of adjacent rectangular columns. These additional round columns must have considerably marred the architectural effect of this building, but at the same time they probably saved the roof from crashing down on the heads of its occupants.

Across the two narrow ends of the portico and along the rear wall is a bench with inclined back, and to the left of the single large doorway in the back wall, there is a sculptured dais similar to those in the Northwest, North, and Northeast Colonnades. The design on this dais is that of two single files of warriors approaching the front, or north face, of this dais, the warriors in each file apparently being bound together by a connecting rope. The cornice of the dais displays four rattle-snakes weaving along its three faces, one each on the east and west sides, and two meeting in the middle of the front or north face of the dais.

Passing through the single wide door at the rear (4 m width), entrance is gained to the peristyle-court behind (Fig. 5.41). Running around all four sides of this court there is a single tier of 25 round columns, each measuring 4.7 m in height, including the square capital, and each being composed of 10 drums. Only the western half of this court has been excavated, and only 15 of its 25 columns, 7 on the west side, and 4 each on the north and south sides, have been re-erected, the remaining 10 lie prostrate on the ground, their respective drums fallen in wind-rows.

The sunken court surrounded by this peristyle is 9.4 sq m square. Drains at the middle point of its eastern and western sides carried off the rainfall, which otherwise would have had no outlet. In excavations carried on under the level of the court-floor a box-like enclosure of masonry was found, about 0.6 m square at the top but with a deeper central section 76 cm long by 60 cm wide. On the bottom of this enclosure were found a few jade ornaments, and 113 shell beads. The best piece of jade is a pendant carved to represent a human head; it is irregular in shape and measures 3.2 cm wide by 3.8 cm tall.

The long colonnade in front of the peristyle-court, in fact this entire construction, dates from the Toltec period as is indicated by the presence of the sloping basal apron, the roof-grill, here in the form of the letter G like those which ornamented the roof of the Castillo, and finally the dais itself, built against the back wall of the colonnade, decorated with files of Toltec warriors and plumed rattle-snakes. Both parts of this building, the front colonnade and the peristyle-court behind, were excavated and repaired by Karl Rupert in 1932 and 1934.

This square structure anchors the southern end of the Temple of Warriors complex. It is so named for the shelf

Figure 5.40. Temazcalli (Sweatbath) no. 2. Looking east

of stone that surrounds a large gallery and patio that early explorers theorized was used to display wares as in a marketplace. Today, archaeologists believe that its purpose was more ceremonial than commerce.

Sweat Bath no. 2 (Fig. 5.40)

Behind the high feathered-serpent column temple to the east of the Court of the Thousand Columns, but located outside the latter, is the Sweat Bath no. 2, excavated and repaired by Karl Ruppert and P. N. Fontaine in 1935. It is composed on an outer room with four round columns in its front or west face and masonry benches against its north and south end walls; only the north end of this outer room has been completely restored, even including the roof.

In the back, or east, wall there is a low doorway only 0.8 m high and 0.7 wide, which leads into the sweat-room proper. In the north and south ends is a low oven for heating the stones which were used in generating the steam for the sweat-bath. These stones were heated in the oven and then drawn out onto the flag-stone floor of the space between the two end benches. Here water was thrown on them, making steam. Round holes at the ends of this room, above the benches, carried off the excess vapor.

There is another one of these sweat-baths at Chichén Itzá, just south of the Caracol, but it is much less well-preserved than the one here described. This unusual type of building has been found at the Old Empire city of Piedras Negras and was common in central Mexico during Toltec times, where they were called *temazcalli* (hot houses).

In summary, the buildings on the Great North Terrace probably date from the Toltec period.

Note: The sweat or steam bath, in an enclosed chamber heated with rocks, is a construction found in many places of ancient and modern Mesoamerica. They were used for hygiene and curing. The basic design includes a sweating room, an oven, ventilation openings, flues, and drains.

Well of Sacrifice and the Causeway Leading to It (Fig. 5.41-5.43)

Certainly the most sacred place at Chichén Itzá and probably in all Middle America during the thirteenth and fourteenth centuries of the Christian era was the Well of Sacrifice located about 1.2 km north of the northern edge of the great north terrace and connected to it by an elevated stone causeway.

This causeway is 9.5 m wide on top and from the edge of the north terrace to the Well of Sacrifice 170 m long. At the point where it leaves the north terrace is some 3.6 to 4.9 m above the natural ground-level, but as the Well is approached it descends to nearer the original ground level.

Setting out from in front of the west side of the Castillo, a path leads northward passing Dance Platform no. 1 on the east. Beyond this the path turns to the west and just before arriving at the edge of the great north terrace a small headless Chac Mool figure is passed.

The Well of Sacrifice is a great oval shaped hole 60 m long by 55 m wide, where a collapse of the surface limestone strata has exposed the subterranean water-table

Figure 5.41. Sacred Cenote. The walls are near vertical and measure more than 12 m to the surface of the water

Figure 5.42. Gold Mask. Eye Rings and Mouth Piece. Lothrop (1952:69) describes these objects as "one of the finest examples of the cut-out technique in the Americas." The snakes are rattlesnakes with four rattles each, the feathers radiating from the eyes represent quetzal feathers grouped in four bunches attached to the middle of the body, the side of the neck, abnd the top of the snout. These may portray a deity venerated at Chichén Itzá, and represented on architectural decoration at the site. The proto type seems to have been the moan bird (Lothrop 1952:71)

of the peninsula, here about 23 m below the surface of the ground; the sides are either vertical, or undercut, and sounding operations in the water below indicate a depth, to the bottom of this deep pocket in the limestone, of another 23 m.

According to Landa, the Well of Sacrifice was a place where pilgrims flocked from far and near to offer their most valuable possessions to the rain gods who were supposed to dwell in its depths, into which human victims were also hurled:

> *Into this well they have had, and then [1566] had, the custom of throwing men alive as a sacrifice to the gods in time of drought, and they believed that they did not die though they never saw them again. They also threw into it a great many other things, like precious stones and things which they prized. And so if this economy had possessed gold, it would be this well that would have the greater part of it, so great was the devotion which the Indians showed to it.*

Charles P. Bowditch,[16] of Boston, acting upon Landa's statement that "if this country had gold, it would be this

[16] Charles Pickering Bowditch (1842-1921) was the grandson of Nathaniel Bowditch, an early American mathematician, founder of modern maritime navigation, and author of *The New American Practical Navigator*, first published in 1802. Bowditch is perhaps best known for his pioneering work as an archeologist, specializing in Maya hieroglyphic writing. After a pleasure trip to southern Mexico and Yucatan, in 1888, Bowditch became interested in the ancient Maya. He was a great benefactor of the Peabody Museum at Harvard University between 1888 and 1921. In 1891 the Museum sent its first expedition to Central America. The early work of George Byron Gordon, Marshall H. Saville, and John G. Owens at Copán and the Ulúa Valley, Teobert Maler on the Usumacinta River and Petén, Edward H. Thompson in Yucatan and especially in the Cenote of Chichen Itza, Alfred M. Tozzer, Raymond E. Merwin, and Clarence L. Hay in British Honduras and northern Guatemala, Samuel K. Lothrop in Honduras, the second expedition of Sylvanus G. Morley in Yucatan, and the work of Herbert J. Spinden in southern Yucatan, were financed by Bowditch. His interest in funding expeditions resulted in the accession of several important collections to the Peabody Museum. These include a number of original stone carvings from Copan, molds and casts of the stelae and altars from Copan and Quirigua, lintels and stelae from Yaxchilan and

Figure 5.43. Sacred Cenote. Jade figures. Jade necklace and pendant were found on the Red Jaguar Throne, upper left; jade figure fragment in cache at the base of the stairway beneath El Castillo, upper right; jade head dredged from the Sactred Cenote, profile and frontal views

well that would have the greater part of it," made arrangements to have the Well of Sacrifice dredged. The work was entrusted to Edward H. Thompson, owner of the Hacienda Chichén, and was carried on during four field seasons, 1905-1907, and 1910, operations having been begun in the winter of 1905.

At first a power winch was used to lower and raise the orange-sector dredge, but as Thompson told Morley, the vibrations of its engine jarred loose so much dust from the ledges around the sides, that debris fell into the water faster than the dredge could lift it out.

What a treasure in objects of ancient Maya life was finally recovered from the Well: articles of gold, copper, jade, alabaster, shell. Wood, bone, pottery, fragments of brocaded cloth, several tons of copal incense and many human crania, as well as other human bones. The gold and copper were fashioned into bells, beads, pendants, discs, bracelets and rings; the jade into beads, pendants,

Piedras Negras, sculptured stones from Chichen Itza, pottery and other objects from the Ulúa Valley and Copán, from Holmul, and many of the ruins of Yucatan. Second to none is the collection from the Sacred Cenote of Chichen Itza. This work was planned and financed almost entirely by Bowditch. He also subsidized the publication of six folio volumes of the Memoirs of the Peabody Museum. Bowditch also arranged for the translation of almost the entire works of Eduard Seler, Ernst Forstemann, Paul Schellhas, and other German Mesoamericanists. Bowditch also assembled an impressive collection of documents covering the Maya area. He built up gradually one of the best working libraries on this subject, and afterwards gave it to the Museum. He had the Nuttall Codex copied and published, the Laud Codex in the British Museum copied, and, at the time of his death, he was having prepared a copy of the Sahagun manuscript in Florence with its many colored illustrations. Bowditch purchased from William E. Gates photographic reproductioins of more than 50,000 leaves of manuscripts and rare books on Central America and Mexico. This collection comprises practically everything in manuscript form extant on the languages of Central America and much of the material on Mexican linguistics. These reproductions were bound and given to the Museum. Finally, Bowditch sponsored several fellowships, including the first Fellowship in American Archaeology of the Archaeological Institute of America as well as the Central American Fellowship of the Peabody Museum. He was in great part responsible for the establishment of the Division of Anthropology in Harvard University and an Instructorship in Central American Archaeology, presently held by William L. Fash, was first established by him. The personal papers of Bowditch are at the Massachussets History Society (MS N-846) [eds].

plaques, ear-plugs and discs. The wood was made into spear-throwers, knife handles, and clubs. Many choice ceramic pieces were recovered, bowls, dishes, vases, incense burners, etc., carved human and animal bones, and shells. Innumerable cakes of copal incense in its original pottery platters were dredged up from the well. These were decorated in a general pattern of crossed lines and then painted a bright cerulean blue, the ancient Maya color of sacrifice. Finally some 60 human crania were recovered, thus confirming the traditional view that human sacrifice on a large scale had been made in the well, as described by Landa and others,

> *At this cenote, the lords and chiefs of all the provinces of Valladolid observed this custom, after having fasted for 60 days, without raising their eyes during that time even to look at their wives, not at those who brought them food, they came to the mouth of this cenote and, at the break of day, they threw into it some Indian women, some belonging to each of the lords, and they told the women that they should beg for a good year in all those things which they thought fit, and thus they cast them in unbound, but as they were through headlong, they fell into the water, giving a great blow on it; and exactly at midday she who was able to come out cried out loud that they should throw her a rope to drag her out with, and she arrived at the top half dead, and they made great fires around her and incensed her with copal, and when she came to herself she said that below there were so many of her nation, both men and women, who received her, that raising her head to look at some of them, they gave her heavy blows on the neck, making her put her head down, which was all under water, in which she fancied were many hollows and deeps; and in answer to the question which the Indian girl put to them, they replied to her whether it should be a good or bad year, and whether the devil was angry with any of the lords who had cast in the Indian girls, but they lords already knew that if a girl did not beg to be taken out at midday, it was because the devil was angry with them, and she never came out again. Then, seeing that she did not come out, all the followers of that Lord and the lord himself threw great stones into the water, and with loud cries fled from this place.*

The first year I visited the Maya area as a young man just out of college, Thompson was then on his third season of dredging in the West of Sacrifice. How tensely we used to sit by its edge and watch the dredge come up, each time filled with mud and slimy black organic muck, which so very literally was "pay dirt."

The jelly-like contents of the dredge were dumped upon the edge of the cenote and the eager Maya laborers began combing it with their sensitive fingers, a gold bead here, a copper bell there, and now and then a crumpled gold disc, or broken jade plaque, for most of the objects recovered from the Well seem to have been ceremoniously "killed" before having been thrown into it, as if to liberate their respective spirits so that they too could journey to that other world from whence there is no return.

Great trees were also dragged cut, perfect as the day when they toppled into the Well, many centuries ago, with all the corrugations of their bark perfectly preserved, only to slough away in a short time, literally to dissolve into a slimy black mass which soon lost all semblances to its original form.

Did Thompson remove from the Well of Sacrifice all the treasures the ancient Maya had thrown into it? Thompson himself, at least, never believed he had. The work was interrupted in 1910 after the fourth season of dredging and since then has never been resumed. I believe that in the four seasons he dredged, he succeeded in removing only a relatively small part of this ancient Maya treasure and that an unbelievably rich harvest still awaits the dredge of some future archaeologist, beckoning to be rescued from its present oblivion.

However that may, or may not be, it is certain that during the eleventh to fourteenth centuries, Chichén Itzá became a great center of pilgrimage from points not only all over the Maya area, but also from regions as far distant as central Mexico and southern Central America, all of which amply justified my claim for the city as having been the Mecca of the ancient Maya world.

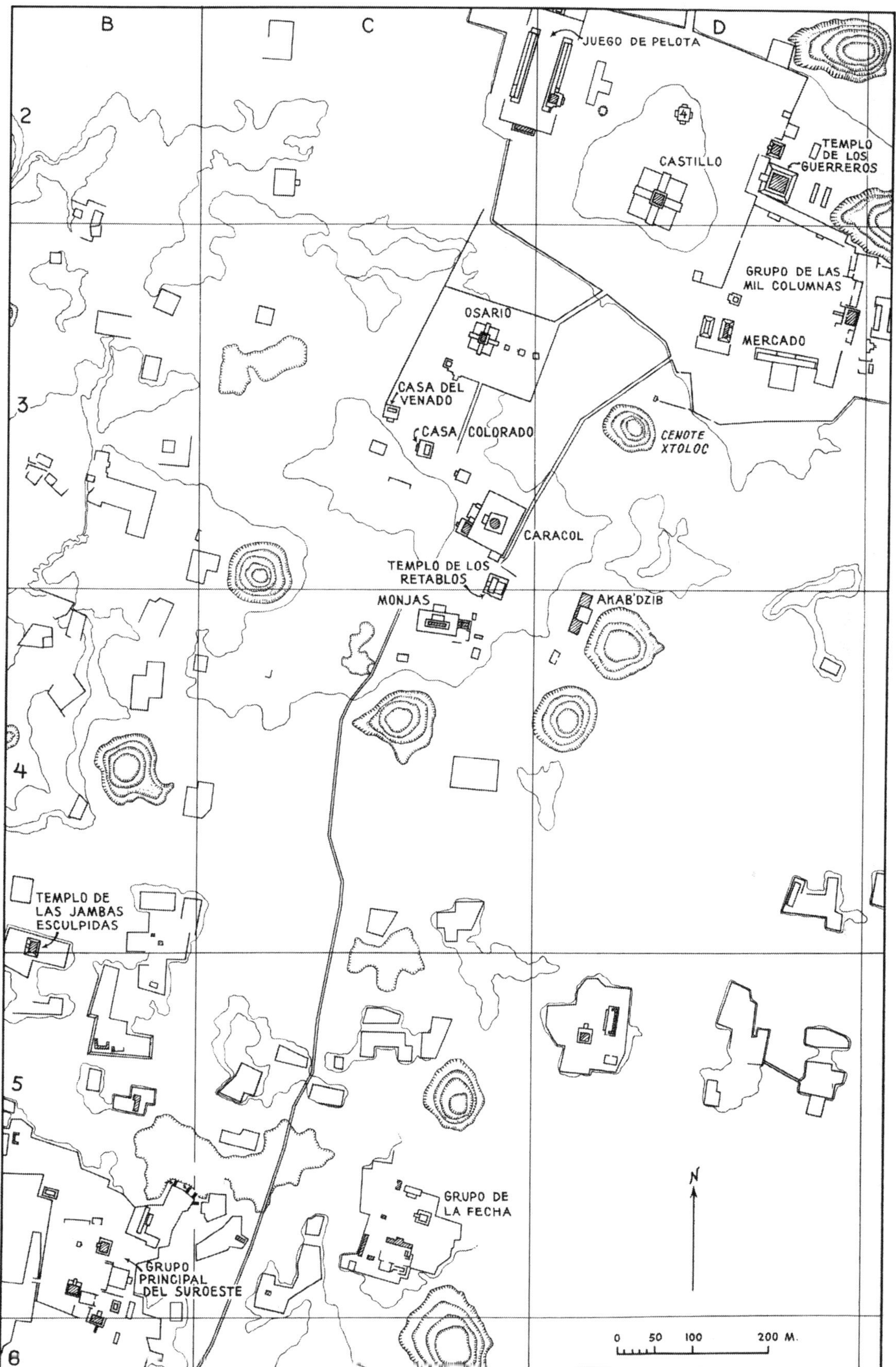

Map 5.1. Chichen Itza. Site plan of central sire area (after Brainerd 1958:355, Map 19)

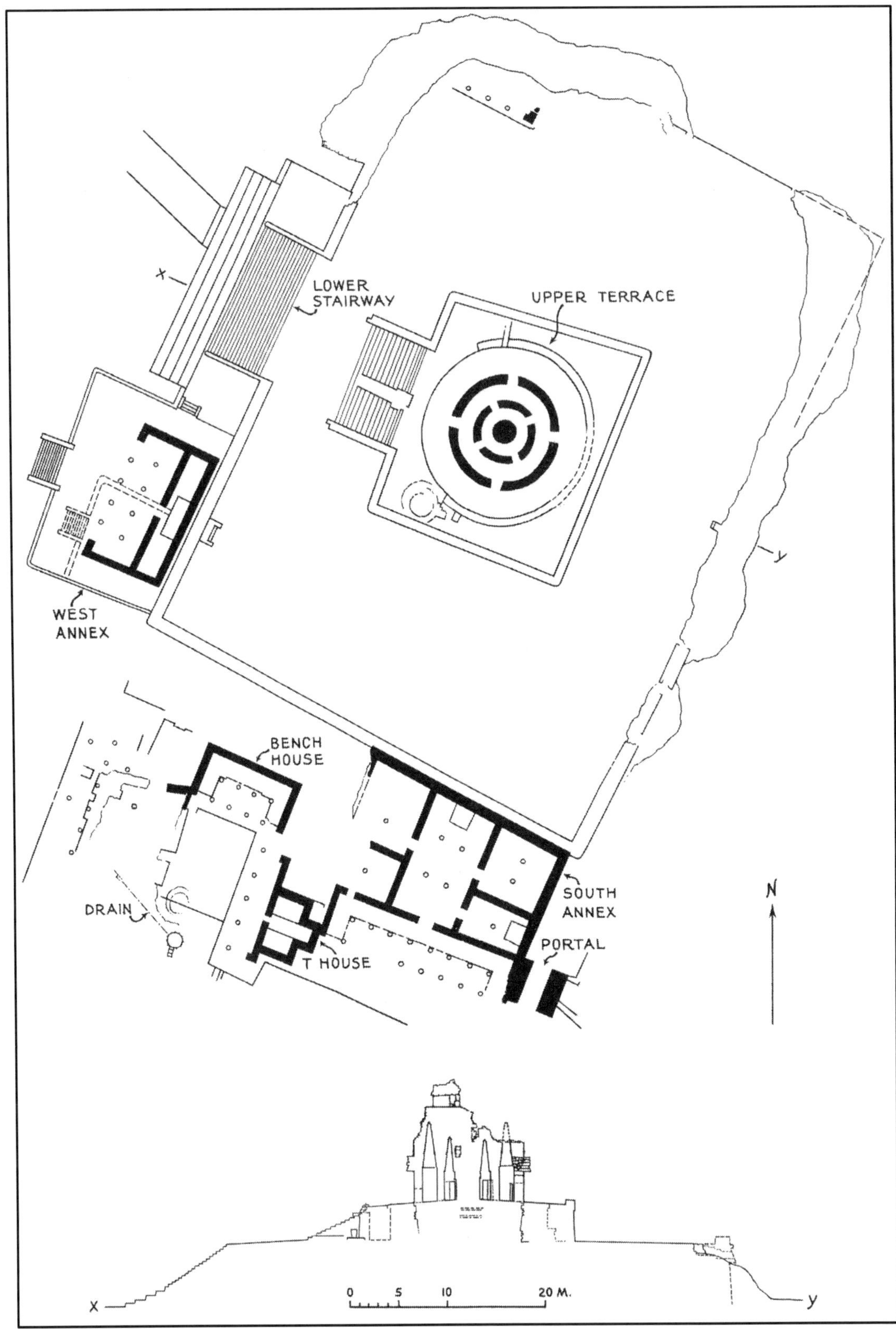

Map 5.2. Chichen Itza. Plan of Caracol Complex (after Brainerd 1958:356, Map 20)

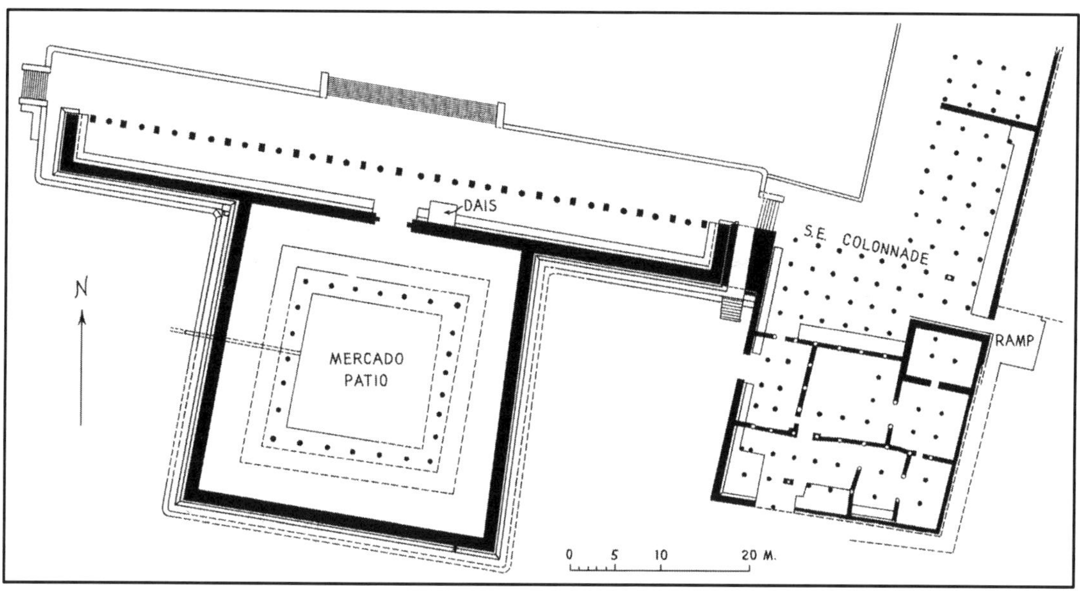

Map 5.3. Chichen Itza. Plan of Mercado and Adjacent Colonnade (after Brainerd 1958:357, Map 21)

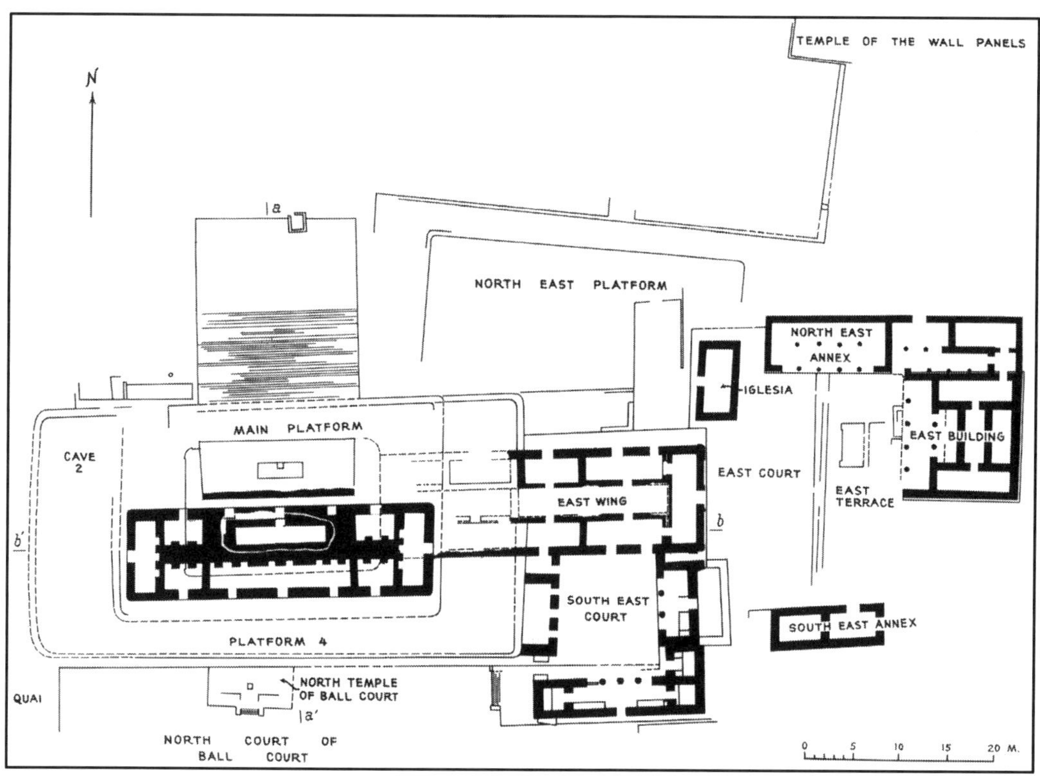

Map 5.4. Chichen Itza. Plan of Monjas Complex (after Brainerd 1958:359, Map 23)

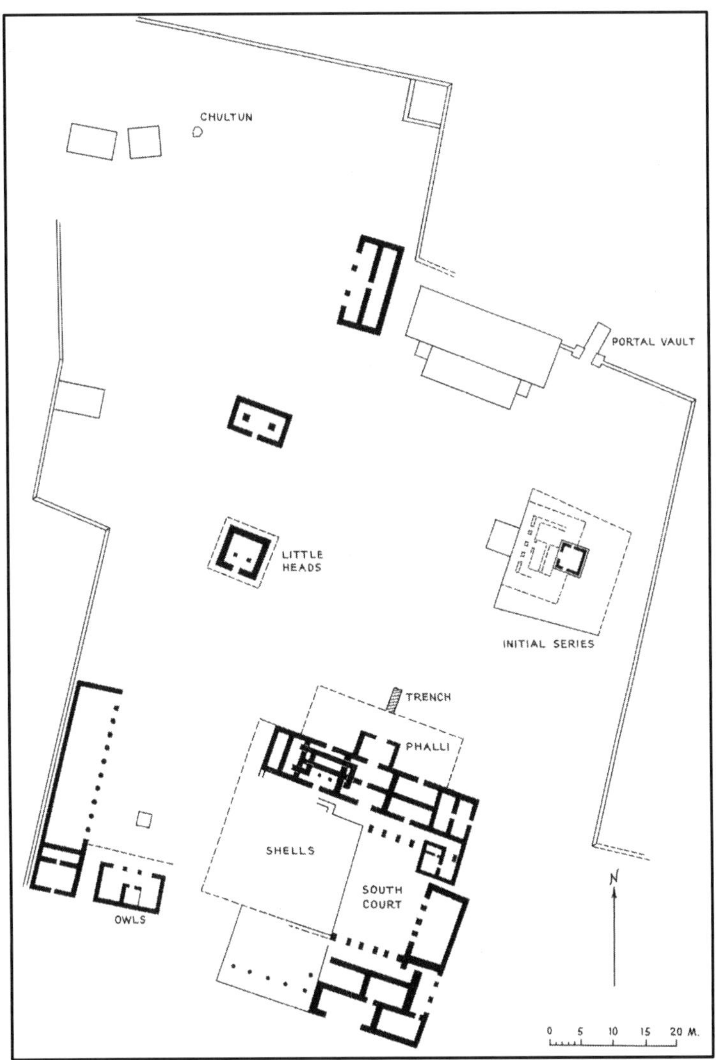

Map 5.5. Chichen Itza. Plan of Initial Series Group (after Brainerd 1958:358, Map 22)

Appendix 1.
CHRONOLOGY OF THE CHICHÉN ITZÁ PROJECT CARNEGIE INSTITUTION OF WASHINGTON

Year	Activity	Personnel
1923	Contract signed between government of Mexico Secretaria de Agricultura y Fomento of Mexico and the Carnegie Institution of Washington	
1923	Group of the Thousand Columns, clearing	
1924	Colonnade, northeast, excavation and repair	E.H. Morris; M. Amsden
1924, 1929, 1932	Base map of Chichén Itzá	J.P. Kilmartin; J.P. O'Neill
1925	Temple at Xtoloc cenote, excavation and repair	A. Morris
1925	Temple of the Four Lintels	O.G. Ricketson
1925-1928	Colonnade, northwest, excavation	E.H. Morris; G. Strömsvik
1925-1928	Temple of the Warriors, excavation and repair	E.H. Morris; G. Strömsvik
1926	Architectural resoration drawings	K.J. Conant
1926	Oil paintings of various buildings	J.L. Smith
1926	Hieroglyphic inscriptions	H.J. Spinden
1926	Group of the Initial Series, gateway, excavation	G.C. Vaillant
1926	Portico of the Atlantean Columns, excavation	G.C. Vaillant
1926	Temple of the Initial Series, excavation	G.C. Vaillant
1926	Temple of the Little Heads, excavation	G.C. Vaillant
1926	Temple of the Warriors, removal of frescoes	C. Hay; A. Austen
1926	Studies on murals	W. Lehmann
1926-1928	Temple of the Warriors, copies of frescoes	J. Charlot; A. Morris
1926, 1933	House of the Phalli, excavation	G.C. Vaillant; G. Strömsvik
1927	House of the Grinding Stones, excavation	
1927	Temple of the Interior Atlantean Columns, excavation	P. S. Martin
1927	Temple of the Wall Panels, excavation and repair	K. Ruppert
1927, 1928	Colonnade, north, excavation and repair	H.B. Roberts
1927, 1928	Colonnade, west, excavation and repair	E.H. Morris
1928	Exploration of outlying sections of Chichén Itzá	K. Ruppert
1928	Temple of the Three Lintels, excavation and repair	P.S. Martin
1928, 1932, 1934	Mercado, excavation and repair	K. Ruppert
1930-1935, 1940	Ceramic Survey	H.B. Roberts; G.W. Brainerd
1931	Round House, repair and excavation	H.E.D. Pollock
1932	Hieroglyphic inscriptions, rubbings	J.H. Denison
1932	Hieroglyphic inscriptions, analysis	H. Beyer
1932-1934	Monjas, excavation and repair	J.S. Bolles; R.T. Smith
1932, 1934-1937, 1940	Architectural survey	H.E.D. Pollock

Year	Activity	Personnel
1934	Renewal of contract signed between government of Mexico and the Carnegie Institution of Washington (CIW) for five years with option for an additional five year renewal	
1936	Sweat Bath, no. 2, excavation	K. Ruppert; P.F. Fontaine
1937	Study of Nahua influences in Chichén Itzá architecture	K. Ruppert
1940	Termination of the Chichén Itzá Project and final withdrawal from Chichén Itzá, May, 1940	
1940	Dance Platform, no. 1, excavation	E.T.P. Kennedy
1935-1938	Agronomic Survey	G.N. Collins; R. Emerson; J.M. Kempton; W. Popenoe; R. Stadelman
1927, 1931-1938	Anthropometric Survey	M. Steggerda; T.J. Hill; G.D. Williams
1930, 1931, 1933, 1937	Biological Survey	H.H. Bartlett; F.M. Gaige; A. Greaser; F.G. Hall; A.L. Lundell; A. Murie; A.S. Pearse; J. Van Tyne
1930-1938, 1940	Ethnological Survey	R. Redfield; A. Hansen; A. Villa Rojas
1934	House Type Survey	R. Wauchope
1931, 1933-1935. 1937, 1938	Linguistic Survey	M. Andrade
1931, 1933, 1935-1940	Documentary History of Yucatán	R.L. Roys
1931, 1934-1940	History of Yucatán	F. Scholes; E.B. Adams; R.S. Chamberlain; J.I. Rubio Mañe
1929-1931	Medical Survey	B.L. Bennett; J.C. Bequaert; F.H. Connell; K. Goodner; J.H. Sandground; G.M. Saunders; G.C. Shattuck
1928-1931	Clinic for the care of Maya laborers	K. MacKay

Appendix 2.
COMMON NAMES AND GRID CORRESPONDENCES OF STRUCTURES AT CHICHÉN ITZÁ

Common Name	Grid
Akabdzib	4D1
Ball Court, Great	2D1
Ball Court, Red House	3C10
Ball Court, Thompson's	3E2
Ball Court, Warriors	2D9
Caracol	3C15
Casa Colorada	3C9
Castillo	2D5
Castillo, Old Chichén	5B18
Chichanchob	3C9
Columnes Confundidos	2C3
Gymnasium	2D1
High Priest's Grave	3C1
House of Grinding Stones	3C5
House of the Dark Writing	4D1
House of the Deer	3C7
House of the Phalli	5C14
House of the Shells	5C5
Iglesia	4C1
Maudslay's no. 6	3C11
Mausoleum I	2D3
Mausoleum II	2D2
Mausoleum III	2D4
Mercado	3D11
Monjas	4C1
North Colonnade	2D10
North Temple of the Big Ball Court	2D1
Northeast Colonnade	3E1
Northwest Colonnade	2D8
Nunnery	4C1
Observatory	3C15
Osario	3C1
Palace	4C1
Portal Vault, General South Annex	3C15
Portal Vault, Initial Series	5C16
Red House	3C9
Round Tower	3C15

Common Name	Grid
Snail	3C15
South Temple of the Big Ball Court	2D1
Southeast Annex of Monjas	4C1
Southeast Colonnade	3D10
Sweat House	3E3
Sweat House, Caracol South Annex	3C15
Temple of Four Lintels	7B4
Temple of Initial Series	5C4
Temple of Kukulcan	2D5
Temple of Quetzalcoatl	2D5
Temple of the Atlantean Columns	5C15
Temple of the Brid Cornice	5A1
Temple of the Big Tables	2D7
Temple of the Chac Mool	2D8
Temple of the Hieroglyphic Jambs	6E3
Temple of the Interior Atlantean Columns	3C6
Temple of the Jaguar Atlantean Columns	5B21
Temple of the Jaguars	2D1
Temple of the Jaguars and Shields	2D1
Temple of the Little Heads	5C3
Temple of the Little Tables	3D8
Temple of the One Lintel	7B1
Temple of the Owls	5C7
Temple of the Sculptured Jambs	4B1
Temple of the Three Lintels	7B3
Temple of the Turtle	5B2
Temple of the Wall Panels	3C16
Temple of the Warriors	2D8
Tennis Court	2D1
Terrace, Temple, or Platform of Cones	2D4
Terrace, Temple, or Platform of Eagles	2D3
Terrace, Temple, or Platform of the Skulls	2D2
Thompson's Temple	3D9
Tomb of the Chac Mool	2D4
Tzompantli	2D2
Tzumpelche	3E3
West Colonnade	3D1

Appendix 3.
SITE PLAN OF CHICHÉN ITZÁ

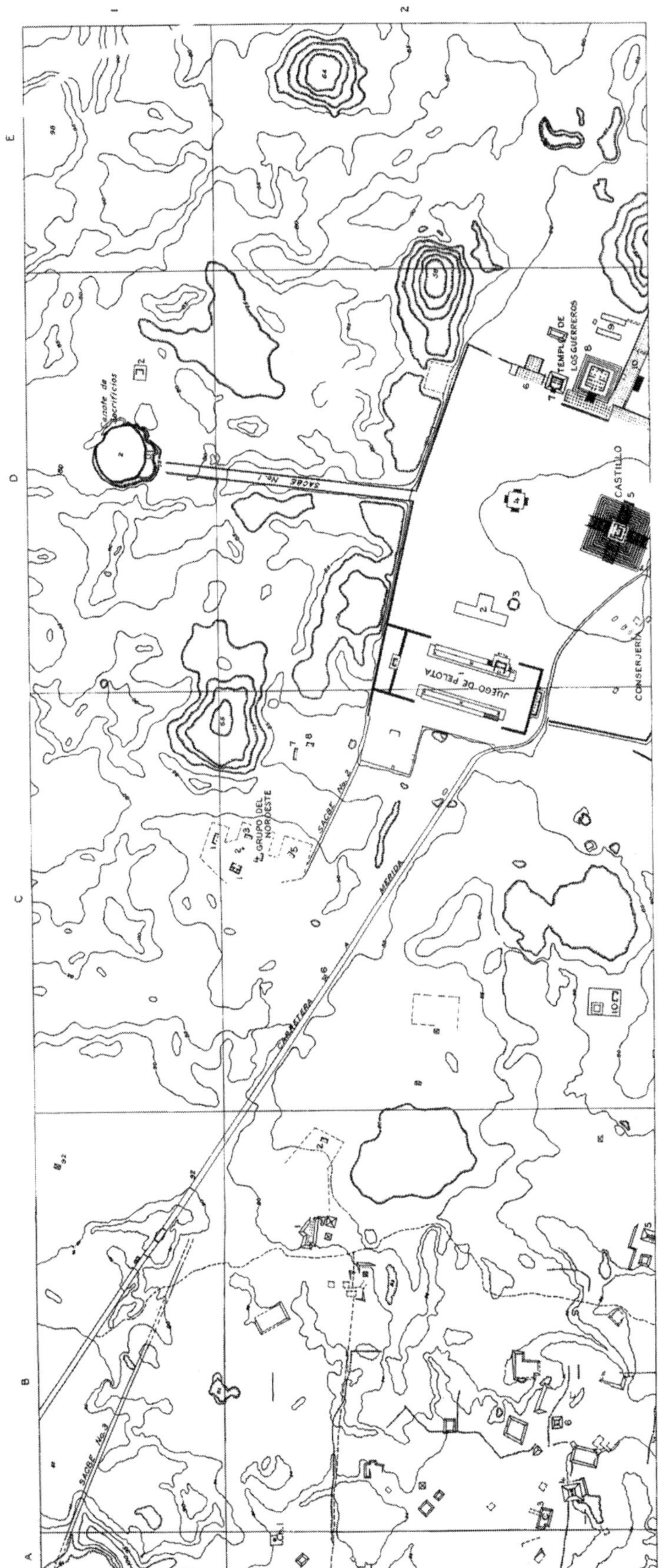

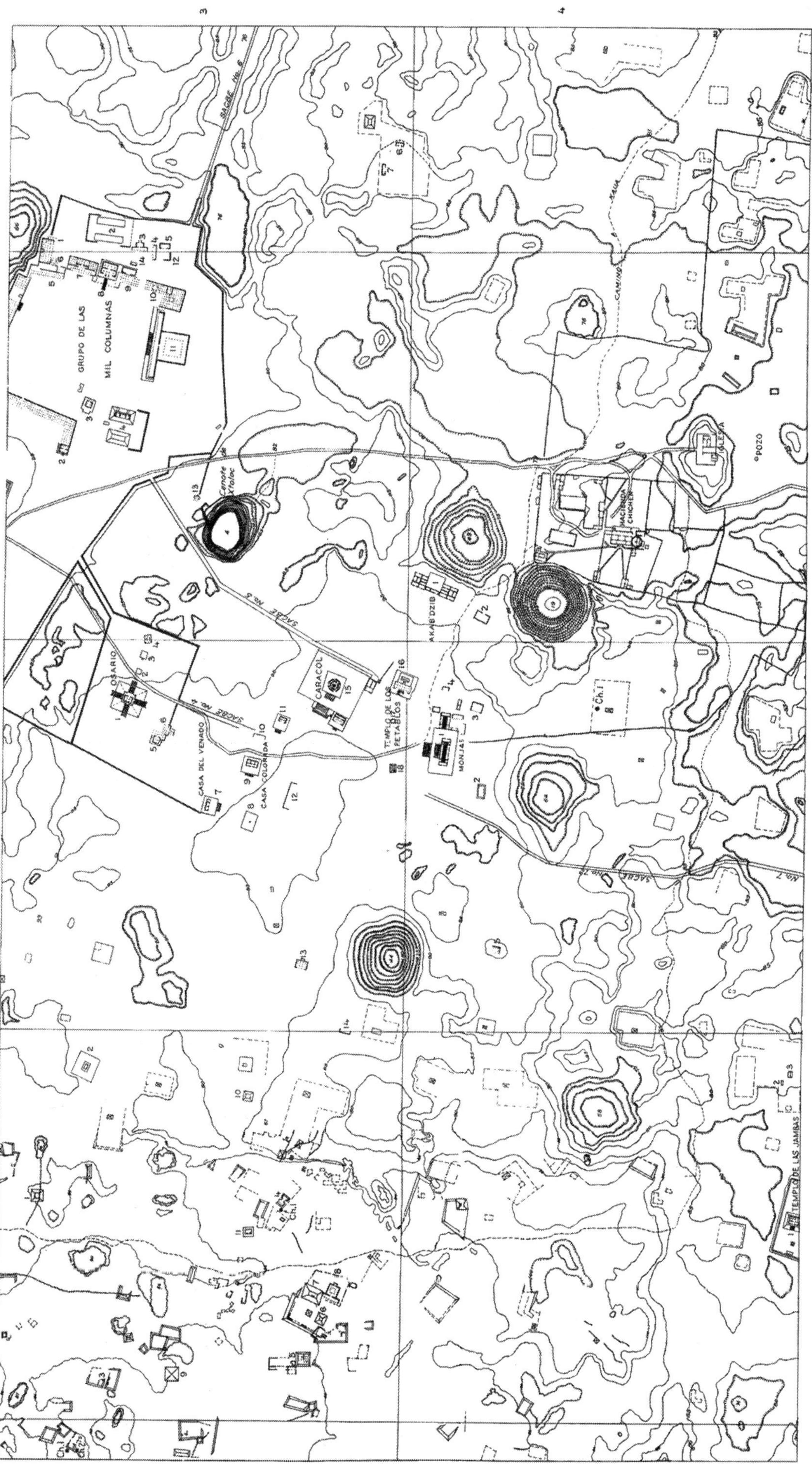
GRUPO DE LAS
MIL COLUMNAS
OSARIO
CARACOL
MONJAS
AKAB DZIB
CASA COLORADA
CASA DEL VENADO
TEMPLO DE LOS
RETABLOS
Cenote
Xtoloc
HACIENDA
CHICHEN
IGLESIA
POZO
CAMINO
TEMPLO DE LAS JAMBAS

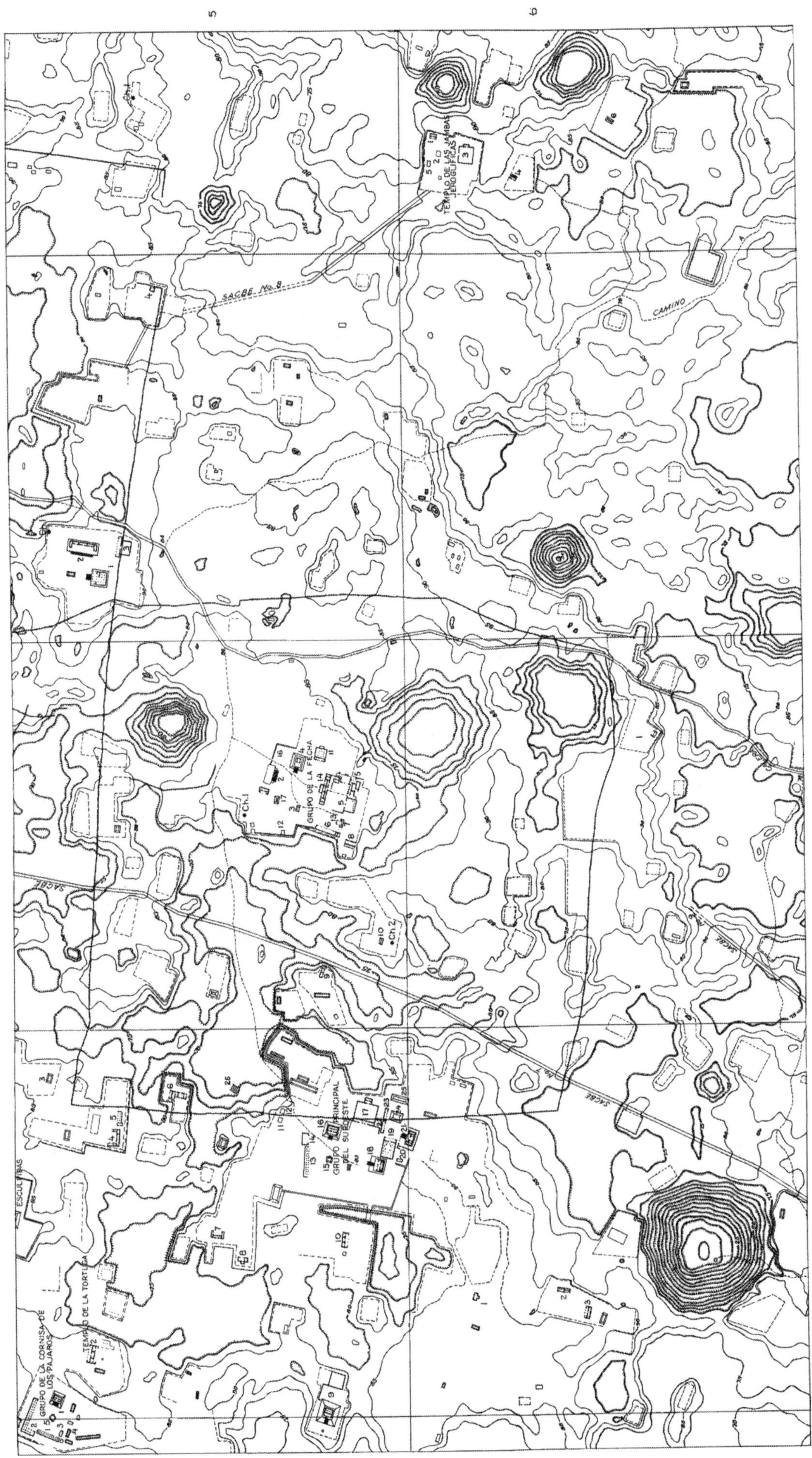
SACBE No. 8
CAMINO
TEMPLO DE LAS JAMBAS JEROGLIFICAS
GRUPO DE LA FECHA
SACBE
GRUPO PRINCIPAL DEL SUDESTE
TEMPLO DE LA TORTUGA
GRUPO DE LA CORNISA DE LOS PAJAROS

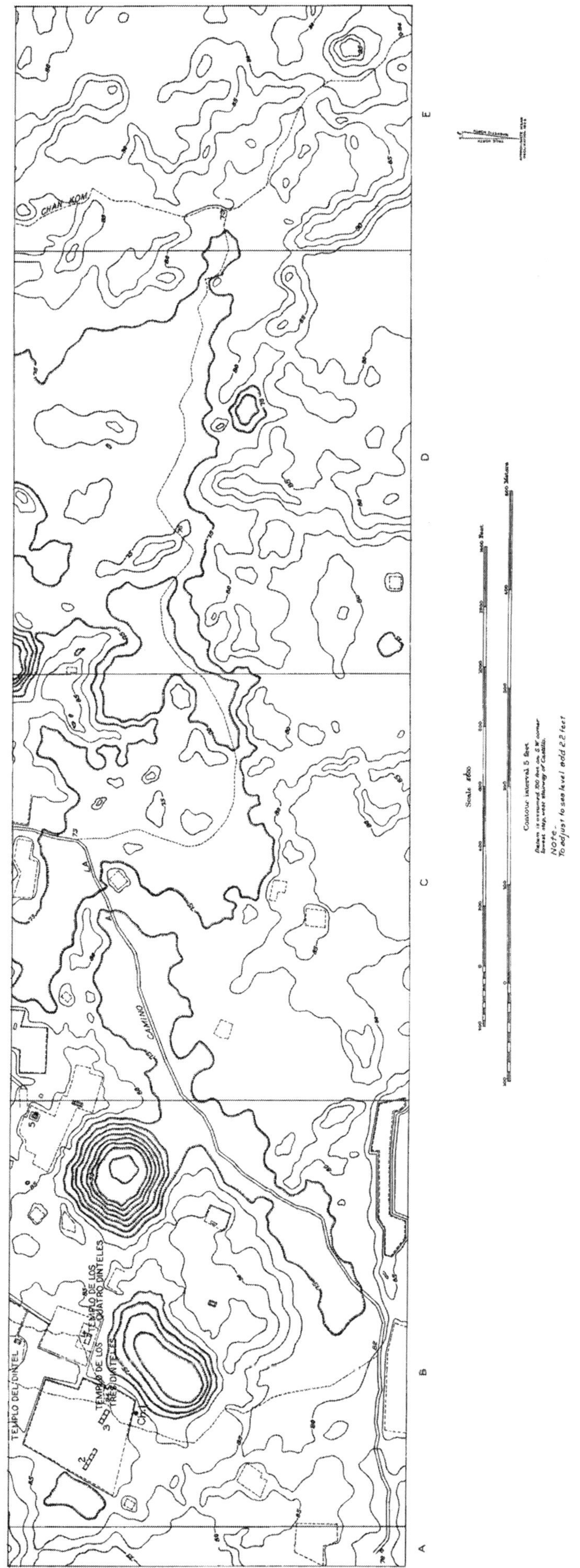
TEMPLO DEL DINTEL
TEMPLO DE LOS QUATRO DINTELES
TEMPLO DE LOS TRES DINTELES
CHAN KOM
CAMINO
A
B
C
D
E
Contour interval 5 feet
Note-
To adjust to sea level add 22 feet

Appendix 4.
FOR FURTHER READING ABOUT CHICHÉN ITZÁ

Acosta, J.R. 1954. Exploraciónes arqueológicos efectuadas en Chichén Itzá, Yucatán, 1951. *Anales del Instituto Naciónal de Antropología e Historia* 6(34):27-40.

Albright, E. 2009. Excavation underway at Chichén Itzá building dated to ninth century. www.americanegypt.com/blog/?p=679.

Amábilis Domínguez, M. 1923. La última estatua descubierta en Chichén Itzá. *El Agricultor* 10(6):28-31.

Amábilis Domínguez, M. 1963. *Los Atlantes en Yucatán*. Mexico: Editorial Orion.

Amrhein, Laura M. 1997. Iconography of the Ritual Platform Benches at Chichén Itzá. M.A. thesis, Virginia Commonwealth University, Department of Anthropology.

Ancient Maya city in Yucatán: Chichén Itzá. *Science* 60(1540), 1924.

Ancona, E. 1878. *Historia de Yucatán: desde la época mas remota hasta nuestros días*. Mérida: M. Heredia Argüelles.

Anda Alanis, G. de. 2007a. Los huesos del Cenote Sagrado. Chichén Itzá, Yucatán. *Argueología mexicana 14*(83):54-57.

Anda Alanis, G. de. 2007b. Sacrifice and ritual body mutilation in Postclassical Maya society: taphonomy of the human remains from Chichén Itzá's Cenote Sagrada. In *New Perspectives on Human Sacrifice and Ritual Body Treatments in Ancient Maya Society*. V. Tiesler and A. Cucina, eds. pp. 190-208. New York: Springer.

Anderson, P.K. 1994. Interpretations of conflict at Chichén Itzá. In *Seventh Palenque Round Table, 1989*. V.M. Fields, ed. pp. 33-38. Palenque Round Table (7 session, 1989). San Francisco: Pre-Columbian Art Research Institute.

Anderson, P.K. 1998a. Yula, Yucatán, Mexico: terminal classic Maya settlement and political organization in the Chichén Itzá polity. Doctoral dissertation, University of Chicago.

Anderson, P.K. 1998b. Yula, Yucatán, Mexico: Terminal Classic Maya ceramic chronology for the Chichén Itzá area. *Ancient Mesoamerica* 9(1):151-165.

Andrews V, E.W., and J.A. Sabloff. 1986. Classic to Postclassic: A Summary Discussion. *Late Lowland Maya Civilization: Classic to Postclassic.* J.A. Sabloff and E.W. Andrews V, eds. pp. 433-456. Albuquerque: University of New Mexico Press.

Andrews, A.P. 1990. Fall of Chichén Itzá: a preliminary hypothesis. *Latin American Antiquity* 1(3):258-267.

Andrews, A.P., and F. Robles Castellanos. 1985. Chichén Itzá and Cobá: An Itzá-Maya standoff in early Postclassic Yucatán. In *The Lowland Maya Postclassic*. A.F. Chase and P.M. Rice, eds. pp. 62-72. Austin: University of Texas Press.

Archaeological drama at Chichén Itzá. *El Palacio* 27(1-4):24, 1930.

Arochi, L.E. 1991. Concordancia cronológica arquitectónica entre Chichén Itzá y Mayapán. In *Arqueoastronomía y etnoastronomía en Mesoamérica*. J. Broda, S. Iwaniszewski and L. Maupomé, eds. pp. 97-112. Mexico: Universidad Naciónal Autónoma de Mexico.

Arochi, L.E. 1994. *Ciudades del México prehispánico: Tula, Teotihuacan, Monte Albán, Tajín y Chichén Itzá*. Mexico: Panorama Editorial.

Aveni, A.F., S. Milbrath, and C. Peraza Lope. 2004. Chichén Itzá's legacy in the astronomically oriented architecture of Mayapán. *Res: Anthropology and Aesthetics* 45:123-144.

Aznar Gutiérrez, J. 1942. *La sucesión de Mr. Edward Herbert Thompson: las ruinas mayas de Chichén Itzá y las antigüedades mexicanas*. Mexico.

Ball, J.W., and J.M. Ladd. 1992. Ceramics. In *Artifacts from the Cenote of Sacrifice, Chichén Itzá, Yucatán.* C.C. Coggins, ed. pp. 191-233. Memoirs, 10(3). Harvard University, Peabody Museum of Archaeology and Ethnology, Cambridge, MA.

BALUTET, N. 2002. Jeu dangereux a Chichén Itzá. *Ulysse* 82:46-48.

BALUTET, N. 2003. Le jeu de balle dans la peninsula du Yucatán (Mexique): quelques remarques sur les panneaux du terrain 2D1 de Chichén Itzá. *Histoire et Anthropologie* 27.

BANZER-ZUNICH, M.L. 1971. Chichén Itzá, Maya-Toltec: a review of current scholarship and appraisal. M.A. thesis, California State University, Long Beach, Department of Anthropology.

BARRERA RUBIO, A. 1978. Trabajos de conservación en el Chichan Chob de Chichén Itzá. *Revista de la Universidad de* Yucatán 20(120):36-46.

BARRERA Y ALVÁREZ, G. de la. 1950. *Chichén Itzá, Uxmal, y Kabah en el arte maya*. Mexico: Talleres Gráficos de la Nación.

BARTHEL, T.S. 1955. Versuch über die Inschriften von Chich'en Itzá Viejo. *Baessler Archiv* 3:5-33.

BARTHEL, T.S. 1964. Comentarios a las inscripciónes clásicas tardias de Chichén Itzá. *Estudios de cultura maya* 4:223-244.

BAUDEZ, C.-F. 2000. Arquitectura y culto marcial en Chichén Itzá. In *Memoria de la Mesa Redondo de Palenque; arquitectura e ideologia de los antiguos mayas*. S. Trejo, ed. pp. 177-194. Mexico: Instituto Naciónal de Antropología y Historia.

BECK, L.A., and A.K. SIEVERT. 2005. Mortuary pathways leading to the cenote at Chichén Itzá. In *Interacting with the Dead: Perspectives on Mortuary Archaeology for the New Millenium*. G.F.M. Rakita, *et al*., eds. pp. 290-304. Gainesville: University Press of Florida.

BEY, G.J. and W.M. RINGLE. 2007. From the bottom up: the timing and nature of the Tula - Chichén Itzá exchange. In *Twin Tollans: Chichén Itzá, Tula, and the Epiclassic to Early Postclassic Mesoamerican World*. J.K. Kowalski and C. Kristan-Graham, eds. pp. 377-428. Dumbarton Oaks Research Library and Collection, Washington, DC.

BEYER, H. 1937. Studies on the inscriptions of Chichén Itzá. *Carnegie Institution of Washington, Contributions to American archaeology* (21):29-175.

BEYER, H. 1941. A discussion of J. Eric Thompson's interpretations of Chichén Itzá hieroglyphs. *American Antiquity* 6(4):327-338.

BEYER, H. 2001. Studies on the inscriptions of Chichén Itzá. In *The Decipherment of Ancient Maya Writing*. Stephen Houston, Oswaldo Chinchilla Mazariegos and David Stuart, eds. pp. 168-172. Norman: University of Oklahoma Press.

BOLAÑOS Q.J.J. 1975. Civilización maya; Uxmal, Chichén Itzá. *Anuario de estudios centroamericanos* 2:403-406.

BOLLES, J.S. 1934. Monjas. *Carnegie Institution of Washington, Year Book* 33:90-91.

BOLLES, J.S. 1963. *La Iglesia, Chichén Itzá, Yucatán*.

BOLLES, J.S. 1977. *Las Monjas: A Major Pre-Mexican Architectural Complex at Chichén Itzá*. Norman: University of Oklahoma Press.

BOOT, E. 1996. Recent epigraphic research on the inscriptions at Chichén Itzá, Yucatán, Mexico. *Yumtzilob* 8(1):5-27.

BOOT, E. 1997. Classic Maya paradigm of power at Chich'en Itsa: K'ak'upakal as paramount ruler? In *U Mut Maya VI*. C. Jones and T. Jones, eds. pp. 165-174. Arcata, CA: T. Jones.

BOOT, E. 1997. Preliminary notes on the 'hieroglyphic band' fragments of the Caracol, Chichén Itsa, Yucatán, Mexico. *Yumtzilob* 9(1):69-86.

BOOT, E. 2000. Architecture and identity in the Northern Maya lowlands: the Temple of K'uk'ulkan at Chichén Itsa, Yucatán, Mexico. In *The Sacred and the Profane: Architecture and Identity in the Maya Lowlands*. P.R. Colas, K. Delvendahl, M. Kuhnert, and A. Schubart, eds. pp. 183-204. Acta Mesoamericana, 10. Markt Schwaben: Verlag Anton Saurwein.

BOOT, E. 2003. The great ballcourt in Chichén Itzá, Yucatán, Mexico; perpetuation of rulership of the Itzá Maya. In *Coleciónes latinoamericanas/ Latin American Collections: Essays in Honour of Ted J.J. Leyenaar*. D. Krop Jansen, and E.K. de Bock, eds. pp. 95-124. Leiden: Gegevens Koninklije Biblioteek.

BOOT, E. 2005. *Continuity and Change in Text and Image at Chichén Itzá, Yucatán, Mexico: A Study of the Inscriptions, Iconography, and Architecture at a Late Classic to Early Postclassic Maya Site*. Leiden: CNWS Publications.

BRAINERD, G.W. 1953. On the design of the Fine-Orange pottery found at Chichén Itzá. *Revista mexicana de estudios antropológicos* 13 463-473.

BRAINERD, G.W. 1958. *The Archaeological Ceramics of Yucatán*. Anthropological Records, 19. Berkeley: University of California, Berkeley.

BRASWELL, G.E. 1998. El Epiclásico, Clásico Terminal y Postclásico Temprano: una visión cronológica desde Teotihuacán, Chichén Itzá, Kaminaljuyú y Copán. In *Simposio de Investigaciónes Arqueológicas en Guatemala* (11 session, 1997). pp. 803-806. Ministerio de Cultura y Deportes; Instituto de Antropologia e Historia; Asociación Tikal, Guatemala.

BRASWELL, G.E. 2002. Northern Yucatán Obsidian Finds: Mérida and Chichén Itzá. FAMSI website.

BRASWELL, G.E. 2012. Reinterpreting the past of the northern Maya lowlands. In *The Ancient Maya of Mexico: Reinterpreting the Past of the Northern Maya*. G.E. Braswell, ed. pp. 1-40. Bristol: Equinox Publishing.

BREGLIA, L.C. 2005. Keeping world heritage in the family: a genealogy of Maya labour at Chichén Itzá. *International Journal of Heritage Studies* 11(5):385-398.

BRETON, A.C. 1907. Wall paintings at Chichén Itzá. In *Proceedings of the International Congress of Americanists* (15 session, Quebec, 1906). v. 2, pp. 165-169. Quebec.

BRETON, A.C. 1909. Arms and accoutrements of the ancient warriors at Chichén Itzá. *Man* 9(12):188.

BRETON, A.C. 1911. *Ancient Frescoes at Chichén Itzá.* Portsmouth: British Association.

BRETON, A.C. 1917. Preliminary study of the North Building (Chamber C), Great Ball Court, Chich'en Itzá, Yucatán. In *Proceedings of the International Congress of Americanists* (19 session, Washington, DC, 1915). pp. 187-194. Washington, DC.

BRETON, A.C. 1989. Wall paintings at Chichén Itzá. In *The Art of Ruins: Adela Breton and the Temples of Mexico.* Sue Giles and Jennifer Stewart, eds. pp. 55-57. Bristol: City of Bristol Museum and Art Gallery.

BRETON, A.C., and Sue GILES. 1989. Caryatid figures from the Temple of the Jaguars. In *The Art of Ruins: Adela Breton and the Temples of Mexico.* Sue Giles and Jennifer Stewart, eds. pp. 48-51. Bristol: City of Bristol Museum and Art Gallery.

BRICKER, V.R., and H.M. BRICKER. 1995. An astronomical text from Chichén Itzá, Yucatán, Mexico. *Human Mosaic* 28(2):91-105.

British Museum. 1923. *Guide to the Maudslay Collection of Maya Sculptures (Castes and Originals) from Central America.* London: Trustees of the British Museum.

Buildings found within Mexican pyramid; Toltec relic covers still other structures. *New York Times*, April 6, p. 21, 1932.

BUNKER, F.F. 1927. Art of the Maya as revealed by excavations at the Temple of the Warriors, Chichén Itzá, Yucatán. *Art and Archaeology* 23:2-10.

BURKE, S. 2011. Envoy: from deep to dark. http://the harvardadvocate.com/content/envoy-deep-dark?page =show.

BUSH ROMERO, P. 1972. Sacred well of Chichén Itzá and other freshwater sites in Mexico. *Museums and Monuments* 13:147-151

CANO, O. 2002. Guía de viajeros: Chichén Itzá, Yucatán. *Arqueología mexicana* 9(53):80-87.

CANUL, G. 2003. La Estructura 5C2 del conjunto de la serie inicial, Chichén Itzá, Yucatán: la columnata del yugo. In *Simposio de Investigaciónes Arqueologicas en Guatemala* (17 session, 2003). pp. 1015-1024. Ministerio de Cultura y Deportes; Instituto de Antropología e Historia, Guatemala.

Caracol; a perplexing Maya ruin. *Carnegie Institution of Washington, News Service Bulletin* 3:211-226, 1935.

CARLSON, J.B. 1999. Pilgrimage and the equinox Serpent of Light and Shadow phenomenon at the Castillo, Chichén Itzá, Yucatán. *Archaeoastronomy* 14(1):136-152.

CASTAÑEDA, Q.E. 1991. An "archaeology" of Chichén Itzá: discourse, power, and resistance in a Maya tourist site. Doctoral dissertation, State University of New York at Albany.

CASTAÑEDA, Q.E. 1995. La economia escritual y las invenciones de las culturas mayas en el Museo de Chichén Itzá. *Revista española de antropología americana* 25:181-203.

CASTAÑEDA, Q.E. 1996. *In the Museum of Maya Culture: Touring Chichén Itzá.* Minneapolis: University of Minnesota Press.

CASTAÑEDA, Q.E. 1997. Chichén Itzá y la invanción del mundo maya. *Cultura de Guatemala* 1:11-28.

CASTAÑEDA, Q.E. 1997. On the correct training of indios in the handicraft market at Chichén Itzá: Tactics and tactility of gender, class, race and state. *Journal of Latin American Anthropology* 2(2):106-143.

CASTAÑEDA, Q.E. 2004. Art-writing in the modern Maya art world of Chichén Itzá. *American Ethnologist* 31(1):22-42.

CASTAÑEDA, Q.E. 2005. Community collaboration and ethnographic intervention: Dialogues in the Piste Maya art world of Chichén Itzá. *Practicing Anthropology* 27(4):31-34.

CASTILLO BORGES, V.R. 1998. Liberación y restauración de la Estructura 2D7 o Templo de Las Grandes Mesas de Chichén Itzá. Tesis de licenciatura, Universidad de Yucatán.

CASTILLO TEJERO, N. 1987. El desarrollo urbano en Tula y Chichén Itzá. In *Memorias del Primer Coloquio Internacional de Mayistas: 5-10 de agosto de 1985.* M. de la Garza, *et al.*, eds. pp. 111-122. Mexico: Universidad Nacional Autónoma de México, Centro de Estudios Mayas.

Chacmool at Chichén Itzá. *El Palacio* 24:80-81, 1928.

Chacmool figure from Chichén Itzá. *El Palacio* 39:43, 1935.

CHARLOT, J. 1927. Report of Jean Charlot on the sculptures and paintings in the North and Northwest Colonnades (Stations 8 and 10). *Carnegie Institution of Washington, Year Book* 26:246-248.

CHARLOT, J. 1928. Report of Jean Charlot on the sculptures of the Temple of the Warriors and the Temple of the Chac Mool. *Carnegie Institution of Washington, Year Book* 27:300-302.

CHARLOT, J. 1931. Bas-reliefs from the Temple of Warriors. *Art and Archaeology* 31:311-315.

CHARLOT, J. 1935. *Mayan Murals from Chichén-Itzá, Yucatán.* New York: Florence Cane School of Art.

CHARNAY, D. 1863. *Cités et ruines américaines, Mitla, Palenqué, Izamal, Chichén-Itzá, Uxmal.* Paris: Gide.

CHARNAY, D. 1885. *Les anciennes villes du Nouveau monde; voyages d'explorations au Mexique et dans l'Amérique Centrale.* Paris: Hachette.

CHARNAY, D. 1887. *The Ancient Cities of the New World; Being Voyages and Explorations in Mexico and Central America from 1857-1882.* New York: Harper.

Chichén Itzá World Heritage Site. http://.whc.unesco.org/en/list/483.

Chichén Itzá, guide officielle. Mexico: Instituto Nacional de Antropología e Historia, 1964.

Chichén Itzá, official guide. Mexico: Instituto Nacional de Antropología e Historia, 1958.

Chichén Itzá. Mexico: Ediciones Orto, n.d.

Chichén-Itzá (del Dicciónario histórico de Yucatán). *Yikal maya than* 9:54-57; 70-71, 1948.

Chilam Balam. Chumayel. 1986. *Heaven Born Merida and Its Destiny: The Book of Chilam Balam of Chumayel*. Munso S. Edmonson, ed. Austin: University of Texas Press.

Chilam Balam. Na. 2000. *The Book of Chilam Balam of Na*. R. Gubler and D. Bolles, eds. Lancaster, CA: Labyrinthos.

Chilam Balam. Tizimin. 1982. *The Ancient Future of the Itza: The Book of Chilam Balam of Tizimin*. M.S. Edmonson, ed. Austin: University of Texas Press.

Chilam Balam. Tuzik. 1996. *Chilam Balam de Tuzik*. Mexico: Grupo Dzibil.

CIREROL SANSORES, M. 1940. *El Castillo (The Castle): Mysterious Mayan Pyramidal Temple of Chichén Itzá*. Mérida.

CIREROL SANSORES, M. 1948. *Chi Cheen Itzá, Archaeological Paradise of America*. Mérida.

COBOS, R. 1989. *Shelling in; marine molusca at Chichén Itzá. In Coastal Maya Trade*. H. McKillop and P.F. Healy, eds. pp. 49-58. Occasional Papers in Anthropology, 8. Peterborough: Trent University.

COBOS, R. 1997. Katún y ahua: fechando el fin de Chichén Itzá. In *Identidades Sociales en Yucatán*. M.C. Lara C., ed. pp. 19-40. Merida: Universidad Autónoma de Yucatán.

COBOS, R. 1997. Patrones de asentamiento de la comunidad Clasico Terminal de Chichén Itzá. In IV *Coloquio Pedro Bosch Gimpera*. E. Vargas Pacheco, ed. pp. 845-864. Mexico: Universidad Nacional Autónoma de México.

COBOS, R. 1998. Chichén Itzá y el Clásico Terminal en las tierras bajas mayas. In *Simposio de Investigaciones Arqueológicas en Guatemala* (11 session, 1997). pp. 791-802. Guatemala: Ministerio de Cultura y Deportes; Instituto de Antropología e Historia; Asociación Tikal.

COBOS, R. 1999. Chichén Itzá: nuevas perspectivas sobre el patrón de asentamiento de una comunidad maya. In *Trabajos de Investigación Arqueológica en Puerto Rico*. pp. 57-66. San Juan.

COBOS, R. 1999. Fuentes históricas y arqueología: convergencias y divergencias en la reconstrucción del período Clásico Terminal en Chichén Itzá. *Mayab* 12:58-70.

COBOS, R. 2000. The Settlement Patterns of Chichén Itzá, Yucatán. FAMSI website.

COBOS, R. 2001. Chichén Itzá. In *The Oxford Encyclopedia of Mesoamerican Cultures: The Civilizations of Mexico and Central America*. D. Carrasco, ed. v. 1, pp. 183-187. Oxford, England: Oxford University Press.

COBOS, R. 2001. El centro de Yucatán: de area periferica a la integración de la comunidad urbana en Chichén Itzá. In *Reconstruyendo la ciudad Maya: el urbanismo en las sociedades antiguas*. A.C. Ruiz, M.I. Ponce de León, and M. Martínez Martínez, eds. pp. 253-304. Madrid: Sociedad Española de Estudios Mayas.

COBOS, R. 2003. The Settlement Patterns of Chichén Itzá, Yucatán, México. Doctoral dissertation, Tulane University.

COBOS, R. 2003. Ancient community form and social complexity at Chichén Itzá, Yucatán. In *El Urbanismo en Mesoamerica; Urbanism in Mesoamerica*. W.T. Sanders, A.G. Mastache, and R.H. Cobean, eds. v. 1, pp. 451-472. Mexico: University Park: Instituto Nacional de Antropología e Historia; Pennsylvania State University.

COBOS, R. 2004. Chichén Itzá: settlement and hegemony during the Terminal Classic period. In *The Terminal Classic in the Maya Lowlands: Collapse, Transition, and Transformation*. A.A. Demarest, P.M. Rice, and D.S. Rice, eds. pp. 517-544. Boulder: University Press of Colorado.

COBOS, R. 2005. Los Patrones de Asentamiento de Chichén Itzá, Yucatán. FAMSI website.

COBOS, R. 2005. Jaguares y pumas de Tula y Chichén Itzá. *Arqueología mexicana* 12(72):34-39.

COBOS, R. 2007. El Cenote sagrado de Chichén Itzá, Yucatán. *Argueologia mexicana* 14(83):50-53.

COBOS, R. 2007. Multepal or centralized kingship? New evidence on governmental organization at Chichén Itzá. In *Twin Tollans: Chichén Itzá, Tula, and the Epiclassic to Early Postclassic Mesoamerican World*. J.K. Kowalski and C. Kristan-Graham, eds. pp. 315-344. Washington, DC: Dumbarton Oaks Research Library and Collection.

COBOS, R, and T.L. WINEMILLER 2001. Late and terminal Classic-period causeway systems of Chichén Itzá, Yucatán, Mexico. *Ancient Mesoamerica* 12(2):283-291.

COGGINS, C.C. 1987. New fire at Chichén Itzá. In *Memorias del Primer Coloquio Internacional de Mayistas: 5-10 de agosto de 1985*. Mercedes de la Garza, *et al*., eds. pp. 427-484. Mexico: Universidad Nacional Autónoma de México, Centro de Estudios Mayas.

COGGINS, C.C. 1992a. *Artifacts from the Cenote of Sacrifice, Chichén Itzá, Yucatán: Textiles, Basketry, Stone, Bone, Shell, Ceramics, Wood, Copal, Rubber, Other Organic Materials and Mammalian Remains*. Memoirs, 10(3). Cambridge, MA: Harvard University, Peabody Museum of Archaeology and Ethnology.

COGGINS, C.C. 1992b. Conclusions. In *Artifacts from the Cenote of Sacrifice, Chichén Itzá, Yucatán*. C.C. Coggins, ed. pp. 387-389. Memoirs, 10(3). Cambridge, MA: Harvard University, Peabody Museum of Archaeology and Ethnology.

COGGINS, C.C. 1992c. Dredging the cenote. In *Artifacts from the Cenote of Sacrifice, Chichén Itzá, Yucatán*. C.C. Coggins, ed. pp. 9-31. Memoirs, 10(3). Cambridge, MA: Harvard University, Peabody Museum of Archaeology and Ethnology.

COGGINS, C.C. 1994. El Cenote Sagrado. *Arqueología mexicana* 2(7):47-50.

COGGINS, C.C. 2001a. Chichén Itzá. In *Archaeology of Ancient Mexico and Central America: An Encyclopedia*. S.T. Evans and D.L. Webster, eds. pp. 127-133. New York: Garland.

COGGINS, C.C. 2001b. A soft economy: perishable artifacts offered to the Well of Sacrifice, Chichén Itzá. In *Enduring Records: The Environmental and Cultural Heritage of Wetlands*. B.A. Purdy, ed. pp. 83-91. Oxford, England: Oxbow Books.

COGGINS, C.C. 2002. Toltec. *Res* 42:34-85.

COGGINS, C.C., and J.M. LADD. 1992a. Copal and resin offerings. In *Artifacts from the Cenote of Sacrifice, Chichén Itzá, Yucatán*. C.C. Coggins, ed. pp. 345-357. Memoirs, 10(3). Cambridge, MA: Harvard University, Peabody Museum of Archaeology and Ethnology.

COGGINS, C.C., and J.M. LADD. 1992b. Wooden artifacts. In *Artifacts from the Cenote of Sacrifice, Chichén Itzá, Yucatán*. C.C. Coggins, ed. pp. 235-344. Memoirs, 10(3). Cambridge, MA: Harvard University, Peabody Museum of Archaeology and Ethnology.

COGGINS, C.C., and O.C. SHANE. 1984. *Cenote of Sacrifice: Maya Treasures from the Sacred Well of Chichén Itzá*. Austin: University of Texas Press.

COGGINS, C.C., and O.C. SHANE. 1989. *El Cenote de los Sacrificios: tesoros mayas extraídos del cenote sagrado de Chichén Itzá*. Mexico: Fondo de Cultura Económica.

COHODAS, Marvin. 1974. Great Ball Court of Chichén Itzá, Yucatán, Mexico. Doctoral dissertation, Columbia University.

COHODAS, M. 1978. *The Great Ball Court at Chichén Itzá, Yucatán, Mexico*. New York: Garland.

Concesión otorgada por el Gobierno Mexicano a la Carnegie Institution of Washington para exploraciónes arqueológicas en Chichén Itzá, Yucatán. Publicaciónes, Departamento de Antropología, 3(8). Mexico: Secretaria de Educación Pública, Dirección Editorial, 1925.

Conference of archaeological staff at Chichén Itzá. *Carnegie Institution of Washington, News Service Bulletin* 2:177, 1931.

DÁVALOS HURTADO, E. 1961. Return to the sacred cenote. *National Geographic* 120(4):540-549.

DAVOUST, M. 1977. *Les premiers chefs mayas de Chichén Itzá, and Etude des glyphes de filiation*. Paris.

DAVOUST, M. 1980. Les primiers chefs mayas de Chichén Itzá. *Méxicon* 2(2):25-29.

DAVOUST, M. 1989-1990. Nuevas lecturas de los textos mayas de Chichén Itzá. *Anuario Centro de Estudios Indígenas 3*:139-164.

DEHARPORT, D.L. 1953. Sculpture at Chichén Itzá. *Carnegie Institution of Washington, Year Book* 52:283-284.

DESMOND, L.G. 1994. Application of close-range photogrammetry to archaeology: Chichén Itzá and Uxmal, Yucatán, Mexico, 1989. In *Seventh Palenque Round Table*, 1989. V.M. Fields, ed. pp. 43-48. Palenque Round Table (7 session, 1989). San Francisco: Pre-Columbian Art Research Institute.

DESMOND, L.G. 1996. A geophysical survey of the Great Plaza and Great Ball Court at Chichén Itzá, Yucatán, Mexico. In *Eighth Palenque Round Table*, 1993. M.J. Macri and J. McHargue, eds. pp. 271-280Palenque Round Table (8 session, 1993). San Francisco: Pre-Columbian Art Research Institute.

DESMOND, L.G. 2008. Excavation of the Platform of Venus, Chichén Itzá, Yucatán, México: the pioneering fieldwork of Alice Dixon Le Plongeon and Augustus Le Plongeon. In *Tributo a Jaime Litvak King*. P. Schmidt, E. Ortiz Diaz, and J. Santos Ramírez, eds. pp. 155-166. México: Instituto de Investigaciones Antropológicas, UNAM.

DESMOND, L., and P. MESSENGER. 1988. *A Dream of Maya: Augustus and Alice LePlongeon in Nineteenth Century Yucatan*. Albuquerque: University of New Mexico Press.

DÍAZ BOLIO, J. 1972. *Guía instructiva (estudio) a las ruinas de Chichén Itzá*. Mexico.

DÍAZ BOLIO, J. 1982. *La serpiente de luz de Chichén Itzá*. Merida: Area Maya.

Dr. S.G. MORLEY, 65, an archaeologist; specialist in Maya hierioglyphic writing dies; had directed Chichén Itzá Project. *New York Times*, September 3, p. 19, 1948.

Duck-bill pipe from Yucatán: A remarkably well preserved Chac Mool figure uncovered at Chichén Itzá, Yucatán. *Art and Archaeology* 24:47, 1927.

DUMOND, D.E. 1997. *The Machete and the Cross: Campesino Rebellion in Yucatán*. Lincoln: University of Nebraska Press.

DÜTTING, D. 1992. Hieroglyphic texts of Chichén Itzá. *Baessler Archiv* 40(1):101-160.

DUTTON, B.P. 1952. Toltecs and Their Influence on the Culture of Chichén Itzá. Doctoral dissertation, Columbia University, Department of Anthropology.

DUTTON, B.P. 1956. A brief discussion of Chichén Itzá. *El Palacio* 63:203-232.

EDIGER, Donald. 1971. *Well of sacrifice*. Garden City, NY: Doubleday and Company.

EFFLER, Louis R. 1935. *Ruins of Chichén Itzá; a Tourist Guide*. Toledo.

El Castillo, pyramid-temple of the Maya god, Kukulcan. *Carnegie Institution of Washington, News Service Bulletin* 4:106-116, 1937.

El Castillo, templo piramidal del dios Kukulcán. Supplementary Publication, 32. Washington, DC: Carnegie Institution of Washington, 1937.

El templo-piramide de Kukulcan en Mexico; la Institución Carnegie de Washington ha estudiado las ruinas de ese monumento en los mismos, descubierto en el territorio de Yucatán. *La Prensa*, May 8, 1938.

EROSA PENICHE, J.A. 1937. *Guía para visitar las ruinas de Chichén-Itzá*. Merida: Tipografía Yucateca.

EROSA PENICHE, J.A. 1946. *Guía para visitar las ruinas de Chichén-Itzá*. 2 ed. Merida: Imprenta Oriente.

EROSA PENICHE, J.A. 1947a. Descubrimiento y exploración arqueológica de la subestuctura del Castillo en Chichén-Itzá. In *Proceedings of the International Congress of Americanists* (27 session, Mexico, 1939). v. 2, pt. 1, pp. 229-248. Mexico.

EROSA PENICHE, J.A. 1947b. *Guide to the Ruins of Chichén-Itzá*. Merida: Editorial Yikal Maya Than.

EROSA PENICHE, J.A. 1949. *Guide to the ruins of Chichén Itzá*. Merida: Yikal Maya Than.

EWING, M.R. 1972. A history of the archaeological activity at Chichén Itzá, Yucatán, Mexico. M.A. thesis, Kent State University.

FERGUSON, W.M. 1977. *Maya ruins of Mexico in color; Palenque, Uxmal, Kabah, Sayil, Xlapak, Labna, Chichén Itzá, Labna, Cobá, Tulum*. Norman: University of Oklahoma Press. 246 p.

FERNÁNDEZ SOUZA, L. 2001. Representaciones de Venus en Chichén Itzá. *Temas antropológicas, revista científica de investigaciones regionales* 23(2):181-200.

FERNÁNDEZ SOUZA, L. 2006. Death and memory in Chichén Itzá. In *Jaws of the Underworld: Life, Death, and Rebirth Among the Ancient Maya*. P.R. Colas, G. LeFort, and B. Liljefors Persson, eds. pp. 21-34. Acta Mesoamericana, 16. Markt Schwaben: Verlag Anton Saurwien.

FOLAN, W.J. 1961. Sacred cenote of Chichén Itzá. *National Geographic Society Research Reports*, pp. 77-98.

FOLAN, W.J. 1966. Sacred cenote of Chichén Itzá, Yucatán, Mexico. M.A. thesis, Southern Illinois University.

FOLAN, W.J. 1968. *El cenote sagrado de Chichén-Itzá. Departamento de Monumentos Prehispánicos*. Informes, 15. Mexico, Instituto Nacional de Antropología e Historia.

FOLAN, W.J. 1972. Kukulkan y un culto fálico en Chichén Itzá, Yucatán, Mexico. *Estudios de cultura* maya 8:77-82.

FOLAN, W.J. 1974. Cenote sagrado of Chichén Itzá, Yucatán, Mexico, 1967-68; the excavation, plans, and preparations. *International Journal of Nautical Archaeology and Underwater* Exploration 3(2):283-293.

FOLAN, W.J. 1978. *Chichén Itzá*. Ediciones Orto, 238. Mexico: Xicontencatl.

FOLAN, W.J. 1980. Chichén Itzá, el Cenote Sagrado y Xibalbá: una nueva vision. *Boletín de la Escuela de Ciencias Antropológicas de la Universidad de Yucatán* 9(44):70-76.

FOLAN, W.J. 1990. Chichén Itzá, el Cenote Sagrado y Xibalba: una revision. *Boletín de la Escuela de Ciencias Antropológicas de la Universidad de Yucatán* 15(86):53-54.

FORSHAW, F.C. 1984. Cosmography at the Caracol, Chichén Itzá, Yucatán, Mexico. Doctoral dissertation, University of Oregon, Department of Anthropology. 194 leaves.

FOSTER, L., and L. WREN. 1996. World Creator and World sustainer: God N at Chichén Itzá. In *Eighth Palenque Round Table*, 1993. Martha J. Macri and Jan McHargue, eds. pp. 259-269. San Francisco: Pre-Columbian Art Research Institute.

FOURNIER, P., and V.H. BOLAÑOS. 2007. The Epiclassic in the Tula region beyond Tula Chico. In *Twin Tollans: Chichén Itzá, Tula, and the Epiclassic to Early Postclassic Mesoamerican World*. J.K. Kowalski and C. Kristan-Graham, eds. pp. 481-530. Washington, DC: Dumbarton Oaks Research Library and Collection.

FOX, J.A. 1997. Phoneticism, dates, and astronomy at Chichén Itzá. In *The Language of Maya Hieroglyphs*. Martha J. Macri and Anabel Ford, eds. pp. 13-32. San Francisco: Pre-Columbian Art Research Institute.

FREIDEL, D. 2007. War and statecraft in the northern Maya lowlands: Yaxuna and Chichén Itzá. In *Twin Tollans: Chichén Itzá, Tula, and the Epiclassic to Early Postclassic Mesoamerican World*. J.K. Kowalski and C. Kristan-Graham, eds. pp. 345-376. Washington, DC: Dumbarton Oaks Research Library and Collection.

GALINDO Y VILLA, J. 1934. El Codice Troano: El Templo de los Guerreros en Chichén Itzá. *Memorias y revista de la Sociedad Científica Antonio Alzate* 53:161-169.

GALLENKAMP, C.B. 1968. Une exploration mouvementée a Chichén Itzá le puits des sacrifices. *Archéologia* 22:40-51.

GARCÍA CAMPILLO, J.M. 1996. Sufijo verbal -ki# en las inscripciones de Chichén Itzá. *Mayab* 10:50-58.

GARCÍA CAMPILLO, J.M. 1999a. Estudio Introductoria del Lexico de las Inscripciones de Chichén Itzá. Thesis, McMicken College of Arts and Science, University of Cincinnati, Ohio.

GARCÍA CAMPILLO, J.M. 1999b. Implicaciones de un aniversario de doce años túnicos en las inscripciones de Chichén Itzá. *Revista española de antropología americana* 29:131-157.

GARCÍA CAMPILLO, J.M. 2000a. *Estudio introductorio del léxico de las inscripciones de Chichén Itzá, Yucatán,*

México. International Series, 831. Oxford, England: British Archaeological Reports; Hadrian Books.

GARCÍA CAMPILLO, J.M. 2000b. Linguistic Study: Chichén Itzá Inscriptions. FAMSI website.

GARCÍA CAMPILLO, J.M. 2001. Santuarios urbanos: casas para los antepasados en Chichén Itzá. In *Reconstruyendo la ciudad Maya: el urbanismo en las sociedades antiguas*. A.C. Ruiz, M.I. Ponce de León, and M. Martínez Martínez, eds. pp. 403-426. Madrid: Sociedad.

GARCÍA CAMPILLO, J.M. 2005. Estudio Lingüístico: Las Inscripciones de Chichén Itzá. FAMSI website.

GARCÍA LAXCURÁIN V.G. 1989. Conservación de tejidos mayas procedentes del cenote sagrado de Chichén Itzá. In *Memorias del Segundo Coloquio Internacional de Mayistas*, 1. Alain Breton, ed. pp. 333-376. Mexico: Universidad Nacional Autónoma de México, Instituto de Investigaciones Filologicas.

GARCÍA MOLL, R., and R. COBOS. 2009. *Chichén Itzá: patrimonio de la humanidad*. México: Grupo Azabache.

GIBB, D. 1938-1939. Cities of the Mayas: Palenque, Copán, Uxmal, and Chichén Itzá. *Geographical Magazine* 8:97-104,187-202, 237-252.

GILLESPIE, S.D. 2007. Toltecs, Tula and Chichén Itzá: The development of an archaeological myth. In *Twin Tollans: Chichén Itzá, Tula, and the Epiclassic to Early Postclassic Mesoamerican World*. J.K. Kowalski and C. Kristan-Graham, eds. pp. 85-128. Washinghton, DC: Dumbarton Oaks Research Library and Collection.

GILPIN, L. 1948. *Temples in Yucatán: A Camera Chronicle of Chichén Itzá*. New York: Hastings House.

GONZÁLEZ DE LA MATA, R. 2003. Actividades cotidianas en Chichén Itzá: El conjunto alrededor del Chultun 1 del Grupo de la Serie Inicial. In *INAH: una historia*. J.C. Oliveì Negrete and B. Cottom, eds. v. 2, pp. 651-658. Mexico: Instituto Nacional de Antropologiìa e Historia.

GONZÁLEZ DE LA MATA, R. 2006. Agua, agricultura y mitos: el caso de tres rejolladas de Chichén Itzá. In *Simposio de Investigaciones Arqueológicas en Guatemala*, (XIX session, 2005). pp. 279-290. Guatemala: Museo Nacional de Arqueología y Etnología.

GORDON, G.B. 1911. A trip to Chichén Itzá. *Museum Journal* 2(1):10-21.

GRAHAM, I. 2002. *Alfred Maudslay and the Maya: A Biography*. London: British Museum.

GRAÑA-BEHRENS, D., C. PRAGER, and E. WAGNER. 1999. Hieroglyphic inscription of the High Priest's Grave at Chichén Itzá, Yucatán, Mexico. *Méxicon* 21(3):61-66.

GRAULICH, M. 2002. Los reyes de Tollan. *Revista española de antropología americana* 32:87-114.

GRUBE, N., and R.J. KROCHOK. 2007. Reading between the lines: hieroglyphic texts from Chichén Itzá and its neighbors. In *Twin Tollans: Chichén Itzá, Tula, and the Epiclassic to Early Postclassic Mesoamerican World*. J.K. Kowalski and C. Kristan-Graham, eds. pp. 205-250. Washington, DC: Dumbarton Oaks Research Library and Collection.

Guía oficial de Chichén Itzá. Mexico: *Instituto Naciónal de Antropología e Historia*. 1978.

GUZMÁN PEREDO, M. 1974. Exploring the Sacred Well. *Américas* 26(8):17-23.

HABERLAND, W. 1954. Golden battle discs of Chichén Itzá. *Ethnos* 19:94-104.

HAGAR, S. 1928. Jaguar and serpent mural at Chichén Itzá. In *Proceedings of the International Congress of Americanists* (20 session, Rio de Janeiro, 1922). v. 2, pt. 1, pp. 75-78. Rio de Janeiro.

Hallazgo arqueológico. *El Universal*, January 13, 1940.

Hand-ball palace of the Mayas; new pictures of the ruins of Chichén Itzá, Mexico. *Sphere* 141(1839):103, 1935.

HARTUNG, H. 1969. Consideraciones urbanísticas sobre los trazos de los centros ceremoniales de Tikal, Copán, Uxmal y Chichén Itzá. In *El proceso de urbanización en América desde sus orígenes hasta nuestros días*. J. Hardoy, ed. pp. 121-125. Buenos Aires.

HARTUNG, H. 1984. Alignments in architecture and sculpture of Maya centers; notes on Piedras Negras, Copán and Chichén Itzá. *Ibero-Amerikanisches Archiv* 10(2):223-240.

HARTUNG, H., and A.F. AVENI. 1978. Los observatorios astronómicos en Chichén Itzá, Mayapán, y Paalmul. *Boletín de la Escuela de Ciencias Antropológicas de la Universidad de Yucatán* 6(32):2-13.

HARTZELL-SCOTT, P. 1990. Warfare and the iconography of Chichén Itzá, Mexico. *Human Mosaic* 24(1-2):43-49.

HARVEY, W. 1952. Metallographic examination of gilded sheet copper and wire-like bells. In *Metals from the Cenote of Sacrifice, Chichén Itzá, Yucatán*. S.K. Lothrop, ed. pp. 117-118. Memoirs, 10(2). Cambridge, MA: Harvard University, Peabody Museum of Archaeology and Ethnology.

HATT, R.T. 1972. Chichén remembered. *Explorer* 14(1):6-12.

HAYWARD, K. 1994. Oyohualli: a prominent symbol at Chichén Itzá. *Pre-Columbian Art Research Institute Newsletter* 18:2.

HEADRICK, A. 1991. Chicomoztoc of Chichén Itzá. M.A. thesis, University of Texas at Austin.

HEALAN, D.M. 2007. New perspectives onTula's obsidian industry and its relationship to Chichén Itzá. In *Twin Tollans: Chichén Itzá, Tula, and the Epiclassic to Early Postclassic Mesoamerican World*. J.K. Kowalski and C. Kristan-Graham, eds. pp. 429-448. Washington, DC: Dumbarton Oaks Research Library and Collection.

HERNÁNDEZ, Juan J. 1841. Ruinas de Chichén Itzá. *El Museo Yucateco* 1:270-276.

HOLMES, W.H. 1895-1897. *Archaeological Studies among the Ancient Cities of Mexico*. Publication, 8, 16. Chicago: Field Museum of Natural History. 2 v.

HOOTON, Earnest A. 1940. Skeletons from the cenote of sacrifice at Chichén Itzá. In *The Maya and Their Neighbors*. C. Hay, ed. pp. 272-280. New York: Appleton-Century.

HOPKINS, M.R. 1992. Mammalian remains. In *Artifacts from the Cenote of Sacrifice, Chichén Itzá, Yucatán*. Clemency C. Coggins, ed. pp. 369-385. Memoirs, 10(3). Cambridge, MA: Harvard University, Peabody Museum of Archaeology and Ethnology.

HOUWALD, G. von. 1984. *Mapa y descripción de la montaña del Petén e Ytzá: Interpretación de un documentos de los años un poco después del la conquista de Tayasal*. Indiana, 9. Berlin: Ibero-Americanisches Institut.

HUONDER, A. 1907. *La fuente sagrada de Chichén Itzá: narracion del antiguo Yucatán*. Barcelona: Maria Herder. 138 p.

HUTSON, S. 2005. Ways of seeing: Chichén Itzá landscape portraiture and Maya archeologists. In *Art for Archaeology's Sake: Material Culture and Style across the Disciplines*. A/. Waters-Rist, C. Cluney, C. McNamee, and L. Steinbrenner, eds. pp. 228-238. Chacmool Conference, 33. Calgary: University of Calgary, Archaeological Association.

ICHIKAWA, S. 1931. La restauración del mosaico de turquesas. In *Los mayas de la region central de America*. pp. 13-16. Supplementary Publication, 4. Washington, DC: Carnegie Institution of Washington.

ICHIKAWA, S. 1931. Restoration of the turquoise mosaic plaque (in the Temple of the Warriors, Chichén Itzá). *Art and Archaeology* 31(6):306-310.

Inferencias sobre distintivos sociales en Chichén Itzá a través del estudio de la cerámica Pizarra Chichén (Chichén Slate Ware). In *Religión y sociedad en el área maya*. C.V. Torrecilla, J.L.B. Villarejo, and Y.F. Marquínez, eds. pp. 177-195. Publicaciónes de la S.E.E.M., 3. Madrid: Instituto de Cooperación Iberoamericana.

Isla Cerritos, un importante puerto prehispanico de Chichén Itzá. *Novedades de Yucatán*, March 15, 1986.

JOHNSON, R.E. 1989. Chichén Itzá dates and planetary events. In *U Mut Maya* II. T. Jones and Carolyn J., eds. pp. 157-168. Arcata: T. Jones.

JOHNSON, R.E. 1989. Inscriptions of Chichén Itzá. In *U Mut Maya* II. T. Jones and C. Jones, eds. pp. 145-156. Arcata: T. Jones.

JONES, G.D. 1998. *The Conquest of the Last Maya Kingdom*. Stanford: Stanford University Press.

JONES, L.R. 1989. Hermeneutics of Sacred Architecture: A Reassessment of the Similitude Between Tula, Hidalgo, and Chichén Itzá, Yucatán. Doctoral dissertation, University of Chicago, Department of Religion. 757 leaves.

JONES, L.R. 1993. Hermeneutics of sacred architecture: a reassessment of the similitude between Tula, Hidalgo and Chichén Itzá, Yucatán. II. *History of Religions* 32(4):315-342.

JONES, L.R. 1995. *Twin City Tales: A Hermeneutical Reassessment of Tula and Chichén Itzá*. Niwot: University Press of Colorado. 482 p.

JONES, L.R. 1997. Conquests of the imagination: Maya-Mexican polarity and the story of Chichén Itzá. *American Anthropologist* 99(2):275-290.

JUÁREZ COSSÍO, D., M.A. PÉREZ JUÁREZ. 1994. *Guía oficial: Chichén Itzá*. Mexico: Instituto Nacional de Antropología e Historia. 83 p.

KELLEY, D.H. 2009. *Dates from the Well of Time, Chichén Itzá, Yucatán, Mexico*. Research Reports on Ancient Maya Writing, 58. Bernardsville, NC: Center for Maya Research.

KEPECS, S. 2007. Chichén Itzá, Tula and the Epiclassic/Early Postclassic Mesoamerican world system. In *Twin Tollans: Chichén Itzá, Tula, and the Epiclassic to Early Postclassic Mesoamerican World*. J.K. Kowalski and C. Kristan-Graham, eds. pp. 129-150. Washington, DC: Dumbarton Oaks Research Library and Collection.

KEPECS, S., *et al*. 1994. Chichén Itzá and its hinterland: a world-systems perspective. *Ancient Mesoamerica* 5(2):141-158.

KIDDER, A.V. 1930. Conference at Chichén Itzá. *Science* 71:391-392.

KIDDER, A.V. 1930. Division of Historical Research. *Carnegie Institution of Washington, Year Book* 29:91-119.

KIDDER, A.V. 1931. Division of Historical Research. *Carnegie Institution of Washington, Year Book* 30:101-158.

KIDDER, A.V. 1943. Spindle whorls from Chichén Itzá, Yucatán. *Carnegie Institution of Washington, Notes on Middle American Archaeology and Ethnology* 1(16):92-99.

KILMARTIN, J.O. 1924. Report on the survey and base-map at Chichén Itzá, Mexico. *Carnegie Institution of Washington, Year Book* 23:213-217.

KILMARTIN, J.O. 1924. Report on the survey and base-map at Chichén Itzá, Mexico. In *Research in Middle American Archaeology*. S. G. Morley, ed. pp. 213-217. Washington, DC: Carnegie Institution of Washington.

KILMARTIN, J.O. 1929. Report of J.O. Kilmartin on information surveys at Chichén Itzá. *Carnegie Institution of Washington, Year Book* 28:312-315.

KING, P. 1937. *Reliquias de los sacrificios mayas; han sido descubiertas por los exploraciones cientificos en las ruins del Viejo Castillo*. Los Angeles.

KNOWLTON, T.W. 2010. Nahua Vocables in a Maya Song of the Fall of Chichén Itzá: Music and Social Memory in the Construction of Yucatecan Ethnicities. In

Astronomers, Scribes, and Priests: Intellectual Interchange between the Northern Maya Lowlands and Highland Mexico in the Late Postclassic Period. G. Vail and C. Hernandez, eds. pp. 241-261. Washington, DC: Dumbarton Oaks.

KOONTZ, Rex A., *et al.* 1994. A Group of Related Titles from Structure 6E1 at Chichén Itzá. In *U Mut Maya* V.C. Jones and T. Jones, eds. pp. 191-195. Arcata: T. Jones.

KOWALSKI, J.K. 1985. Lords of the northern Maya; dynastic history in the inscriptions of Uxmal and Chichén Itzá. *Expedition* 27(3):50-60.

KOWALSKI, J.K. 1992. Las deidades astrales y la fertilidad agrícola: temas fundamentales en el simbolismo del juego de pelota mesoamericano en Copán, Chichén Itzá y Tenochtitlan. In *El Juego de pelota en Mesoamérica: raíces y supervivencia.* M.T. Uriarte, ed. pp. 305-333. Mexico: Siglo Veintiuno Editores.

KOWALSKI, J.K. 1993. Astral Deities and Agricultural Fertility: Fundamental Themes in Mesoamerican Ballgame Symbolism at Copán, Chichén Itzá, and Tenochtitlan. In *The Symbolism in the Plastic and Pictorial Representations of Ancient Mexico: A Symposium of the 46th International Congress of Americanists, Amsterdam 1988.* J. de Durand-Forest, and M. Eisinger, eds. pp. 49-72. Bonn: Holos Verlag.

KOWALSKI, J.K. 2003. Collaboration and conflict: an interpretation of the relationship between Uxmal and Chichén Itzá during the terminal Classic/Early Posclassic periods. In *Escondido en la selva: arqueología en el norte de Yucatán.* H.J. Prem, ed. pp. 235-272. Mexico: Instituto Nacional de Antropología e Historia; Universidad de Bonn.

KOWALSKI, J.K. 2007. What's "Toltec" at Uxmal and Chichén Itzá? Merging Maya and Mesoamerican worldviews and world systems in Terminal Classic to Early Postclassic Yucatán. In *Twin Tollans: Chichén Itzá, Tula, and the Epiclassic to Early Postclassic Mesoamerican World.* J.K. Kowalski and C. Kristan-Graham, eds. pp. 251-314. Washington, DC: Dumbarton Oaks Research Library and Collection.

KOWALSKI, J.K., and C. KRISTAN-GRAHAM. 2007. *Twin Tollans: Chichén Itzá, Tula, and the Epiclassic to Early Postclassic Mesoamerican World.* Washington, DC: Dumbarton Oaks Research Library and Collection.

KOWALSKI, J.K., R.B. SILVERSTEIN, and M. FOLLANSBEE. 2002. Seats of power and cycles of creation: continuities and changes in iconography and political organization at Dzibilchaltun, Uxmal, Chichén Itzá and Mayapán. *Estudios de cultura maya* 22:87-111.

KRISTAN-GRAHAM, C.B. 1989. Art, rulership and the Mesoamerican body politic at Tula and Chichén Itzá. Doctoral dissertation, University of California, Los Angeles.

KRISTAN-GRAHAM, C.B. 2001. A sense of place at Chichén Itzá. In *Landscape and Power in Ancient Mesoamerica.* Rex Koontz, Kathryn Reese-Taylor, and Annabeth Headrick, eds. pp. 317-368. Boulder: Westview Press.

KRISTAN-GRAHAM, C. 2007. Structuring identity at Tula: the design and symbolism of colonnaded halls and sunken spaces. In *Twin Tollans: Chichén Itzá, Tula, and the Epiclassic to Early Postclassic Mesoamerican World.* J.K. Kowalski and C. Kristan-Graham, eds. pp. 531-578. Washington, DC: Dumbarton Oaks Research Library and Collection.

KRISTAN-GRAHAM, C.B., and J.K. KOWLASKI. 2007. Chichén Itzá, Tula, and Tollan: Changing perspectives on a recurring problem in Mesoamerican archaeology and art history. In *Twin Tollans: Chichén Itzá, Tula, and the Epiclassic to Early Postclassic Mesoamerican World.* J.K. Kowalski and C. Kristan-Graham, eds. pp. 13-84. Washingtion, DC: Dumbarton Oaks Research Library and Collection.

KROCHOCK, R.J. 1988. Hieroglyphic Inscriptions and Iconography at the Temple of the Four Lintels and Related Monuments, Chichén Itzá, Yucatán. M.A. thesis, University of Texas at Austin.

KROCHOCK, R.J. 1989. *Hieroglyphic Inscriptions at Chichén Itzá, Yucatán, Mexico: The Temples of the Initial Series, The One Lintel, The Three Lintels, and The Four Lintels.* Research Reports on Ancient Maya Writing, 23. Washington, DC: Center for Maya Research.

KROCHOCK, R.J. 1991. Dedication Ceremonies at Chichén Itzá: The Glyphic Evidence. In *Sixth Palenque Round Table, 1986.* V.M. Fields, ed. pp. 43-50. Norman: University of Oklahoma Press.

KROCHOCK, R.J. 1994. Ballcourts and the evolution of political rhetoric at Chichén Itzá. In *Hidden Among the Hills: Maya Archaeology of the Northwest Yucatán Peninsula.* H.J. Prem, ed. pp. 359-375.Acta Mesoamericana, 7. Möckmühl: Verlag von Flemming.

KROCHOCK, R.J. 1997. *A New Interpretation of the Inscriptions on the Temple of the Hieroglyphic Jambs, Chichén Itzá.* Texas Notes on Precolumbian Art, Writing, and Culture, 79. Austin: University of Texas at Austin, Center of the History and Art of Ancient American Culture.

KROCHOCK, R.J. 1998. The Development of Political Rhetoric at Chichén Itzá, Yucatán, México. Doctoral dissertation, University of Texas, Austin. 2 v.

KROCHOCK, R.J. 2000. Recording the Political History of Chichén Itzá: Photography of the Denison Rubbings and Archival Research at the Peabody Museum. FAMSI website.

KROCHOCK, R.J. 2002. Women in the hieroglyphic inscriptions of Chichén Itzá. In *Ancient Maya Women.* T. Ardren, ed. pp. 152-170. Walnut Creek, CA: Altamira Press.

KROCHOCK, R.J. 2003. Registrando la Historia Política de Chichén Itzá: Fotografía de los Calcos de Denison e

Investigación de Archivo en el Museo Peabody. FAMSI website.

KUBLER, G.A. 1961. Chichén Itzá and Tula. *Estudios de cultura maya* 1:47-80.

KUBLER, G.A. 1982. Serpent and Atlantean columns: symbols of Maya-Toltec polity. *Journal of the Society of Architectural Historians* 41(2):93-115.

KURJACK, E.B. 1992. Conflicto en el arte de Chichén Itzá. *Mayab* 8:88-96.

KURJACK, E.B., and Merle G. ROBERTSON. 1994. Politics and art at Chichén Itzá. In *Seventh Palenque Round Table, 1989*. Virginia M. Fields, ed. pp. 19-24. San Francisco: Pre-Columbian Art Research Institute.

KUTSCHER, Gerdt. 1944. Cobá y Chichén Itzá, relación de Teobert Maler. *Ensayos y estudios* 4:1-40.

KUTTNER, R. 1937. Mexikanische Pyramiden geben Geheimmisse preis; El Castillo, der Pyramidentempel Kukulcans, des Gottes der Maya. *Wissen und Fortschrift* 11(10):819-825.

La profanación del Cenote Sagrado. *El Naciónal*, July 9, 1926.

LANDA, D. de. 1941. *Relación de las cosas de Yucatán*. A.M. Tozzer, ed. Papers, 18. Cambridge: Peabody Museum of American Archaeology and Ethnology, Harvard University.

LANZ TRUEBA, J. 1936. Chichén Itzá y su verdadera historia. *El Universal*, July 13.

LARSEN, H. 1964. Trip from Chichén-Itzá to Xcacal. *Ethnos* 29(1-2):5-42.

LEHMANN, W. 1934. El pozo de los Itzá; las maravillas de una ciudad antigua en la tierra de los mayas de Yucatán. *Anales de la Sociedad de Geografía e Historia de Guatemala* 11:45-49.

LEPLONGEON, A. 1881. *Vestiges of the Mayas, or, Facts Tending to Prove That Comminications and Intimate Relations Must Have Existed, In Very Remotre Times, Between the Inhabitants of Mayab and Those of Asia and Africa*. New York: J. Polhemus.

LEPLONGEON, A. 1896. *Queen M'oo and the Egyptian Sphinx*. New York: The Author.

LERNER, J. 2008. Chichén Itzá: ruinas en construcción. *Dimensión antropológica* 15(42): 165-188.

LINCOLN, C.E. 1983. Chichén Itzá: Clásico Terminal o Postclásico Temprano? *Boletín de la Escuela de Ciencias Antropológicas de la Universidad de Yucatán* 10(59):3-29.

LINCOLN, C.E. 1986. The Chronology of Chichén Itzá: A Review of the Literature. In *Late Lowland Maya Civilization: Classic to Postclassic*. J.A. Sabloff and E.W. Andrews V, eds. Pp. 141-196. Albuquerque: University of New Mexico Press.

LINCOLN, C.E. 1990. Ethnicity and social organization at Chichén Itzá, Yucatán, Mexico. Doctoral dissertation, Harvard University. 2 v.

LINCOLN, C.E. 1990b. Proyecto Arqueológico Chichén Itzá. *Boletín de la Escuela de Ciencias Antropológicas de la Universidad de Yucatán* 15(86):3-43.

LINCOLN, C.E. 1994. Structural and philological evidence for divine kingship at Chichén Itzá, Yucatán, Mexico. In *Hidden Among the Hills: Maya Archaeology of the Northwest Yucatán Península*. H.J. Prem, ed. pp. 164-196. Acta Mesoamericana, 7. Möckmühl: Verlag von Flemming.

LIZARDI RAMOS, C. 1936. Los secretos de Chichén Itzá. *Excélsior*, December 21.

LIZARDI RAMOS, C. 1937. New discoveries of Maya culture at Chichén Itzá: fresh examples from Yucatán: Art relics, including reliefs representing fertility rites of a cruel and picturesque religion. *Illustrated London News*, July 3, pp. 12-15.

LLOYD, Robin. 1994. A child's eye view of Chichén Itzá. *Washington Post*, September 25, p. E1.

LÓPEZ DE COGOLLUDO, D. 1867-1868. *Historia de Yucatán, escrito en el siglo XVII*. Mérida: Imprenta de M. Aldana Rivas. 2 v.

LÓPEZ MARTÍNEZ, B. 1939. Interesante conferencia del Dr. S.G. Morley en Chichén. *Diario de Yucatán*, May 8.

Los descubrimientos del arqueologo Edward Thompson en Mexico. *Revista de Revistas*, June 3, 1923.

LOTHROP, J.M. 1992. Textiles. In *Artifacts from the Cenote of Sacrifice, Chichén Itzá, Yucatán*. C.C. Coggins, ed. pp. 33-90. Memoirs, 10(3). Cambridge, MA: Peabody Museum of Archaeology and Ethnology, Harvard University.

LOTHROP, S.K. 1952. *Metals from the Cenote of Sacrifice, Chichén Itzá, Yucatán*. Memoirs, 10(2), Cambridge, MA: Harvard University, Peabody Museum of American Archaeology and Ethnology. 139 p.

LOVE, B. 1989. *The hieroglyphic lintels of Yulá, Yucatán, México*. Research reports on ancient Maya writing, 24. Washington, DC: Center for Maya Research.

LOVE, B. 1990. Proyecto de Mapeo de Yula: Chichén Itzá. *Boletín de la Escuela de Ciencias Antropológicas de la Universidad de Yucatán* 15(86):44-52.

LOVE, B. 2002. Inscripciones jeroglificas mayas del Osario (Estr. 3C1) en Chichén Itzá: informe preliminary. *Los investigadores de la cultura maya* 10:140-145.

LUNARDI, E. 1975. L'antico e il nuovo a Chichén Itzá il Castillo e le modificazioni del calendario. *Terra ameriga* 12(37-40):41-64.

M.A.M. 1929. Temple maya de Chichén-Itzá. *Journal de la Sociéte des Américanistes de Paris* 21:431.

MACKAY, K. 1929. Report of Miss Katheryn MacKay on the Chichén Itzá clinic. *Carnegie Institution of Washington, Year Book* 28:315-316.

MALDONADO CÁRDENAS, R. 1994. Chichén Itzá en numerous. *Arqueología mexicana* 2(7):52.

MALDONADO CÁRDENAS, R. 1997. Las intervenciones de restauración arqueológica en Chichén Itzá (1926-1980). In *Homenaje al profesor César A. Sáenz*. Angel García Cook, *et al*., eds. pp. 103-132. Mexico: Instituto Nacional de Antropología e Historia.

MALDONADO CÁRDENAS, R. 1998. Los relieves del Juego de Pelota de Chichén Itzá. *Arqueología mexicana* 5(30):41.

MALER, T. 1910. *Historia de las ruinas de Chichén Itzá*. 63 p.

MALER, T. 1932. *Impresiones de viaje a las ruinas de Cobá y Chichén Itzá*. Merida: Imprenta del Editor, José E. Rosado E.

MALKUS, A.S. 1930. *Dark Star of Itzá: The Story of a Pagan Princess*. New York: Harcourt Brace.

MANAHAN, T.K., A. Alonso OLVERA, and T. ARDREN. 2008. Apuntando hacia un modelo regional de desarrollo de Chichén Itzá: historia de una plataforma Sotuta en Xuenkal, Yucatán. *Investigadores de la cultura maya* 16(2): 93-104.

Map of the Ruins of Chichén-Itzá, Yucatán, Mexico. Washington, DC: Williams-Webb Co., 1924.

MARISCAL, M. 1937. Los relieves de la banqueta del juego de pelota de Chichén-Itzá. *Revista de Revistas*.

MARTIN, P.S. 1928. Report of Paul S. Martin on the Temple of the Two Lintels (Station 7). *Carnegie Institution of Washington, Year Book* 27:302-305.

MARTINEZ DEL RIO, P. 1931. El Instituto Carnegie y el Templo de los Guerreros. *Universidad de Mexico* 2(10):326-332.

MARTÍNEZ PAREDES, D. 1955. Que significa Ch'ich'en Itzám? *Historia mexicana* 4:393-397.

MATTHEWS, P. 1999. Chichén Itzá. In *Encyclopedia of Archaeology: History and Discoveries*. Tim Murray, ed. v. 1, pp. 299-300. Santa Barbara: ABC-Clio.

MAUDSLAY, A.M. 1889-1902. *Archaeology: Biologia Centrali-Americana; or, Contributions to the Knowledge of the Fauna and Flora of Mexico and Central America*. London: R.H. Porter and Dulau. 4 v.

Maya conference at Chichén Itzá. *El Palacio* 32:169-170, 1932.

Maya mosaic is found: beautiful disk contains 1,000 pieces of polished turquoise. *New York Times*, March 8, p. 41, 1928.

Maya tomb under Castillo stairway. *El Palacio* 34(19-20):151, 1937.

MAYER, K.H. 1983. Eine phallische Statue aus Chichén Itzá. *Mexicon* 5(5):78-79.

MAYER, K.H. 1986. Chichén Itzá: a wooden phallus effigy. *Mexicon* 8(3):42.

MAYER, K.H. 1998. A stone phallus at Chichén Itzá. *Mexicon* 20(4):65-67.

MCCAFFERTY, G.G. 2007. So what else is new? A Cholula-centric perspective on lowland/highland interaction during the Classic/Postclassic transition. In *Twin Tollans: Chichén Itzá, Tula, and the Epiclassic to Early Postclassic Mesoamerican World*. J.K. Kowalski and C. Kristan-Graham, eds. pp. 449-480. Washington, DC: Dumbarton Oaks Research Library and Collection.

MCVICKER, M.F. 2005. *Adela Breton: A Victorian Artist Amid Mexico's Ruins*. Albuquerque: University of New Mexico Press.

MEANS, P.A. 1917. *History of the Spanish Conquest of Yucatan and of the Itzas*. Papers, 7. Cambridge: Peabody Museum of American Archaeology and Ethnology, Harvard University.

MEDÍZ BOLIO, A. 1950. El tesoro del Cenote Sagrado. *Yikal maya than* 11:183-186.

MEFFORD, J.J. 1992. Basketry, twined sandal soles, and cordage. In *Artifacts from the Cenote of Sacrifice, Chichén Itzá, Yucatán*. C.C. Coggins, ed. pp. 91-97. Memoirs, 10(3). Cambridge, Peabody Museum of Archaeology amnd Ethnology, Harcard University.

MEMENZA CASTILLO, R. 1938. Salamanca Chichén Itzá. *Ah-kin-pech* 2(17):13.

MENÉNDEZ, O. 1926. *Observaciones arqueográficos sobre la cultura maya (particularmente Chichén-Itzá y Uxmal): guía de las 200 proyecciones (dibujos y fotografías) que ilustran el ciclo de conferencias*. Mexico: Talleres Gráficos de la Nación.

MENÉNDEZ, O. 1936. *Outline of a cycle of conferences to the knowledge of the Mayan culture (especially Chichén Itzá and Uxmal)*. Mexico.

Merida, Chichén-Itzá, Uxmal y Dzibilchaltun. Merida: La Literaria, 1960.

Mexican state of Yucatán buys archaeologixcal site of Chichén Itzá from private loandowner. http://artdaily.com/index.asp?int_new=3717&int_sec=11&int_modo=1.

MILBRATH, S. 1988. Representación y orientación astronómica en la arquitectura de Chichén Itzá. *Boletín de la Escuela de Ciencias Antropológicas de la Universidad de Yucatán* 15(89):25-40.

MILLER LLANA, S. 2007. Ownership fight erupts over Maya ruins. http://www.csmonitor.com/2007/21017.p.20S01-woam.html.

MILLER, A.G. 1977. Captains of the Itzá: unpublished mural evidence from Chichén Itzá. In *Social Process in Maya Prehistory: Studies in Honor of Sir Eric Thompson*. N. Hammond, ed. pp. 197-225. New York: Academic Press.

MILLER, M.E. 1985. A re-examination of the Mesoamerican chacmool. *Art Bulletin* 67(1):7-17.

MILLER, M.E. 2007. Tula and Chichén Itzá: a historical afterward. In *Twin Tollans: Chichén Itzá, Tula, and the Epiclassic to Early Postclassic Mesoamerican World*. J.K. Kowalski and C. Kristan-Graham, eds. pp. 619-640. Washington, DC: Dumbarton Oaks Research Library and Collection.

MILLER, V.E. 1989. Star warriors at Chichén Itzá. In *Word and Image in Maya Culture: Explorations in Language, Writing, and Representation*. W.F. Hanks and D.S. Rice, eds. pp. 287-305. Salt Lake City: University of Utah Press.

MILLER, V.E. 2002. Representaciones de sacrificio en Chichén Itzá. In *Antropología de la eternidad: la muerte en la cultura maya*. A. Ciudad Ruiz, M.H. Ruz Sosa, and M.J.I. Ponce de Leon, eds. pp. 383-404, Madrid: Sociedad Espanola de Estudios Mayas.

MILLER, V.E. 2007. Skeletons, skulls, and bones in the art of Chichén Itzá. In *New Perspectives on Human Sacrifice and Ritual Body Treatments in Ancient Maya Society*. V. Tiesler and A. Cucina, eds. pp. 165-189. New York: Springer.

MIMENZA CASTILLO, R. 1925. Chichén Itzá el Egipto americano. *El Universal Ilustrado,* October 15.

MIMENZA CASTILLO, R. 1932. De cuando y por que dieron los españoles el nombre de Salamanca a Chichén Itzá. *Anales de la Sociedad de Geografía e Historia de Guatemala* 9:228-230.

MOHOLY-NAGY, H., and J.M. LADD. 1992. Objects of stone, shell, and bone. In *Artifacts from the Cenote of Sacrifice, Chichén Itzá, Yucatán*. C.C. Coggins, ed. pp. 99-151. Memoirs, 10(3). Cambridge, MA: Harvard University, Peabody Museum of Archaeology and Ethnology.

MOHOLY-NAGY, H., C.C. COGGINS, and J.M. LADD. 1992. Miscellaneous: Palm nut artifacts, decorated gourds, leather, and stucco. In *Artifacts from the Cenote of Sacrifice, Chichén Itzá, Yucatán*. C.C. Coggins, ed. pp. 359-368 Memoirs, 10(3). Cambridge, MA: Harvard University, Peabody Museum of Archaeology and Ethnology.

MOLINA SOLIS, J.F. 1896. *Historia del descubrimientio y conquista de Yucatán, con una reseña de la historia de esta peninsula*. Mérida: Imprenta y Lit. R. Caballero.

MONTGOMERY, J. 1991. Observations on name clauses at Chichén Itzá: Part 1. In *U Mut Maya* III. T. Jones and C. Jones, eds. pp. 141-146. Arcata: T. Jones.

MORLEY, S.G. 1911. Ancient temples and cities of the New World: Chichén Itzá. *Bulletin of the Pan American Union* 32(3):453-568.

MORLEY, S.G. 1913. Archaeological research at the ruins of Chichén Itzá, Yucatán. In *Reports Upon the Present Condition and Future Needs of the Science of Anthropology*. W.H.R. Rivers, A.E. Jenks, and S.G. Morley, eds. pp. 61-91. Publication, 200. Washington, DC: Carnegie Institution of Washington.

MORLEY, S.G. 1925. Chichén Itzá, an ancient American mecca. *National Geographic* 47:63-95.

MORLEY, S.G. 1931. Report of the Chichén Itzá Project. *Carnegie Institution of Washington, Year Book* 30:104-108.

MORLEY, S.G. 1935. Inscriptions at the Caracol. In *The Caracol at Chichén Itzá, Yucatán, Mexico*. K. Ruppert, ed. pp. 276-293; 336-338. Publication, 454. Washington, DC: Carnegie Institution of Washington.

MORLEY, S.G. 1936. Chichén Itzá. *Carnegie Institution of Washington, Year Book* 35:120-122.

MORLEY, S.G. 1937. Chichén Itzá. *Carnegie Institution of Washington, Year Book* 36:139-141.

MORLEY, S.G. 1938. Chichén Itzá. *Carnegie Institution of Washington, Year Book* 37:141-143.

MORLEY, S.G., K. RUPPERT, and J.S. BOLLES. 1934. Chichén Itzá. *Carnegie Institution of Washington, Year Book* 33:89-90.

MORRIS, A.A. 1928. Report of Ann Axtell Morris on the mural paintings and painted reliefs in the Temple of the Chac Mool. *Carnegie Institution of Washington, Year Book* 27:297-300.

MORRIS, A.A. 1931. Temple of the Warriors murals. Art and Archaeology 31:316-322.

MORRIS, E.H. 1924. Report of Mr. E.H. Morris on the excavations at Chichén Itzá, Mexico. *Carnegie Institution of Washington, Year Book* 23:211-213.

MORRIS, E.H. 1925. Report of E.H. Morris on the Temple of the Northeast Bench of Xtoloc Cenote (Station 3). *Carnegie Institution of Washington, Year Book* 24:263-265.

MORRIS, E.H. 1926. Report of E.H. Morris on the excavation of the Temple of the Warriors and the Northwest Colonnade (Stations 4 and 10). *Carnegie Institution of Washington, Year Book* 25:282-286.

MORRIS, E.H. 1927. Report of Earl H. Morris on the Temple of the Warriors and the Northwest Colonnade (Stations 4 and 10). *Carnegie Institution of Washington, Year Book* 26:240-246.

MORRIS, E.H. 1928a. Report of E.H. Morris on the excavation and repair of the Temple of the Warriors (Station 4). *Carnegie Institution of Washington, Year Book* 27:293-297.

MORRIS, E.H. 1928b. Temple of Warriors rebuilt. *El Palacio* 25:425-426.

MORRIS, E.H. 1931a.Temple of the Warriors. *Art and Archaeology* 31:298-305.

MORRIS, E.H. 1931b. *The Temple of the Warriors; the adventure of exploring and restoring a masterpiece of native American architecture in the ruined Maya city of Chichén Itzá, Yucatán*. New York, London, C. Scribner's sons.

MORRIS, E.H. 1980. *Temple of the Warriors: The Adventure of Exploring and Restoring a Masterpiece of Native American Architecture in the Ruined Maya City of Chichén Itzá, Yucatán*. New York: AMS Press.

MORRIS, E.H., Jean CHARLOT, and Ann AXTELL MORRIS. 1931. *The Temple of the Warriors at Chichén Itzá, Yucatán*. Publication, 406. Washington, DC: Carnegie Institution of Washington.

Mosaic disc found in Chichén Itzá. *El Palacio* 24:206, 1928.

MÜLLER, R. 1980. Der Himmel über der Mayastadt Chichén Itzá. *Naturwissenschaftliche Rundschau* 33(7):273-277.

NAVARIJO ORNELAS, L. 1999. Qué nos dicen las aves de Chichén Itzá? *Boletín informativo; la pintura mural prehispánica en México* 5(10-11):22-25.

NAVARRO, A.G., and P.P.A. FUNARI. 2009. Estudio de caso de la arqueología historica: organizacion espacial y memoria colectiva en Chichén Itzá. In *Arquelogía Colonial Latinoamericana: Modelos de Estudio*. J. Garcia Targa and P. Fournier Garcia, eds. pp. 163-186. International Series, 1988. Oxford, England: British Archaeological Reports.

NORMARK, J. 2007. Lethal encounters: warfare and virtual ideologies in the Maya area. In *Encounters/ Materialities/Confrontations: Archaeologies of Social Space and Interaction*. P. Cornell and F. Fahlander, eds., pp. 165-197. Cambridge, England: Cambridge Scholars Press.

Old tribute to the Maya gods is found in a Yucatán temple. *New York Times*, May 13, p. 126, 1928.

Older pyramid beneath El Castillo. *El Palacio* 32:259-260, 1932.

OSORIO LEÓN, J. 2003. El conjunto de los falos en Chichén Itzá: el reflejo de una vida palaciega. In *Simposio de Investigaciones Arqueologicas en Guatemala* (17 session, 2003). pp. 1025-1034. Guatemala: Ministerio de Cultura y Deportes; Instituto de Antropología e Historia.

OSORIO LEÓN, J. 2004. La Estructura 5C4 (Templo de la Serie Inicial): un edificio clave para la cronología de Chichén Itzá. Tesis de Licenciatura, Universidad de Yucatán.

OSORIO LEÓN, J. 2005. La Sub-estructura de los Estucos (5C4-1): un ejemplo de arquitectura temprana en Chichén Itzá. In *Simposio de Investigaciones Arqueológicas en Guatemala* (XIX session, 2005). v. 1, pp. 836-846. Guatemala: Museo Nacional de Arqueología y Etnología.

OSORIO LEÓN, J. 2006. La presencia del Clásico Tardío en Chichén Itzá (600-800/830 DC). In *Simposio de Investigaciones Arqueológicas en Guatemala* (XIX session, 2005). v. 1, pp. 403-410. Guatemala: Museo Nacional de Arqueología y Etnología.

OSORIO LEÓN, J., and E. PEREZ, 2001. La arquitectura y la cerámica del clasico tardio en Chichén Itzá: excavaciones en el edificio de la Serie Inicial (5C4). *Los investigadores de la cultura maya* 9:327-334.

Palace of the Sculptured Columns, Chichén Itzá. *Pre-Columbian Art Research Institute Newsletter* 20:4, 1995.

PALACIOS, E.J. 1935. *Guía arqueológica de Chichén Itzá: aspectos arquitectónicos, cronológicos y de interpretación*. Mexico: Talleres Gráficos de la Nación.

PAXTON, M.D. 1975. Gold discs from the sacred cenote at Chichén Itzá, Yucatán: stylistic analysis and ethnohistorical interpretation. M.F.A. Thesis, University of New Mexico.

PEÑA CASTILLO, A. 1998. El Castillo de Chichén Itzá. *Arqueología mexicana* 5(30):38-41.

PEÑA CASTILLO, A., S. BOUCHER, H. CHUNG, D. ORTEGÓN ZAPATA, G. EUÁN CANUL, J. OSORIO LEÓN, M. ELENA PERAZA (1991) "Proyecto Chichén Itzá, Informe Preliminar 1990". Informe mecanuscrito, Centro Yucatán-I.N.A.H., Mérida.

PERAZA LÓPEZ, C.A., *et al*. 1989. Una contribución al patrón de asentamiento de Chichén Itzá. *Boletín de la Escuela de Ciencias Antropológicas de la Universidad de Yucatán* 16(97):28-36.

PERAZA LÓPEZ, M.E., *et al*. 1987. La invasion de vendedores de artesanías en la zona arqueológica de Chichén Itzá, Yucatán. *Boletín de la Escuela de Ciencias Antropológicas de la Universidad de Yucatán* 14(82):17-30.

PÉREZ DE HEREDIA PUENTE, E.J. 1999. Chen K'u: La Cerámica del Cenote Sagrado de Chichén Itzá: Estudio de los Fragmentos Cerámicos de las Exploraciones de los Años Sesentas. FAMSI website.

PÉREZ DE HEREDIA PUENTE, E.J. 2005. La secuencia ceramic de Chichén Itzá. *Los Investigadores de la cultura maya* 13:445-466.

PÉREZ DE HEREDIA PUENTE, E.J. 2008. Chen K'u: The Ceramics of the Sacred Cenote at Chichén Itzá: Study of the Ceramic Fragments of the Explorations Conducted in the 60s. FAMSI website.

PÉREZ RUIZ, F. 2003. Perspectivas y desarrollo de plano de Chichén Itzá, desde el siglo XVI hasta el presente. In *Simposio de Investigaciones Arqueologicas en Guatemala* (17 session, 2003). pp. 1007-1014. Guatemala: Ministerio de Cultura y Deportes; Instituto de Antropología e Historia.

PÉREZ RUIZ, F. 2005. Recintos amurallados: una interpretación sobre el sistema defensive. In *Simposio de Investigaciones Arqueologicas en Guatemala* (19 session, 2005). pp. 917-926. Guatemala: Ministerio de Cultura y Deportes; Instituto de Antropología e Historia.

PEREZ-ROCHA, E., *et al*. 1987. Los vendedores de artesanías en Chichén Itzá. *Boletín de la Escuela de Ciencias Antropológicas de la Universidad de Yucatán* 14(82):17-30.

PHILLIPS, C. 2005. *The Aztec and Maya World: Everyday Life, Society and Culture in Ancient Central America and Mexico*. London: Lorenz Books.

PHILLIPS, D. 1932. Turquoise plaque of Chichén Itzá. *Design* 34(2):45;49.

PIÑA CHAN, R. 1968. Exploracion del cenote de Chichén Itzá, 1967-1968. *Boletin del Instituto Nacional de Antropologia e Historia*, 32.

PIÑA CHÁN, R. 1970. *Informé preliminar de la reciente exploración de cenote sagrado de Chichén Itzá*. Mexico: Instituto Nacional de Antropología e Instituto Nacional de Antropología e Historia.

PIÑA CHÁN, R. 1980. *Chichén Itzá; la ciudad de los brujos del agua*. Mexico: Fondo de Cultura Económica.

PIÑA CHÁN, R. 1991. *Chichén Itzá, la ciudad de los brujos del agua*. 4 ed. México: Fondo de Cultura Económica.

POLLOCK, H.E.D. 1929. Report of Harry E.D. Pollock on the Casa Redonda (Station 15). *Carnegie Institution of Washington, Year Book* 28:310-312.

POLLOCK, H.E.D. 1936. The Casa redonda at Chichén Itzá, Yucatán. *Carnegie Institution of Washington, Contributions to American archaeology* 3(17):129-154.

PREM, H.J., P.J. SCHMIDT, and J. Osorio LEON. 2004. Die Stadt der Krieger: Selbstdarstellung in Chichén Itzá, Yucatán, Mexico. *Antike Welt* 35(1):27-35.

PROSKOURIAKOFF, Tatiana. 1952. Glyphs. In *Metals from the Cenote of Sacrifice, Chichén Itzá, Yucatán*. S.K. Lothrop, ed. pp. 33-34. Memoirs, 10(2). Cambridge, MA: Harvard University, Peabody Museum of Archaeology and Ethnology.

PROSKOURIAKOFF, T. 1970. On two inscriptions at Chichén Itzá. In *Monographs and Papers in Maya Archaeology*. W.R. Bullard, ed. pp. 457-467. Papers, 61. Cambridge, MA: Harvard University, Peabody Museum of Archaeology and Ethnology.

PROWE, H. 1897. Neuere Forschungen in Chichén Itzá. *Globus* 72:200-206, 219-223.

Pyramid temple of Kukulcan. *Scientific American*, August, 1937.

Pyramid uncovered near Mérida. *El Palacio* 36(5-6):47-48, 1934.

QUIRARTE, J. 1966. Diferencias arquitectónicas en dos ciudades mayas: Uxmal y Chichén Itzá. *Boletín del Centro de Investigaciones Históricas y Estéticas* 5:51-119.

RAMÍREZ AZNAR, L.A. 1990. *El saqueo del Cenote Sagrado de Chichén Itzá*. Mexico: Producción Editorial Dante.

RANDS, R.L. 1954. Artistic connections between the Chichén Itzá Toltec and the Classic Maya. *American Antiquity* 19(3):281-282.

Rebuilding America's sacred city. *Popular Mechanics* 47:546-552, 1927.

REED, A.M. 1923a. Well of the Maya's human sacrifice. *El Palacio* 14:159-161.

REED, A.M. 1923b. Well of the Maya's human sacrifice. *New York Times*, April 8, p. SM9.

REED, N. 1964. *The Caste War of Yucatán*. Stanford: Stanford University Press.

REH, E. 1932. Site of Chichén Itzá in legal tangle. *El Palacio* 33:182.

REH, E. 1934. Temple within temple at Chichén Itzá. *El Palacio* 36(7-8):58-59.

REJÓN GARCÍA, M. 1942. Disertaciones sobre asuntos mayas; origende Itzámatul, Chichén Itzá e Izamal, voces derivadas de Itzát, que significa sabio, algunas observaciones. *Yikal maya than* 4:191-192.

REYGADAS VÉRTIZ, J. 1928. Chichén Itzá. In *Estado actual de los principales edificios arqueológicos de México*. pp. 237-263. Mexico: Dirección de Arqueología.

REYGADAS VÉRTIZ, J. 1929. Carved stone terrace at Chichén Itzá. *El Palacio* 27:186-187.

RICKETSON, E.B. 1927. Sixteen carved panels from Chichén Itzá, Yucatán. *Art and Archaeology* 23(1):11-15.

RICKETSON, O.G. 1925. Report of O.G. Ricketson, Jr., on the repair of the Caracol (Station no. 5). *Carnegie Institution of Washington, Year Book* 24:265-269.

RINGLE, W.M. 1990. Who was who in ninth-century Chichén Itzá? *Ancient Mesoamerica* 1(2):233-24.

RINGLE, W.M. 2004. On the political organization of Chichén Itzá. *Ancient Mesoamerica* 15(2):167-218.

RINGLE, W.M. 2009. The Art of War: Imagery of the Upper Temple of the Jaguars, Chichén Itzá. *Ancient Mesoamerica* 20(1): 15-44.

RINGLE, W.M., G. BEY, and C. PERAZA L. 1991. "An Itzá Empire in Northern Yucatán?: A Neighborinng View". Paper presented to the 47th International Congress of Americanists, New Orleans.

RIVARD, J.J. 1969. A hierophany at Chichén Itzá. *Katunob* 7(3):51-54.

RIVARD, J.J. 1971. *A Hierophany at Chichén Itzá and Pictures Can Be Glyphs*. Miscellaneous Series, 26. Greeley: University of Northern Colorado, Museum of Anthropology.

RIVAS SALMÓN, A. 1938. Las ruinas de Chichén-Itzá. *Revista geográfica americana* 10:264.

ROBERTS, H.B. 1933. Ceramic research. *Carnegie Institution of Washington, Year Book* 32:86-88.

ROBERTS, H.B. 1935. Ceramics. *Carnegie Institution of Washington, Year Book* 34:126-127.

ROBERTSON, M.G. 1991. Ballgame at Chichén Itzá: an integrating device of the polity in the Post-Classic. In *The Mesoamerican Ballgame*. G.W. van Bussel, P.L. van Dongen and T.J. Leyenaar, eds. pp. 91-110. Leiden: Rijksmuseum voor Volkenkunde.

ROBERTSON, M.G. 1994. Iconography of isolated art styles, that are group supported and individual supported occuring at Chichén Itzá and Uxmal. In *Hidden Among the Hills: Maya Archaeology of the Northwest Yucatán Peninsula*. H. J. Prem, ed. pp. 197-211. Acta Mesoamericana, 7. Möckmühl: Verlag von Flemming.

ROBERTSON, M.G. 1995. A school of sculptors at Chichén Itzá, Yucatán, Mexico. In *Mille ans de Civilisations Mésoaméricaines Des Mayas aux Aztèques: 1. Danse Avec Les Dieux*. J. de Durand-Forest and G. Baudot, eds. pp. 25-54. Paris: Éditions L'Harmattan.

ROBERTSON, M.G. 2002. Chichén-Itzá: The Palace of the Sculptured Columns. FAMSI website.

ROBERTSON, M.G. 2004. Chichén Itzá: El Palacio de las Columnas Esculpidas. FAMSI website.

ROBERTSON, M.G., and Margaret ANDREWS. 1992. Una reevaluación del arte del Templo del Chac Mool y de la Columnata Noroeste en Chichén Itzá: coexistencia y conflicto interior. *Mayab* 8:54-87.

ROBLES C.F., and A.P. ANDREWS (1986) A Review and Synthesis of Recent Postclassic Archaeology in Northern Yucatán. In *Late Lowland Maya Civilization: Classic to Postclassic*. J.A. Sabloff and E.W. Andrews V, eds. pp. 53-98. University of New Mexico Press, Albuquerque.

ROOT, W.C. 1952a. Copper-lead alloys. In *Metals from the Cenote of Sacrifice, Chichén Itzá, Yucatán*. S.K. Lothrop, ed. pp. 15-16. Memoirs, 10(2). Cambridge, MA: Harvard University, Peabody Museum of Archaeology and Ethnology.

ROOT, W.C. 1952b. Mexican bronze. In *Metals from the Cenote of Sacrifice, Chichén Itzá, Yucatán*. S.K. Lothrop, ed. pp. 14-15. Memoirs, 10(2). Cambridge, MA: Harvard University, Peabody Museum of Archaeology and Ethnology.

ROSADO, S. 1937. Breve excursion a la muerta ciudad, Chichén Itzá, Yucatán. *El Universal*, June 1.

ROYS, R.L. 1949. *The Prophecies of the Maya Tuns or Years in the Books of Chilam Balam of Tizimin and Mani*. Contributions to American Anthropology and History, 51. Washington: Carnegie Institution of Washington.

RUGELEY, T. 1996. *Yucatán's Peasantry and the Origins of the Caste War*. Austin: University of Texas Press.

RUPPERT, K. 1925. Report on the secondary constructions in the Court of the Columns. *Carnegie Institution of Washington, Year Book* 24:269-270.

RUPPERT, K. 1927a. Report on the Caracol (Station 5). *Carnegie Institution of Washington, Year Book* 26:249-25.

RUPPERT, K. 1927b. Report on the Temple of the Wall Panels (Station 14). *Carnegie Institution of Washington, Year Book* 26:252-256.

RUPPERT, K. 1928. Report on the outlying sections of Chichén Itzá. *Carnegie Institution of Washington, Year Book* 27:305-307.

RUPPERT, K. 1929. Report on the excavation and repair of the Caracol (Station 5). *Carnegie Institution of Washington, Year Book* 28:303-310.

RUPPERT, K. 1931a. Caracol. *Carnegie Institution of Washington, Year Book* 30:108-109.

RUPPERT, K. 1931b. Temple of the Wall Panels, Chichén Itzá. *Carnegie Institution of Washington, Contributions to American archaeology* 1(3):117-140.

RUPPERT, K. 1934. Mercado. *Carnegie Institution of Washington, Year Book* 33:90.

RUPPERT, K. 1935. *Caracol of Chichén Itzá, Yucatán, Mexico*. Publication, 454. Washington, DC: Carnegie Institution of Washington.

RUPPERT, K. 1943. Mercado, Chichén Itzá, Yucatán. *Carnegie Institution of Washington, Contributions to American Anthropology and History* 8(43):223-260.

RUPPERT, K. 1946. Investigations at Chichén Itzá. *Carnegie Institution of Washington, Year Book* 45:205-206.

RUPPERT, K. 1950. Gallery-patio type structures at Chichén Itzá. In *For the Dean: Essays in Anthropology in Honor of Byron Cummings on His Eighty-Ninth Birthday, September 20, 1950*. E.K. Reed and D.S. King, ed. pp. 249-258. Tucson.

RUPPERT, K. 1952. *Chichén Itzá: Architectural Notes and Plans*. Publication, 595. Washington, DC: Carnegie Institution of Washington.

RUPPERT, K., and A.L. SMITH. 1957. House types in the environs of Mayapán and at Uxmal, Kabah, Sayil, Chichén Itzá, and Chacchob. *Carnegie Institution of Washington, Current Reports* 2(39):573-597.

RUPPERT, K., E.M. SHOOK, A.L. SMITH, and R.E. SMITH. 1954 Chichén Itzá, Dzibiac, and Balam Canché, Yucatán. *Carnegie Institution of Washington, Year Book* 53:286-289.

RUZ LHUILLIER, A. 1948. *Puerta occidental de la muralla de Chichén Itzá*. Mérida: Instituto Nacional de Antropología e Historia S.E.P.; Dirección de Monumentos Prehispánicos, Zona Maya.

RUZ LHUILLIER, A. 1951. Chichén Itzá y Palenque, ciudades fortificadas. In *Homenaje al doctor Alfonso Caso*. pp. 331-342. Mexico: Imprenta Nuevo Mundo.

RUZ LHUILLIER, A. 1955. *Chichén Itzá, guia oficial*. Mexico: Instituto Nacional de Antropología e Historia.

RUZ LHUILLIER, A. 1962. Chichén Itzá y Tula; comentarios a un ensayo. *Estudios de cultura maya* 2:205-220.

RUZ LHUILLIER, A. 1963. *Chichén Itzá*. 3 ed. Cordoba, Argentina: Instituto Nacional de Antropología.

RUZ LHUILLIER, A. 1969. *Chichén Itzá*. 6 ed. Mexico, Instituto Nacional de Antropología e Historia.

RUZ LHUILLIER, A. 1979. *Chichén Itzá en la historia y en el arte*. Mexico: Editoria del Sureste.

RUZ LHUILLIER, A. 1981. *Chichén Itzá*. Mexico: Instituto Nacional de Antropología e Historia.

SALAZAR ORTEGÓN, Ponciano. 1952. El Tzompantli de Chichén Itzá. *Tlatoani* 1(5-6):36-41.

SATTERTHWAITE, L. 1944. Opposed interpretations of dates and hieroglyphs styles at Chichén Itzá. *Revista mexicana de estudios anthropologicos* 4:19-35.

SCHÁVELZON, D. 1985. El jaguar de Chichén Itzá, un monumento olvidado. *Cuadernos de arquitectura mesoamericana* 5:55-57.

SCHÁVELZON, D., and J. TOMASI. 2006. Publicación: La Imagen de América: Los Dibujos de Arqueología Americana de Francisco Mújica Diez de Bonilla. FAMSI website.

SCHMIDT, P.J. 1981. *Chichén Itzá: Apuntes para el Estudio del Patrón de Asentamiento*. Memoria del Primer Congreso Interno, 1979. pp. 55-70. Mérida: Centro Regional del Sureste, I.N.A.H., Mérida.

SCHIMDT, P.J. 1994. Chichén Itzá. *Arqueología mexicana* 2(10):20-25.

SCHIMDT, P.J. 1998. Contacts with Central Mexico and the transition to Postclassic: Chichén Itzá in central Yucatán. In *Maya*. P. Schmidt, M. de la Garza, and E. Nalda, eds. pp. 426-449. New York: Rizzoli International.

SCHIMDT, P.J. 1999a. Chichén Itzá: los contactos con el centro de Mexico y la transición al periodo Postclásico. In *Los Mayas*. P. Schmidt, M. de la Garza, and E. Nalda, eds. pp. 427-449. Mexico: CONACULTA; Instituto Nacional de Antropología e Historia.

SCHIMDT, P.J. 1999b. Chichén Itzá: resultados proyectos nuevos (1992-1999). *Arqueología mexicana* 7(37):32-39.

SCHIMDT, P.J. 2000. Nuevos datos sobre la arqueología e iconografia de Chichén Itzá. *Los investigadores de la cultura maya* 8(1):38-48.

SCHIMDT, P.J. 2003. Siete anos entre los Itzá; nuevas excavaciones en Chichén Itzá y sus resultados. In *Escondido en la selva: arqueologia en el norte de Yucatán*. H.J. Prem, ed. pp. 53-64. Mexico: Instituto Nacional de Antropología e Historia; Universidad de Bonn.

SCHIMDT, P.J. 2006. Nuevos hallazgos en Chichén Itzá. *Arqueología mexicana* 13(76):48-57.

SCHIMDT, P.J. 2007a. Birds, ceramics, and cacao: New excavations at Chichén Itzá, Yucatán. In *Twin Tollans: Chichén Itzá, Tula, and the Epiclassic to Early Postclassic Mesoamerican World*. J.K. Kowalski and C. Kristan-Graham, eds. pp. 151-204. Washington, DC: Dumbarton Oaks Research Library and Collection.

SCHIMDT, P.J. 2007b. Los toltecas de Chichén Itzá, Yucatán. *Arqueología mexicana* 14(85): 64-68.

SCHIMDT, P.J., and R. GONZÁLEZ DE LA MATA. 2006. La Galería de Los Monos, Estructura 5C6 de Chichén Itzá. In *Simposio de Investigaciones Arqueologicos en Guatemala* (20 session, 2006). pp. 477-488. Guatemala: Museo Nacional de Arquología y Etnología.

SCHIMDT, P.J., D. STUART, and B. LOVE. 2008. Inscriptions and iconography of Castillo Viejo, Chichén Itzá. *PARI Journal* 9(2): 1-17.

SCHROTH, S.A. 1986. Murals in the Upper Temple of the Jaguars, Chichén Itzá. M.A. Thesis, University of New Mexico.

SELER, E. 1906. Chich'en Itzá: Kopien aus dem Tempel der Jaguare und der Schilds von Miss Adela Breton. In *Proceedings of the International Congress of Americanists* (14 session, Stuttgart, 1904). v. 1, pp. Lxvii-lxix.

SELER, E. 1910. Die Ruinen von Chich'en Itzá in Yukatan. In *Proceedings of the International Congress of Americanists* (16 session, Vienna, 1908). v. 1, pp. 151-239.

SELER, E. 1915. Die Ruinen von Chich'en Itzá in Yucatán. In *Gesammelte Abhandlungen zur Amerikanischen Sprach-und Alterthumskunde*. v. 5, pp. 197-388. Berlin: A. Asher.

SELER, E. 1998. Ruins of Chichén Itzá in Yucatán. In *Collected Works in Mesoamerican Linguistics and Archaeology*. 2 ed. v. 5, pp. 41-165. Lancaster, CA: Labyrinthos.

SERRANO, J.U. 1997. Tres bloques con pintura mural de Chichén Itzá en el Smithsonian Institution. *Boletín informativo; la pintura mural prehispánica en México* 3(6-7):18-22.

SHEETS, P.D. 1991. Flaked lithics from the Cenote of Sacrifice, Chichén Itzá, Yucatán. In *Maya Stone Tools: Selected Papers from the Second Maya Lithic Conference*. T.R. Hester and H.J. Shafer, eds. pp. 163-188. Monographs in World Archaeology, 1. Madison: Prehistory Press.

SHEETS, P.D., J.M. LADD, and D. BATHGATE. 1992. Chipped-stone artifacts. In *Artifacts from the Cenote of Sacrifice, Chichén Itzá, Yucatán*. C.C. Coggins, ed. pp. 153-179. Memoirs, 10(3). Cambridge, MA: Harvard University, Peabody Museum of Archaeology and Ethnology.

SIEVERT, A.K. 1990. Maya cermonial specialization: lithic tools from the Sacred Cenote at Chichén Itzá, Yucatán. Doctoral dissertation, Northwestern University.

SIEVERT, A.K. 1992. *Maya ceremonial specialization: lithic tools from the Sacred Cenote at Chichén Itzá, Yucatán*. Madison: Prehistory Press.

SKIDMORE, J. 2006. Recent archaeological work at Chichén Itzá. *Mesoweb*. www.mesoweb.com/Chichén/features/work/01.html.

SMITH, A.L. 1955. Two new gallery-patio type structures at Chichén Itzá. *Carnegie Institution of Washington, Notes on Middle American Archaeology and Ethnology* 5(122):59-62.

SMITH, J.G. 2000. Chichén Itzá- Ek Balam Transect Project: An Intersite Perspective on the Political Organization of the Ancient Maya. Doctoral dissertation, University of Pittsburgh.

SMITH, J.G. 2001. Preliminary report of the Chichén Itzá-Ek Balam Transect Project. *Méxicon* 23(2):30-35.

SMITH, M.E. 2007. Tula and Chichén Itzá: Are we asking the right questions? In *Twin Tollans: Chichén Itzá, Tula, and the Epiclassic to Early Postclassic Mesoamerican World*. J.K. Kowalski and C. Kristan-Graham, eds. pp. 579-618. Washington, DC: Dumbarton Oaks Research Library and Collection.

SMITH, R.M. 1971. *The Pottery of Mayapán; Including Studies of Ceramic Material from Uxmal, Kabah, and Chichén Itzá*. Papers, 66. Cambridge, MA: Peabody Museum of Archaeology and Ethnology, Harvard University.

Society group to sail to view Maya ruins; Mrs. G.E. Vincent a member of expedition departing today for Yucatán. *New York Times*, February 6, p. 37, 1929.

SODI MIRANDA, F., and D. ACEVES ROMERO. 2001. La ceiba o yaxche y el origen de los mayas en Balankanché y Chichén Itzá. In *Simposio de Investigaciones Arqueológicas en Guatemala* (14 session, 2000). pp. 969-978. Guatemala: Instituto de Antropología e Historia de Guatemala; Asociacion Tikal.

SODI MIRANDA, F., and D. ACEVES ROMERO. 2003. El juego de pelota de Chichén Itzá. In *Simposio de Investigaciones Arqueologicas en Guatemala* (17 session, 2003). pp. 881-888. Guatemala: Ministerio de Cultura y Deportes; Instituto de Antropología e Historia.

SODI MIRANDA, F., and D. ACEVES ROMERO. 2006. Chichén Itzá, Tula y su impacto en la gran Tenochtitlan, a través de la complejidad cultural en el arte y sus implicaciones en la sociedad. In *Simposio de Investigaciones Arqueológicas en Guatemala* (XIX session, 2005). J.P. Laporte, B. Arroyo, and H.E. Mujía, eds. v. 1, pp. 411-422. Guatemala: Museo Nacional de Arqueología y Etnología.

SPINDEN, H.J. 1925. Holy city of early America revealed; Maya and Toltec ruins at Chichén Itzá in Yucatán, now being restored, have elaborate decorations. *New York Times*, December 6, p. SM8.

SPINDEN, H.J. 1933. Digging in Yucatán, by Ann Axtell Morris. *Saturday Review of Literature*, September 19.

SPOEHR, A. 1949. Restoration of Chichén Itzá, famed ancient Maya city. *Bulletin of the Chicago Natural History Museum* 20(1):3-4.

SPOTA, L. 1940. El saqueo del cenote (de Chichén Itzá); la aventura del gambusino y consul de Estados Unidos Edward Herbert Thompson. *Hoy*, July 27, pp. 48-54.

SQUIER, E.L. 1927. Bride of the Sacred Well, legend. *Good Housekeeping* 85:26-29.

SQUIER, E.L. 1928. *Bride of the Sacred Well, And Other Tales of Ancient Mexico*. New York: Cosmopolitan.

Statue of Chac-Mool, tiger king of the Mayas, is discovered in the ruins of Chichén Itzá. *New York Times*, April 19, p. 1, 1923.

STEGGERDA, M. 1936. Estudios de antropología fisica y geografia humana. *Diario de Yucatán*, August 24.

STEPHENS, J.L. 1841. *Incidents of Travel in Central America, Chiapas, and Yucatan*. London: J. Murray. 2 v.

STEPHENS, J.L. 1843. *Incidents of Travel in Yucatan*. New York: Harper and Brothers. 2 v.

STEVENSON, M. 2008. US Museum head says Mexico should get Mayan jade. http://www.usatrpoday.com/news/topstories/2008-11-18-2204655354_x.htm.

STRÓMSVIK, G. 1931. Notes on the metates of Chichén Itzá, Yucatán. *Carnegie Institution of Washington. Contributions to American archaeology* 1(4):141-157.

STRÓMSVIK, G. 1932. Metates of Chichén Itzá, Yucatán. *Carnegie Institution of Washington, News Service Bulletin* 2:210.

STRÓMSVIK, G. 1933. Temple of the Phalli. *Carnegie Institution of Washington, Year Book* 32:86.

STRÓMSVIK, G. 1935. Notes on metates from Calakmul, Campeche, and from the Mercado, Chichén Itzá, Yucatán. *Carnegie Institution of Washington, Contributions to American archaeology* 3(16):121-127.

STUART, G.E. 1989. Introduction: The Hieroglyphic Record of Chichén Itzá and its Neighbors. *Research Reports on Ancient Maya Writing* 23-25: 1-6.

SUÁREZ, L. 1980. *El Yucatán de los Mayas, Uxmal, Chichén Itzá, Sayil, Kabah, Labna, Dzibilchaltun, Mérida*. Madrid: Everest.

SUTRO, L.D. 1973. Tula, Chichén Itzá, and Qurzalcaotl: a study of the Toltecs and their influence in Mesoamerica. B.A. Thesis, Yale University.

TAUBE, K.A. 1994. Iconography of Toltec period Chichén Itzá. In *Hidden Among the Hills: Maya Archaeology of the Northwest Yucatán Península*. H.J. Prem, ed. pp. 212-246. Acta Mesoamericana, 7. Möckmühl: Verlag von Flemming.

TEMBOUR, F. 1992. Hydration dating of obsidian artifacts from the Sacred Cenote, Chichén Itzá. In *Artifacts from the Cenote of Sacrifice, Chichén Itzá, Yucatán*. C.C. Coggins, ed. pp. 179-181. Memoirs, 10(3). Cambridge, MA: Harvard University, Peabody Museum of Archaeology and Ethnology.

Thinks Maya ruins go back to 450 A.D.; Dr. Morley believes Chichén Itzá civilization was oldest in the Americas; finds signs of great city; reports about 15 square miles of plazas, pyramids, and temples buried in tropical foliage. *New York Times*, April 3, p. 3, 1923.

THOMPSON, E.H. 1913. Temple of the Jaguars. *American Museum Journal* 13:267-282.

THOMPSON, E.H. 1914. Home of a forgotten race: mysterious Chichén Itzá, in Yucatán Mexico. *National Geographic* 25:585-608.

THOMPSON, E.H. 1932. *People of the Serpent: Life and Adventure Among the Mayas*. Boston: Houghton Mifflin.

THOMPSON, E.H. 1938. *The high priest's grave, Chichén Itzá, Yucatán, Mexico; a manuscript, by Edward H. Thompson. Prepared for publication, with notes and introduction by J. Eric Thompson*. Anthropological Series, 27(1). Chicago: Field Museum of Natural History.

THOMPSON, E.H. 1992. Sacred well of the Itzáes. In *Artifacts from the Cenote of Sacrifice, Chichén Itzá, Yucatán*. C.C. Coggins, ed. pp. 1-8. Memoirs, 10(3). Cambridge, MA: Harvard University, Peabody Museum of Archaeology and Ethnology.

THOMPSON, J.E.S. 1937. A new method of deciphering Yucatecan dates with special reference to Chichén Itzá. *Carnegie Institution of Washington, Contributions to American archaeology* 22:177-197.

THOMPSON, J.E.S. 1941. A coordination of the history of Chichén Itzá with ceramic sequences in central Mexico. *Revista mexicana de estudios antropológicos* 5:97-111.

THOMPSON, J.E.S. 1942. Representations of Tezcatlipoca at Chichén Itzá. *Carnegie Institution of Washington,*

Notes on Middle American Archaeology and Ethnology 1(12):48-50.

THOMPSON, J.E.S. 1943. Representations of Tlalchitonatiuh at Chichén Itzá, Yucatán, and at Baul, Escuintla. *Carnegie Institution of Washington, Notes on Middle American Archaeology and Ethnology* 1(12):117-121.

THOMPSON, J.E.S. 1959. Un arquitecto en Chichén Itzá. *Arquitectura México* 15(66):95-100.

Tomb of Mayan kings believed discovered; legends on exterior give clue to identity of crypt found at Chichén Itzá, Yucatán. *New York Times*, May 24, p. 23, 1932.

TOSCANO, Salvador. 1940. La pintura mural precolombina de Mexico. *Boletín Bibliográfico de antropología americana* 4(1):37-51.

TOZZER, A.M. 1922. Toltec architect of Chichén Itzá. In *American Indian Life*. E.W.C. Parsons, ed. pp. 265-271. New York: B.W. Huebsch.

TOZZER, A.M. 1928. Maya and Toltec figures at Chichén Itzá. In *Proceedings of the International Congress of Americanists* (23 session, New York, 1928). pp. 155-164. New York.

TOZZER, A.M. 1932. Figuras mayas y toltecas en Chichén Itzá. *Anales de la Sociedad de Geografía e Historia de Guatemala* 9:182-193.

TOZZER, A.M. 1957. *Chichén Itzá and Its Cenote of Sacrifice; A Comparative Study of Contemporaneous Maya and Toltec*. Memoirs, 11-12. Cambridge, MA: Harvard University, Peabody Museum of American Archaeology and Ethnology. 2 v.

TOZZER, A.M. 1967. Chichén Itzá: Well of sacrifice. In *History Was Buried*. Margaret Wheeler, ed. pp. 175-199. New York.

TYNE, J. Van, and M.B. TRAUTMAN. 1935. Estudio sobre las aves de Yucatán para aclarar la civilizacion maya; dos zoologos de la Universidad de Michigan se trasladan a Chichén Itzá para obtener ejemplares de los pajaros que existen en aquella region. *Excelsior*, February 23.

VAIL, G., and C.L. HERNÁNDEZ. 2010. Astronomers, Scribes, and Priests: Intellectual Interchange Between the Northern Maya Lowlands and Highland Mexico in the Late Postclassic Period. Washington, DC: Dumbarton Oaks.

VAILLANT, G.C. 1933. Hidden history; how a little-known corner of Chichén Itzá adds a page to the story of pre-Columbian Yucatán. *Natural History* 33(6):618-62.

VAILLANT, G.C. 1940. Chichén Itzá: the thrice conquered: out of the jungle of Yucatán rises the ruins of a New World Rome, in eloquent tribute to the architectural genius of aboriginal America. *Natural History* 46(1):9-20.

Valiosas joyas arqueologicas fueron halladas; se encuentran en el cenote mayor de las ruinas de Chichén Itzá; jade, oro y cobre; notables resultados de la exploración realizada por Cicerol Sansores. *Excelsior*, March 29, 1940.

Venus y su importancia en los origenes de la civilización maya: su presencia e influencia en Chichén Itzá. *Simposio de Investigaciónes Arqueológicas en Guatemala* (14 session, 2000). pp. 1037-1043. Guatemala: Instituto de Antropología e Historia de Guatemala; Asociación Tikal, 2001.

VERGARA CALLEROS, M.Á. 1996. *Chichén Itzá: la ruta iniciática de los mayas en Chichén Itzá: la universidad cósmica de los mayas: la casa blanca donde se posa el santo-sol*. Merida: Escuelas de Mérida, Órgano Oficial del Instituto Tecnológico de Hotelería, A.C.

VILLAVERDE, C. 1992. Chichén Itzá, Yucatán. *Institute of Maya Studies Newsletter* 21(9):7.

VILLELA, K.D., and R. KOONTZ. 1993. *A Nose Piercing Ceremony in the North Temple of the Great Ballcourt at Chichén Itzá*. Texas Notes on Precolumbian Art, Writing, and Culture, 41. Austin: University of Texas at Austin, Center of the History and Art of Ancient American Culture.

VOSS, A.W. 2001. Los Itzáes en Chichén Itzá: los datos epigraficos. *Los investigadores de la cultura maya* 9(1):151-173.

VOSS, A.W., and H. KREMER. 2000. K'ak-u-pakal, Hun-pik-tok' and the Kokom: The political organization of Chichén Itzá. In *The Sacred and the Profane: Architecture and Identity in the Maya Lowlands*. Pierre R. Colas, Kai Delvendahl, Marcus Kuhnert, and Annette Schubart, eds. pp. 149-182. Acta Mesoamericana, 10. Markt Schwaben: Verlag Anton Saurwein.

WAGNER, E. 1995. The Dates of the High Priest Grave ("Osario") Inscription, Chichén Itzá, Yucatán. *Mexicon* 17(1):10-13.

WASHINGTON, H.S. 1921. Obsidian from Copán and Chichén Itzá. *Journal of the Washington Academy of Sciences* 11(20):481-487.

WEITZEL, R.B. 1945. Chichén Itzá inscriptions and the Maya correlation problem. *American Antiquity 11*(1):27-3.

WEITZEL, R.B. 1946. Atlantean columns and the lintel of the Initial Series temple at Chichén Itzá. *American Antiquity* 12(1):53-54.

What's on when: Spring Equinox at Chichén Itzá. *Guardian*, March 2, p. 11, 2002.

WILLARD, T.A. 1926. *City of the Sacred Well; Being a Narrative of the Discoveries and Excavations of Edward Herbert Thompson in the Ancient City of Chichén Itzá with Some Discourse on the Culture and Development of the Maya Civilization as Revealed by Their Art*. London: W. Heinemann. 293 p.

WILLARD. T.A. 1930. *Bride of the rain god: princess of Chichén-Itzá, the sacred city of the Mayas; being a hitorical romance of a prince and princess of Chichén-Itzá in that glamorous land of the ancient Mayas, where conflicting human passions dominated the lives of the long-dead past as they do those of today*. Cleveland: Burrows Brothers.

WILSON, T.H. 1976. Architecture and chronology at Chichén Itzá, Yucatán. Doctoral dissertation, University of California, Berkeley.

WINNING, H. von. 1985. *Two Maya Monuments in Yucatán: The Palace of the Stuccoes at Acanceh and the Temple of the Owls at Chichén Itzá.* Los Angeles: Southwest Museum, Frederick Webb Hodge Anniversary Publication Fund.

WRAY, D.E. 1945. Historical significance of the murals in the Temple of the Warriors, Chichén Itzá. *American Antiquity* 11(1):25-27.

WREN, L. 2003. Commemoration, celebration and replication: function and pursuasion in the art of Chichén Itzá. In Esc*ondido en la selva: arqueología en el norte de Yucatán: arqueología en el norte de Yucatán*. H.J. Prem, ed. pp. 65-78. Mexico: Instituto Nacional de Antropología e Historia; Universidad de Bonn.

WREN, L.H. 1989. Composition and content in Maya sculpture: a study of ballgame scenes at Chichén Itzá, Yucatán, Mexico. In *Ethnographic Encounters in Southern Mesoamerica*. V.R. Bricker and G.H. Gossen, eds. pp. 287-302. Studies on Culture and Society, 3. Albány: State University of New York at Albány, Institute for Mesoamerican Studies.

WREN, L.H. 1991. Great Ball Court Stone from Chichén Itzá. In *Sixth Palenque Round Table, 1986*. V. M. Fields, ed. pp. 51-58. Palenque Round Table (6 session, 1986). Norman: University of Oklahoma Press.

WREN, L.H. 1994. Ceremonialism in the reliefs of the North Temple, Chichén Itzá. In *Seventh Palenque Round Table, 1989*. V.M. Fields, ed. pp. 25-32. Palenque Round Table (7 session, 1989). San Francisco: Pre-Columbian Art Research Institute.

WREN, L.H., and L. FOSTER. 1992. Familial and titular patterns in the inscriptions of Chichén Itzá. In *U Mut Maya IV*. T. Jones and C. Jones, eds. pp. 161-167. Arcata: T. Jones.

WREN, L.H., and P. SCHMIDT. 1990. Elite interaction during the terminal Classic period: new evidence from Chichén Itzá. In *Classic Maya Political History: Hieroglyphic and Archaeological Evidence*. T.P. Culbert, ed. pp. 199-225. Cambridge, England: Cambridge University Press.

WREN, L.H., P. SCHMIDT, and R. KROCHOCK. 1989. *The Great Ball Court Stone of Chichén Itzá*. Research Reports on Ancient Maya Writing, 25. Washington, DC: Center for Maya Research.

WREN, L.H., R. KROCHOCK, E. BOOT, L. FOSTER, P. KEELER, R. KOONTZ, and W. WAKEFIELD. 1994. Maya Creation and Re-Creation in the Art, Architecture and Inscriptions of Chichén Itzá. In *U Mut Maya V*. C. Jones and T. Jones, eds. pp. 171-189. Arcata: T. Jones.